Dario Argento |

Contemporary Film Directors

Edited by James Naremore

The Contemporary Film Directors series provides concise, well-written introductions to directors from around the world and from every level of the film industry. Its chief aims are to broaden our awareness of important artists, to give serious critical attention to their work, and to illustrate the variety and vitality of contemporary cinema. Contributors to the series include an array of internationally respected critics and academics. Each volume contains an incisive critical commentary, an informative interview with the director, and a detailed filmography.

A list of books in the series appears
at the end of this book.

Dario Argento |

L. Andrew Cooper

**UNIVERSITY
OF
ILLINOIS
PRESS**
URBANA,
CHICAGO,
AND
SPRINGFIELD

Library of Congress Cataloging-in-Publication Data
Cooper, L. Andrew, 1977–
Dario Argento / L. Andrew Cooper.
p.   cm. — (Contemporary film directors)
Includes bibliographical references and index.
Includes filmography.
ISBN 978-0-252-03709-2 (cloth)
ISBN 978-0-252-07874-3 (pbk.)
1. Argento, Dario—Criticism and interpretation.
2. Argento, Dario—Interviews.
I. Title.
PN1998.3.A74C66   2012
791.4302'33092—dc23   2012018395

Contents |

Acknowledgments |

The thinking behind this book has spanned almost a decade, and thanking everyone who has influenced me through discussions of Dario Argento would stretch these pages and my memory beyond their capacities. First, I'd like to thank the students who took my course Dario Argento in Context at Georgia Tech in the fall of 2010. I hope I influenced their thinking as much as they influenced mine. Colleagues at Georgia Tech also provided substantive input: Jay Telotte gave me several pointers, and after a presentation based on the "Against Interpretation" section of this book, Phil Auslander, Blake Leland, Janet Murray, and Jesse Stommel asked questions that led to refined claims. Janet's suggestion about Argento inhabiting the role of the Italian villain from eighteenth-century British gothic influenced the "Against Criticism" section, and Blake's thoughtful discussion of nihilism influenced "Against Narrative." I especially want to thank Paulette Richards, who reviewed and edited my translations of the French-language interviews at the end of this volume. Élie Castiel's interview is translated and reproduced with the permission of the original author and publisher. Georgia Tech's Library and Information Center, particularly the indefatigable staff handling interlibrary loans, also deserves tremendous credit. During the final phases of manuscript preparation, Tom Byers and my other new colleagues in film studies at the University of Louisville were extremely helpful and encouraging. Above all, without Bryn Gravitt's help as research assistant and reader, this project might not have materialized.

The discussion of *Opera* derives from my essay "The Indulgence of Critique: Relocating the Sadistic Voyeur in Dario Argento's *Opera*" (*Quarterly Review of Film and Video* 22.1 [2005]: 63–72). It appears here by permission of Taylor and Francis Ltd. Wheeler Winston Dixon and others at *QRFV* were very supportive. My first presentation about Argento occurred at the 2002 meeting of the Southwest/Texas Popular Culture Association, where Steffen Hantke and others provided helpful feedback. Throughout the development of this project, my partner James Chakan has been a constant reader, advisor, and editor. Watching and rewatching films, we've come to many of the same conclusions, most of all sharing a conviction that Argento's works contain a genius that others would be fortunate to discover.

Dario Argento |

Doing Violence on Film

Dario Argento's films push the limits of visual and auditory experience; they offend, confuse, sicken, and baffle. Never complacent, Argento approaches each work as an experiment, and over more than four decades of filmmaking, his commitment to innovation has produced a broad range of styles applied almost unwaveringly within two closely related genres—crime thriller and supernatural horror—with results that are sometimes brilliant, sometimes muddled, and sometimes both. The films are not to everyone's taste. Their violence is often so extreme that even hardened horror veterans will avert their eyes. The extremity goes beyond gore, reaching previously unrecorded levels of pain, suffering, and mental anguish. Even more disturbing than the extremity is that Argento makes the combination of carefully arranged details, from the sets' colors and shadows to the cameras' angles and movements, so fundamentally *pretty*. Viewers who can stand to look at one of his films once might very well want to look again.

The problem of looking, of the desire to see, is central to all of Argento's films. From his directorial debut, *The Bird with the Crystal Plumage* (1970), in which a man watches helplessly as a woman is apparently attacked, to *Giallo* (2009), in which cop and killer both appreciate photos of murder victims a little too much, characters watching violence reflect viewers watching the film, and nobody involved in the exchange escapes complicity in the horrific spectacles. Argento's films challenge a viewer's accepted ideas about film spectatorship, meaning, storytelling, and genre. The violence they do reaches beyond their minced murder victims: they do violence to film itself.

Argento has worked as a writer, producer, director, composer, and/or editor on more than forty films. He comments in an interview included on the Blue Underground DVD of *The Bird with the Crystal Plumage*, "I was practically born into the cinema because my father was a producer." His initial exposure to the chaotic world of film production lacked appeal, so he became a film critic instead, a role that taught him "all the theories about cinema" and thus provided a foundation for the critical engagement with cinematic conventions that this book traces throughout his oeuvre. Argento enjoyed working as a critic, but gradually opportunities lured him into screenwriting. His most notable early effort was collaborating with Bernardo Bertolucci on the screenplay for Sergio Leone's classic western *Once upon a Time in the West* (1968). This success helped to create the opportunity for Argento to direct *Bird*, which his father, Salvatore Argento, produced. He continued to collaborate with his father as producer or executive producer on all of his features through 1982's *Tenebre*, and his younger brother, Claudio Argento, has served in production roles in the majority of features since 1973's *The Five Days of Milan*.

Through the production company Opera Film Produzione, Dario and Claudio Argento have produced a number of features that the elder brother did not helm, including the directorial debut of Dario's daughter Asia Argento, *Scarlet Diva* (2000). Asia's own career as an actress began in the Argento-produced film *Demons 2* (1986); she later led the casts of the Argento-directed features *Trauma* (1993), *The Stendhal Syndrome* (1996), *The Phantom of the Opera* (1998), *Mother of Tears* (2007), and *Dracula 3D* (2012, projected). Although she has pursued a career in fashion rather than film, Dario's elder daughter, Fiore, debuted as an actress in the Argento-directed *Phenomena* (1985) and had major roles in the Argento-produced *Demons* (1985) and Argento-directed *The Card Player* (2004). These familial connections suggest a thin, permeable boundary between Dario Argento's personal life and his artistic work. Indeed, he has often commented on the pleasure of seeing his daughters grow up on film, and as this book's discussion of *The Stendhal Syndrome* suggests, Asia's identity as his daughter becomes a crucial aspect of the film's rhetorical challenges to film norms.

While the collaborative roles of his father, brother, and daughters are important aspects to consider when approaching Argento's works as a whole, the most significant collaboration of his career has arguably been with Daria Nicolodi, his onetime girlfriend, Asia's mother, and the star of many of his most successful films, including *Deep Red* (1975), *Tenebre, Phenomena,* and *Opera* (1987). Nicolodi also cowrote *Suspiria* (1977), considered by many to be Argento's masterpiece, taking inspiration from rumors of witchcraft in her own family history. She continued to be a creative influence on *Suspiria*'s sequels *Inferno* (1980) and *Mother of Tears,* both of which feature her as an actress. This book does not focus on the sort of biographical criticism that Argento's collaborative relationships invite, but observing the centrality of collaboration, particularly with family, in Argento's work could help to qualify any illusion of the film director as a solitary author responsible for the works that this book associates pervasively with a possessive form of his name. The works that bear the Dario Argento brand are in some ways profoundly cohesive, which justifies approaching them as a meaningful collection, but the approach of *Dario Argento* should not occlude considering that "Argento's" works contain facets that far exceed the efforts of Dario Argento the man.

To establish the cohesiveness that makes Argento's oeuvre meaningful as such, the critical essay that forms the bulk of this book examines sixteen films that feature Argento as writer and director. While it includes a fairly comprehensive overview, with discussions of stories and performers as well as details about production, it does not attempt exhaustive treatments of these works, all of which deserve further scholarly attention. In focusing on how Argento's films function as rhetorical interventions against dominant views on film criticism, interpretation, narrative, and conventions, the essay aims to open up interpretive possibilities that connect the films to broader tendencies in film history. Even as it shows connections between Argento's works and works by canonical filmmakers, the argument relates the films to a broader turn away from the "high-art" and "high-theory" traditions of film and film studies. Argento's films inhabit the cinematic worlds of the popular director Mario Bava, Argento's closest predecessor in Italian film, and of the canonized artists Michelangelo Antonioni and Federico Fellini. Thus they have helped reevaluate cinema, especially "genre" cinema, in terms derived outside traditional aesthetic and critical paradigms. As this essay demonstrates, the films have strong roots in romanticism and aestheticism, but their relentless self-reflection also makes them distinctly postmodern, so even in their most "traditional" moments of aesthetic flourish, they wield an iconoclastic, deconstructive edge. The present argument differs from other studies that have influenced it, especially Maitland McDonagh's groundbreaking *Broken Mirrors, Broken Minds* and the collection of essays published in the journal *Kinoeye,* through a consistent focus on the films' overarching tendency to challenge the norms of film as an art form. This tendency emphasizes Argento's status as a sensationalist and provocateur whose work uses aesthetic impact to create, comment on, and at times resolve contemporary controversies.

The essay begins where Argento's films depart from some of the normative assumptions that have driven film criticism throughout his career, particularly those derived from psychoanalysis. It then explores the films' aesthetic challenges to narrative structure, and finally, it considers how Argento's later works respond to the new norms that his earlier works helped create. Although the essay explains these norms through emphasis on films bearing the Argento brand, it could just as easily illustrate them through discussion of the many films and filmmakers Argento has influenced, including the acknowledged masters George A. Romero (who has collaborated with Argento on multiple projects), John Carpenter (who pays homage to Argento's 1975 *Deep Red* in 2005's "Cigarette Burns," an episode of the TV show *Masters of Horror*), and Quentin Tarantino (who thanks Argento in the credits of his 2007 film *Death Proof*). Argento's international influence is also clearly visible in the aesthetic excesses of Japanese horror, exemplified in the works of Takashi Miike (*Audition*; 1999), as well as in works by a new generation of filmmakers represented by the French filmmakers Alexandre Aja (*High Tension*; 2003) and Pascal Laugier, who acknowledges his debt to Argento through the dedication of *Martyrs* (2008).

Despite its emphasis on the unity and influence of Argento's oeuvre, this essay eschews a traditional auteur approach: beyond those already mentioned, biographical details are relatively few, as the extent to which the films express Argento's "personal" vision is not a primary question. When the essay cites interviews, it treats Argento as an interpreter rather than the authoritative voice on what his films mean. Implicitly, it demonstrates the usefulness of approaching film as rhetoric and the cinema as a public and intellectual forum, but the essay's construals of specific films should not limit their possibilities for additional or even contradictory significance. Ultimately, the films speak for themselves, but they say things that are often ambiguous, equivocal, and difficult. If they were susceptible to a "final word," they would not be as worthy of consideration as they are.

Against Criticism:
Opera and *The Stendhal Syndrome*

Accusations of sadism have condemned people who create and enjoy horror fiction, no matter the medium, for as long as horror fictions have existed, or at least since the Marquis de Sade put his stamp of approval on Matthew Lewis's eighteenth-century splatterfest novel *The Monk* (Cooper, *Gothic*, 48). Contemporary critics who want to frame horror's viewers as sadistic voyeurs often turn to Laura Mulvey's foundational 1975 article "Visual Pleasure and Narrative Cinema," later incorporated into her book *Visual and Other Pleasures*, which explores "the way the unconscious of patriarchal society has structured film form" (14). Using the films of Alfred Hitchcock as a model, Mulvey describes how, in the representational strategies of many films, "the power to subject another person to the will sadistically or the gaze voyeuristically is turned onto the woman as the object of both" (23). By interrogating ways that film reinforces patriarchal norms that objectify women, Mulvey seeks a "break," an "alternative" that uses the language of patriarchal oppression in a gesture of resistance. She proposes an "alternative cinema [that] must start specifically by reacting against these obsessions and assumptions" (15–16). By reacting against these norms, Mulvey's alternative would expose, condemn, and ultimately replace the perverse gaze of the sadistic voyeur.

Over time, critiques of this kind of "perversion" have risen to a position of dominance through the works of feminists who have taken up Mulvey's call. For example, Mary Ann Doane considers Mulvey's scant treatment of female spectatorship and concludes that certain films by Hitchcock and others summon female subjectivity only to negate it, condemning female spectatorship to a state that is merely virtual, an absence (80–81). Also focusing on Hitchcock and seeking a habitable position for the female spectator, Tania Modleski acknowledges Mulvey's essay as "the founding document of psychoanalytic feminist film theory" but argues for more variable gendered identifications with onscreen violence against women (1). Modleski sees "a thoroughgoing ambivalence about femininity" manifested through "the misogyny and the sympathy [that] actually entail one another" in murderous male characters like Norman Bates in Hitchcock's 1960 film *Psycho* (3–4). Building on her own earlier work, Mulvey provides a more nuanced view of female spectatorship, which she claims is masculinized through identifications with the cinema's endemic male gaze (29–30). While these theoretical approaches to spectatorship suggest possibilities and pleasures beyond the misogynistic sadism Mulvey originally described, they still affirm the dominance of sadistic male voyeurism in representations of violence against women.

In *Men, Women, and Chain Saws*, Carol Clover explains that people rarely challenge claims about sadistic voyeurism in the horror film "because to do [so] would be to take on one of the most entrenched . . . and status-quo-supportive clichés of modern cultural criticism" (226). Clover's work takes on this cliché, arguing that the horror film allows its viewers to identify with both killer and victim, sadistically and masochistically, regardless of gender; she does "not, however, believe that sadistic voyeurism is the first cause of horror," favoring instead both male and female masochistic identification with the victim (19). In keeping with Clover's assertion, Dario Argento's films contradict anyone who claims that they predominantly rely on the audience's sadistic identification with the violence his camera captures. Two years before Clover first published her ideas about sadistic and masochistic identification, Argento made a similar argument in the 1985 documentary *Dario Argento's World of Horror*. Speaking of his point-of-view cinematography, he explains, "I want the spectator sucked into the scene. I want him to approach objects, or people. In the end it is you, the spectator, who kills or who is murdered." Argento expects his audiences to identify with his films in varying and multiple ways that go beyond simple determinations of gender. Discussing how Argento's films reflect on gender through the identities of their killers, Adam Knee concludes, "Argento's killers, in their variety and obscurity, tend to frustrate most such generalizations about gender" (215). With his characters as well as his camera, Argento's films represent gender and gendered identifications self-consciously, seldom making them simple or predictable.

Critical responses to Argento's work provide one explanation of this self-consciousness. As Chris Gallant states, "Accusations of misogynist characterizations . . . have surrounded Argento's output since the beginning of his career" (65). Increasing self-consciousness does not, of course, exculpate Argento from charges of misogyny. Though she gives Argento little specific treatment, even Clover includes him in the company of Hitchcock and Brian De Palma as an artist who has made misogynistic statements about the roles of women in his art. Argento's own words seem particularly damning and have reappeared in many critical assessments of his work—Clover takes them from William Schoell's *Stay Out of the Shower* (1985): "'I like women, especially beautiful ones. If they have a good face and figure, I would much prefer to watch them being murdered than an ugly girl or man'" (Clover 42). Argento might very well have been thinking of one of his heroes, Edgar Allan Poe, who, after considering the importance of beauty in poetry as well as the supremacy of melancholy as a poetic quality, concludes, "[T]he death, then, of a beautiful woman is, unquestionably, the most poetical topic in the world" ("Philosophy" 425). The idea that a man attracted to women would prefer to represent beautiful women is not necessarily misogynistic, but having roots in Poe's aesthetic philosophy does not make Argento's representations of women's death (and what Julia Kristeva would call women's abjection) any less problematic. However, Argento's *awareness* of his critics' charge of misogyny serves as a starting point for considering how his 1987 film *Opera* works against such criticism and responds to horror's detractors.

Opera

Opera's storyline is partially a reimagining of Gaston Leroux's 1910 novel *The Phantom of the Opera*. It centers on the experiences of Betty, a young opera singer who unwittingly rises from the rank of understudy to a lead role through the intervention of a killer. On the night of her successful debut, after an aborted attempt at sex with her boyfriend Stefan, Stefan steps out to fetch some tea. Seconds later, a hand grabs Betty's mouth from behind; the killer binds her hands and places tape over her mouth. He ties her to a pillar and takes out two sets of needles held together by strips of tape. When he fastens the needles beneath Betty's eyes, they extend perfectly from lower to upper eyelids. Wide with terror, her eyes, in extreme close-up, dart back and forth behind the almost evenly spaced rows of needles (figure 1).

"Take a good look," the killer says, brandishing a mirror. "If you try to close your eyes, you'll tear them apart, so you'll just have to watch everything." When she hears Stefan returning, Betty squeals an ineffective warning; blood drips down the needles in places where they have scratched her upper eyelids. Taking Betty's point of view from behind the needles, the camera shows Stefan approaching, and the killer's arm

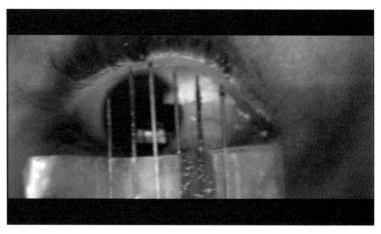

Figure 1. In *Opera*, the opera singer Betty (Cristina Marsillach) watches in terror as needles taped to her lower eyelids force her to witness her boyfriend being stabbed to death.

shoots from the side of the frame and drives a blade into the flesh beneath Stefan's jaw. A close-up shows the bloody tip of the blade emerge inside Stefan's gaping mouth. The sequence cuts back and forth between Betty's face, which registers each of the killer's vicious stabs as the needles force her to watch, and the stabbings themselves. Finally, a shot through the needles shows Stefan's gouged, motionless corpse. The killer sets Betty free and exits.

In this scene the murder victim is, contrary to Argento's preference, a beautiful young man who appears shirtless and vulnerable before the phallic blade penetrates him. In the choice of an eroticized male victim, the scene makes a gruesome counterpoint to the charge that the pleasures of the horror film are inherently or exclusively misogynistic. Though emphasizing female abjection may or may not make Argento himself complicit in patriarchal oppression, this instance of male abjection offers an alternative to an exclusively patriarchal structuration that depends on the subjugation and destruction of female bodies. At the most basic level of the gendered appearance of its characters, *Opera* begins its response to the tradition of criticism that labels horror enthusiasts as sadistic voyeurs.

Stefan's murder challenges critical norms through his gender. The scene's other victim, Betty, offers a critique through her position as witness to the brutality—like the film's audience, she passively watches the carnage unfold. Knee observes this correspondence of Betty with the audience and remarks, "The opera singer's situation in particular appears structured as an allegory for that of the modern horror film spectator, compelled to witness scenes of unspeakable gore, truly pained by the act of looking, horrified yet also complicit" (229 n.12). Chris Gallant refers to her simply as "the captive audience, our diegetic stand-in" (16). Betty's allegorical significance makes her gender another refutation of the primacy critics give to male sadistic identification. The scene's cinematography privileges Betty's point of view and her emotional responses: formally and thematically, the film's viewers are identified as female and strongly connected to the victim, not the killer.

Betty reacts to the murder in a way that also reflects on the film's viewers. Terrified and confused, she feels guilty because she believes her place as a spectator has resulted directly from the killer's interest in her success at the opera. Referring to her performance as Lady Macbeth in

Verdi's opera *Macbeth,* the role of a sadist who watches from the sidelines, Betty wonders, "Why did I sing that role? I shouldn't have. It was my fault." As witness to the attacks, she feels morally responsible, so she accepts the blame that horror's critics often assign to horror's audiences. Jonathan Lake Crane observes, "Enjoying endless reels of gratuitous ultraviolence is taken by critics of recent shockers to mean that . . . woefully impressionable viewers endorse the heinous acts committed by countless avaricious psychos" (3). Betty falls victim to the same logic that conflates watching something violent with a wholesale endorsement of violence; her psychological distress testifies to the damage such criticism can do.

Whatever she might feel, Betty is not at fault for the scene she witnesses: her choice is either to watch or to go blind (and probably be murdered as a result), which is not really a choice at all. Betty's lack of a choice complicates viewers' identification with her. While Betty *must* watch, the filmgoer *chooses* to watch. The critics who condemn horror's creators and fans, then, could keep making their judgments, proclaiming Betty's innocence while excoriating the audience. The similarity between Betty's position and the filmgoer's is not perfect; there are no needles over the audience's eyes. However, emphasizing the difference between Betty and the filmgoer in order to maintain the innocence of the former and the guilt of the latter constitutes a refusal of masochistic identification with Betty, the audience's stand-in. The argument necessary to maintain a condemnation of the film's audience on the grounds of this difference must ignore the point-of-view shots that encourage this identification. It must forego a metaphorical approach to the image of Betty's compulsion that would enable the viewer's complete identification in favor of a highly literal and exacting approach to how identification *must* operate. The critic who makes such an argument dismisses the possibility that Betty's compulsion stands for the inevitability of seeing horrors in everyday life, or that, as Argento claims, it allows audiences a "'positive confrontation with their fears'" (qtd. in Jones 158). To support the judgment of sadistic voyeurism, the critic must close off every alternative to identifying as a sadistic voyeur.

Opera's presentation of Betty as a figure for film spectatorship suggests that critics in effect dictate viewers' sadism in order to condemn it. Following the scene's logic, critical condemnation would distance the critic from Betty by refusing masochistic identification and from viewers by judging them from the height of critical authority. The critic seems to exercise a destructive and arbitrary power, seeking control of the scene and its viewer. The viewer is, in a sense, the victim of the critic's power just like Betty is the victim of her attacker. At a distance from the two victims in the scene, one analog remains for the critic: *Opera*'s sadistic psychokiller, Inspector Santini.

Aligning the monstrous psychokiller with normative criticism is not one of *Opera*'s innovations. Indeed, the subversion or enforcement of norms is a central concern in many horror films—one might even claim that it provides a formative impetus for the entire genre. In his essay "An Introduction to the American Horror Film," Robin Wood "offer[s] a simple and obvious basic formula for the horror film: normality is threatened by the Monster" (175). Wood's formula applies best to early horror films like F. W. Murnau's *Nosferatu* (1922) and James Whale's *Frankenstein* (1931), which "can be claimed as implicitly (on certain levels) identifying their monsters with repressed homosexuality" (172). Antagonists like Frankenstein's monster threaten the function of normative sexuality. The protagonist, often with the help of her or his community, tracks down the monster and destroys it so that normative forces can prevail. With the advent of slasher films like those in the *Halloween* and *Friday the Thirteenth* series, in which the monsters are usually psychokillers who dispatch miscreant teens, the forces of normativity changed orientations. In "Returning the Look," Wood describes

> a sinister and disturbing inversion of the significance of the traditional horror film: there the monster was in general a "creature from the id," not merely a product of repression but a protest against it, whereas in the current cycles the monster, while still "produced by" repression, has become essentially a superego figure, avenging itself on liberated female sexuality or the sexual freedom of the young. What has not changed (making the social implications even more sinister) is the genre's basic commercial premise: that the customers continue to pay, as they always did, to enjoy the eruptions and depredations of the monster. But where the traditional horror film invited—however ambiguously—an identification with the "return of the repressed," the contemporary horror film invites an identification (either sadistic or masochistic or both simultaneously) with punishment. (80)

In these films the monster punishes people who defy the demands of "traditional" normativity. The monster is no longer the disruptor of norms in the slasher film, of which Argento's *Opera* is a close relative; it is the enforcer. While the transformation of the monster from a protest against normative repression to an advocate for such repression signifies a shift of emphasis in the direction of punishment, this shift is not necessarily as disturbing as Wood claims. After all, slasher films represent the enforcers of norms as monstrous. While murderous acts of enforcement may provide the majority of the films' pleasures, their telos, and arguably their greatest pleasure, is still the destruction of the monster. If in the earlier films the destruction of the monster is the (usually temporary) triumph of repression, then in these later films the destruction of the monster is the (almost always temporary) triumph of liberation. The return of the repressed gives way to the return of the repressor. Frankenstein's monster and *Halloween*'s Michael Myers are both likely to come back again in a sequel, and in doing so they demonstrate two sides in the same cycle of repression and liberation. The protagonist of the traditional horror film and the antagonist of this new form of horror are both enforcers of oppressive norms. The enforcer who polices people's pleasures to make sure they fall within normative constraints, then, can correspond figuratively with the critic who hurls condemnations to maintain the status quo.

Opera's human psychokiller, Inspector Santini, does not fit the vaguely supernatural mold of slashers like Michael Myers. Though he stages his death and is thus able to return in what seems like a resurrection for the film's final showdown, like most of Argento's killers, he is mortal, which makes him a weak cipher for an endless cycle of psychic repression and liberation. Though Santini carries on the new horror-film tradition of linking normative critics and psychokillers, the ways in which he resembles the normative critic differ from the ways of his mostly American slasher cousins. While the typical slasher is a figurative policeman who punishes perverts for their illicit pleasures, Inspector Santini is literally a police detective. He is assigned to solve the murders he has committed, which gives him a chance to forestall his detection and strengthen his control over Betty, the main target of his crimes. The inspector abuses his power as a policeman, and if he is an analog for the critic, he suggests that critics abuse their power as well.

A short conversation between Betty and the inspector held before he is revealed as the killer makes explicit the link between policeman and critic. When Betty learns of the inspector's profession after he has expressed admiration of her debut performance, she remarks, "So you're a policeman, not a fan." He responds, "Can't a policeman be a fan?" Considering the inspector's question in light of his attacks on Betty, the answer is not the implied "yes" but a resounding "no." Contrasting a policeman with a fan suggests that a policeman is a more hostile kind of viewer—like a condemning critic. The policeman, or the condemning critic, is not a fan but an attacker. From his first intervention in Betty's life, disabling the lead opera singer so that Betty can take her place, the inspector tries to control who and what Betty will be. When he wants her on stage, he puts her on stage; when he wants her tied to a pillar, he ties her to a pillar. The inspector watches Betty not to enjoy her performance but to shape and evaluate her as a person. By analogy, the critic who denounces sadistic voyeurism joins the audience to judge it, assuming mastery over a horde of contemptible sadists. Early in the film, the inspector's binoculars—which he uses to scrutinize Betty—are splashed with blood, figuring the violence of his critical gaze. Unlike the typical slasher, the inspector's critical emphasis is not punishment but the power he wields over the witness to scenes of horror.

Santini uses his power to prove a critical commonplace related to the claim that people who enjoy horror in fiction will enjoy horror in real life. Crane provides another concise synopsis: "Present-day horror films, if one believes the public guardians, stimulate the desire for real bloodshed as they enthrall witless audiences" (vii). If viewers are exposed to enough horrifying images, the images will supposedly infect them with a desire to create actual violence. Santini's attacks on Betty add up to a critical experiment that would affirm this infectious view of violent imagery. As Leon Hunt remarks, "The spectator is placed as the object of sadistic instruction" (73). The inspector's own bloodlust began when Betty's mother, his lover and a self-avowed voyeur, encouraged him to kill for her pleasure. He believes that by forcing Betty to watch enough murders, he will awaken the mother's bloodlust in the daughter, achieving what critics promise will result from horror enthusiasts' exposure to violent imagery. If he can turn Betty into a sadist by exposing her to violent imagery, the inspector will prove the claim of critics who condemn horror for its destructive influence.

Critical anxiety about the effects of violent imagery has a history that goes far beyond the present-day horror film. Concern about the degradation of character that could result from exposure to violent entertainment predates the history of the cinema, earning a mention in Plato's *Republic* (Cooper, *Gothic*, 2–3). A common strategy in contemporary arguments for and against horror's evil influence is to refer to scientific studies that demonstrate, or fail to demonstrate, such causality. Michael Medved claims that "more than two hundred recent studies show that prolonged exposure to brutal imagery in the media leads to more hostile, violent, and aggressive attitudes and behavior on the part of those who consume such material" (23). Joan Smith questions this claim:

> Even the much-vaunted studies "proving" the link between screen violence and criminal acts turn out, when you look at them more closely, to establish something rather different: that violent offenders, like many law-abiding citizens, enjoy recreational violence at the cinema and in the comfort of their own homes. Who can say which came first? (202–3)

In addition to claiming that violent art stimulates violent behavior, detractors of screen violence have denounced it for desensitizing viewers and creating "mean world syndrome," a perception of real-world violence that "reinforces the worst fears and apprehensions and paranoia of people" (Gerbner). While scholars such as Jonathan Freedman would debunk claims about the conclusiveness of studies that correlate media violence with real-world violence, scholars such as George Comstock now take this correlation as a given (Cooper, *Gothic*, 162–75).

Examining *Opera*'s rhetorical position does not need to involve the Sisyphean task of arguing either side of this debate. The point is that Inspector Santini, and through him Argento's film, *does take such a position*. The inspector's intent becomes clear when Betty catches on to his design. Frustrated by his failure to change her and by the threat of imminent capture, the inspector tries to kill her. Betty wards off Santini's final attack by claiming, "I am like my mother . . . I realize it now," implying that his experiment has worked. The inspector lowers his weapon—and his guard—and for the moment, at least, he and Betty walk side by side, a happy sadistic couple. The policeman-critic finds satisfaction in thinking that his murders have finally proven his assumption about the effects of horror on its viewers.

Moments after she saves herself by convincing the inspector that his experiment has worked, Betty turns on him, and after Santini is apprehended, she triumphantly shouts, "It's not true! I'm not like my mother, not at all!" An American cut of *Opera*, known as *Terror at the Opera*, ends shortly after Betty's claim. Douglas Winter finds Betty's claim in this cut to be "less than convincing" in contrast to the "optimistic" ending of the original Italian cut, in which Betty "falls to the ground and, on hands and knees, embraces the flowers, the grass, the dirt, finally urging a salamander to 'go free'" (283–84). Indeed, Argento's original finale is almost *too* convincing: its sincerity approaches the absurd. If the hyper-sincerity reads more like irony, then the scene becomes opaque, a nod toward the difficulty of reaching a conclusion about the influence of violent imagery. If, however, the optimism of the scene is sincere, then the film argues strongly that violent imagery need not create sadists. Betty has seen horrors beyond description, but she still embraces flowers, showing that she retains an appreciation for nonviolent aesthetics; she has literally watched a ruthless killer without blinking, but she still pities the wee things of the earth, showing that, if anything, her ordeal of violence has awakened deeper feelings of sympathy.

The inspector's experiment—his attempt to prove critics' assumptions about the infectiousness of violent images in horror films—backfires. The end result of his violent attacks is a sense that critical biases against horror films are questionable, if not entirely wrong. By aligning the assumptions of horror's detractors with the mission of a murderous madman, *Opera* suggests not only a potential for brutality within the critical enterprise but also the desperate measures necessary for maintaining the critical status quo against the evolution of new ideas. On the one hand, the battle between Santini and Betty dramatizes the battle between the critics and horror's enthusiasts; on the other hand, it suggests the struggle of entrenched critical assumptions with an artistic sensibility that refuses to be cowed by criticism.

Like the critic and the viewer, the artistic sensibilities behind *Opera* also have a diegetic stand-in. Inspector Santini's test of his critical assumptions fails, but not before he takes his final victim: Marco, the director of the opera at the center of *Opera*, Verdi's *Macbeth*. While Santini's staging of the murders for Betty to watch gives him qualities in common with a film director as well as a film critic, the presence of a director-character whose life directly mirrors Argento's mutes the inevitable resonance between the perpetrator of violence and the creator of violent art. In 1985, Argento was invited to direct Verdi's *Rigoletto*, but scandalous reports of his innovative plans led to his ouster in favor of a director with "a more classical adaptation" (Jones 159). In *Opera*, Marco's girlfriend (one of them, anyway) reads from a newspaper, "Advice to the director: go back to horror films—forget opera." Like Marco, Argento tried to move from horror films to opera and got an icy reception. After Marco's girlfriend finishes reading the terrible review of his take on Verdi, she exclaims, "They're pulling you to pieces!" Marco ironically responds, "At least it's only on paper," foreshadowing his fate: the critical inspector slices and dices him in the final reel. The cost of normative criticism registers highly with the director, who either dies at a policeman-critic's hands or, more likely, ends up facing a different horror, such as a reporter's suggestion that Argento might have been a serial killer had he not gone into the movies (Mietkiewicz D19). Marco's fate suggests that criticism has consequences, and while they may not be as ghastly as murder, they can nevertheless take a heavy toll on artists and their art.

The ultimate power of the condemning critic is containment: the critic maintains the status quo by attacking those who would challenge it, trying to lock them within a derogated status by declaring them unworthy of anything else. *Opera* represents critics' efforts of containment directly in the newspaper critic who would block Marco from moving into the high-art terrain of opera as well as in Inspector Santini, the policeman recognized as anything but a fan. The film allegorizes the critic's effort of containment in the image of a viewer bound, gagged, and placed at the mercy of someone who wants to prove critical assumptions about sadistic voyeurism. The film's strategies for representing critical violence are, of course, extremely violent. It is a critique of critics in their own terms, a violent demonstration of how watching horror films to condemn the art and its fans can itself become a kind of sadistic voyeurism.

The Stendhal Syndrome

Although *Opera* makes a strong statement about sadistic voyeurism and the potential of violent spectacles to create violent spectators, it is not Argento's final word on the subject of art's influence on its audiences, which has been a lifelong interest. In an interview translated for this volume, Argento describes a childhood experience visiting the Parthenon in Athens. Surrounded by sublime art from a bygone era, he felt so overwhelmed that he became ill. Many years later, while casting for *Two Evil Eyes* (1990), a project he shared with the American director George A. Romero, he came across *The Stendhal Syndrome* by the Italian psychoanalyst Graziella Magherini, which describes a psychological condition triggered by exposure to art, an experience of overwhelmingly powerful emotions. Magherini and her colleagues named it after the French writer Stendhal, who wrote about such an experience in one of his early nineteenth-century journals. In an interview on the Blue Underground Blu-ray of Argento's *The Stendhal Syndrome* (1996), Magherini associates the condition with "fear of death . . . feelings of alienation . . . forms of depression, excitement, or also 'misperception' of reality." Across cases, she points to an underlying "crisis of identity, a loss of one's self" due to the "power of images." The book helped Argento to name his potent childhood experience, an influence that has stayed with him throughout his life.

Magherini's book also inspired Argento's *The Stendhal Syndrome*, which he made with his daughter Asia in the lead role of Anna Manni, a police detective who suffers from the titular condition. Argento has described the allure of the syndrome's danger: "'The possibility of Art being deadly really interested me. Violent images in film and on television are supposed to cause violence in viewers. The opening of *Suspiria* is often cited as causing people to faint, yet this is art too. These are the questions I raise in *The Stendhal Syndrome*'" (qtd. in Jones 228–29). His emphasis on raising questions reflects his refusal to provide a definite answer about the veracity of claims about violent art causing real-world violence. The film uses wild visuals—such as spinning shots of classic paintings and CGI doorways that appear inside artworks and draw the heroine in—to establish that art has powerful effects, but it leaves questions about the causation of violence, and related questions about the culpability of art, at least partially unanswered.

What is clear, however, is that the misperception of reality depicted in *The Stendhal Syndrome* stems from a disorder: the Stendhal syndrome is an illness confined to a small minority of people who suffer in the presence of art. Argento's film reflects on the illness by taking it to the utmost extremes. When Anna Manni travels from Rome to Florence to pursue a serial rapist and murderer, she visits the Accademia Gallery as well as the Uffizi Gallery, where, in front of Brueghel's *The Fall of Icarus* (which is perhaps on loan from the Musées Royaux des Beaux Arts in Belgium), she falls into a trance and collapses. She merges into the painting's depiction of the sea that engulfs tiny Icarus, and swimming through the water, she encounters and kisses a large fish. She regains consciousness at the center of a curious crowd, her lip bleeding from the impact of her fall. Dazed, she exits the museum, leaving her purse, which carries her gun, inside. The man who turns out to be the killer retrieves the purse, returns it to Anna sans weapon, introduces himself as Alfredo, and asks her name. When the question puzzles her, he says, "It was the paintings, wasn't it? Works of art have power over us. Great works of art have great power. Most of them, they'll never understand, but I do, and I think you do, too." Alfredo connects with Anna over her illness, suggesting that the two of them have an understanding of art from which the majority of people are barred.

The killer uses this understanding to exploit Anna's weakness. He attacks her twice. The first attack occurs while she is still disoriented from her experience at the Uffizi. Back in her hotel room, her Stendhal syndrome draws her into a reproduction of Rembrandt's *The Night Watch*. She enters the world of the painting, which blends with her own memory of the events leading up to her trip to Florence. Crossing into this blended world brings her back to her identity as a detective; the painting's crowd becomes a crowd gathered around the scene of one of Alfredo's murders. Her interactions provide exposition about who she is and why she is in Florence, and then she returns to her hotel room, where Alfredo is waiting for her. This scene illustrates that the Stendhal syndrome causes not only a misperception of reality but a blurring of the border between the real world and the world of art: Anna passes from the hotel, through the art, into her own memory, back through the art, and back to the hotel room as if they all have the same status as reality. In the Uffizi Gallery and in her hotel room, this blurring causes a loss of self, a loss of identity and memory that she struggles to regain after Alfredo tortures and rapes her during the debilitation that her illness causes. Alfredo's second attack illustrates how well he understands the impact of Anna's illness. As part of her recovery, Anna takes up painting, creating abstract works (actually created by Asia Argento) that express her anguish and victimization and that do not trigger her Stendhal syndrome. The second attack begins when she enters a room where her own works are displayed. Over Anna's images, Alfredo has placed prints of Brueghel's *The Fall of Icarus*, which immediately trigger the disorientation that begins an episode of her illness. For Anna, art becomes a trap. Alfredo kidnaps her, takes her to a remote area, ties her to a mattress, and again tortures and rapes her. He confines her in an outdoor area where concrete-reinforced walls are covered with grotesque graffiti. The graffiti supports Anna's imprisonment: when Alfredo leaves her alone, it triggers an episode of her illness with overwhelming chatter from the images and one image in particular—a demonic figure with a giant, bloody phallus—that comes out of the graffiti to menace her. Art and Alfredo work together to make Anna a victim.

Each of these attacks destabilizes Anna's identity. After the first, as she works to recover the sense of self she has lost, she cuts off all of her long dark hair. During an awkward family reunion, Anna's father mentions the haircut, and her brother observes, "You look like a boy!" This physical transformation reflects an emotional change as well. She tells her boyfriend Marco, "I'm not your woman anymore," and when he persists in trying to initiate sex, she becomes aggressive. She unfastens his belt, turns him around so that his back is to her, and shoves him against a wall as if she intends to rape him from behind. He resists, and she continues to abuse him physically until he flees her apartment. These changes in her appearance and personality suggest that as a result of her traumatic encounter with Alfredo, she is identifying with her attacker and becoming a sadistic rapist. After the second attack, she kills Alfredo and escapes. She changes again, adopting exaggerated femininity symbolized by a long blonde wig that she wears as she pretends to be an art student. In her new guise, she begins a romantic relationship with Marie, a Frenchman whose androgynous name becomes a subject of conversation. The confusion of identity encapsulated by his name reflects Anna's own confusion. She believes Alfredo is still alive, and when Marie and her psychiatrist are murdered, she blames Alfredo. The film ultimately reveals that Anna has become Alfredo, developing a split personality that makes her both man and woman and leads her to kill. Her identification with Alfredo, begun after the first attack, is thus complete.

If art and Alfredo are accomplices in Anna's victimization, and if Anna's victimization transforms her into a murderer, then through a causal chain that begins with exposure to art, *The Stendhal Syndrome* might seem to suggest that art can lead to murder. If this film makes such a claim, then it agrees with *Opera*'s Inspector Santini, turning Anna into the sort of killer that Santini seeks in Betty. This line of reasoning would seem to incriminate Argento and other creators of violent art: if art creates murderers, are artists not culpable for the influence of their art? Worse yet (following this line of reasoning), Argento's film risks doing to its viewers what the art in the film does to Anna. About *The Stendhal Syndrome* Argento has said, "'It's my intention to try and engender the same accumulation of weird sensations and unsettling emotions in the audience that Anna is feeling. How can I do that without going to visually shocking extremes?'" (qtd. in Jones 230). The visual shocks of this film are indeed some of the most extreme in Argento's oeuvre. At one point during Alfredo's first protracted assault on Anna, she lies helplessly bound while, right beside her, Alfredo rapes and murders another woman. The violence culminates in Alfredo shooting the other woman in the face. The bullet passes in slow motion through one cheek, across the interior of the woman's mouth, and out through the other cheek; Anna is splashed by the blood that spews from the exit wound. In a disturbing close-up, Alfredo looks at Anna through the line of sight created by the bullet holes in the woman's face.

The violence is not the only extreme to which Argento exposes his audience. Beginning with the opening credits, which show a scrolling strip of some of the Western world's best-loved paintings, *The Stendhal Syndrome* barrages viewers with potent imagery. Even relatively mundane actions receive extreme representation: for example, when Anna takes pills, they tumble in extreme close-up through the interior of her esophagus. Worse still (from the perspective that blames art for murder), the film's greatest extreme arguably lies in its casting. By the time of the film's release, Asia Argento, who plays Anna, had a growing international reputation as the actress daughter of one of Italy's best-known filmmakers. Even viewers who do not know that Asia Argento is Dario Argento's daughter might draw conclusions from the similarity of names in the opening credits. While watching Anna being raped and tortured, viewers might be unable to escape contemplating that these atrocities are being committed *against the director's own daughter.* Argento's camera shows his own daughter's body stripped and violated. The artist behind the film not only works to subject audiences to the artistic barrage that, according to a line of reasoning that the film suggests, makes people into murderers; he also makes his own daughter a victim. What sort of monster is he?

Through the combination of disturbing elements that is *The Stendhal Syndrome,* Dario Argento seems to become the sort of person that the reporter who asked if he might have been a serial killer would have him be. He inhabits the monstrosity of the gothic villain, perhaps one of the Italians vilified in the aforementioned eighteenth-century novel by Matthew Lewis or by Ann Radcliffe's sinisterly named 1797 novel *The Italian.* In an interview with Francesco Locane on the Argento fan Web site Dark Dreams, Argento explains about the inclusion of nude scenes in his films: "I am not embarrassed in shooting them, not even when they involve my daughter Asia." On the Blue Underground Blu-ray of *The Stendhal Syndrome,* Argento discusses his working relationship with his daughter and how it developed on this film:

> I had no problems before, but I did while we were shooting. That is, the film is very strong, graphic, expressive, and it features nudity. She suffered at times for this. I didn't try to do anything. If I did, I'd have reduced the drama in the scene. I explained the scene and said, "We need to do it, as it is important for the film." So we did it. She did it, then cried, sometimes.

Dario had "problems," which his tone frames as personal rather than logistical, treating his daughter in the ways his script required; Asia's tears suggest that she suffered as well. While what Asia endured suggests that, during filming, art became a higher priority than the well-being of his daughter, Argento's "problems" contradict the image of him as a monster like the killers in his films.

Asia's reflections on her father's work offer further contradiction. In an interview with Billy Chainsaw reproduced on the Dark Dreams Web site, Asia explains, "I watched my father's films when I was very young, I started when I was six. . . . I wasn't so scared by my father's films. I never had so-called bad dreams . . . when I was a kid I wanted to watch them again and again." In an interview by Nick Dawe on the Dark Dreams site, Asia says of her father, "We are very close. We are able to work together and create something as eternal as film." From a very young age, Asia came into contact with her father's films, and she understood them as stories to be enjoyed repeatedly, phenomena separate from the reality of her everyday life with her father. If the claims of this successful actress, writer, and director who has worked on more than forty films are true, she was not ruined by exposure to her father's films or to his camera. She appreciates his works *as films*.

The monstrosity that Dario Argento risks associating with himself by subjecting his audiences and his daughter to extremes of film violence depends on an inability to distinguish art from life, film from fantasy— an inability of the sort associated with Stendhal syndrome, which *The Stendhal Syndrome* clearly marks as an exploitable illness. To condemn *The Stendhal Syndrome* for damaging audiences by exposing them to the conditions of Anna's illness is to suggest that all audiences have this rare illness. To condemn Dario Argento for the rape of his daughter is to assume the illness's symptoms; ultimately, Argento exposes his audience and his daughter not to rape and violence but to *representations* of rape and violence. In effect, the critics who condemn Argento and his works either see the Stendhal syndrome's unique pathology everywhere or, more likely, fall victim to a version of the syndrome themselves, going so far into the world of artistic representations that they begin to confuse them with reality. Once again, a member of the police force— Detective Anna Manni, following Inspector Santini's example—stands in for the critic. Here, however, the critic is also the victim, a sufferer from a horribly confusing condition that afflicts only a small number of viewers when exposed to violent art. In being about a condition that blurs the boundaries of art and life, *The Stendhal Syndrome* is about the misguided critics who condemn horror fictions for creating horrific realities. The film argues that only viewers as unstable as Anna run the risk of becoming killers in her footsteps.

Nevertheless, *The Stendhal Syndrome* does not close down that risk completely. Like *Opera*'s doubled ending, which first suggests that Betty has succumbed to the critical imperative of sadistic voyeurism and then suggests that she has not, *The Stendhal Syndrome*'s fantastic imagery makes the titular phenomenon accessible to all, so just as anyone might succumb to the disease, anyone might confuse art and reality. Argento's film attacks critical assumptions about the sadism and dangerousness of violent cinema, but it does not make cinema safe, and it does not provide easy answers to the questions it raises. In Argento's films, interpretation is always vexed. Although *The Stendhal Syndrome* uses the ideas of a psychoanalyst at the heart of its story, psychoanalytic interpretation—long the dominant critical approach to horror films, a dominant approach to film in general, and the basis of theories about sadistic voyeurism—is no more a key to a clear "truth" in Argento's films than any other approach.[1] *The Stendhal Syndrome* reflects Argento's long-standing interest in psychoanalysis, which supplies another object for his films' oppositional strategies.

Against Interpretation: The First Five *Gialli*

Ready for release in 1969 but held back until 1970, Argento's directorial debut, *The Bird with the Crystal Plumage*, entered the cinema world under the shadow of a film that had hit a decade earlier, Alfred Hitchcock's *Psycho*. Hitchcock's work demonstrated that films focused on maniacs who kill beautiful women could reach artistic heights and also thrive outside the B-movie circuit, and in doing so, it redefined the thriller and horror genres. For years, producers around the globe searched for the movie that would be the next *Psycho* and the director who might be the next Hitchcock. If a thriller had a comparable premise, critics rushed to make the comparison, so when ABC-TV remarked in a review of *Bird*, "Remember *Psycho*? There are scenes with that kind of impact!" the adulation found its way to movie posters and other ads hoping to win some of Hitchcock's mainstream audience. After *Bird* became an international success, Argento quickly earned the title of "The Italian Hitchcock," which still appears in promotional materials for his films today. The marketing of Argento as a Hitchcock-like figure went as far as a television show in the model of *Alfred Hitchcock Presents*; the miniseries *Dario Argento's Door into Darkness* ran for four episodes on Italian television in 1973, with Argento giving eerie intros to stamp each episode with his brand. A bit of Internet lore even claims that Hitchcock once said in response to Argento's *Deep Red*, "This Italian guy is starting to worry me" ("Alfred"). If the claim is true, then Hitchcock gave the title "Italian Hitchcock" an indirect stamp of approval. If it is untrue, then the comparison has become so powerful that fans have fantasized the relationship between the two directors into history.

Comparisons of Hitchcock's works, especially *Psycho*, with Argento's *Bird, Deep Red,* and other *gialli* (plural for *giallo* [yellow]; the *giallo* film is an Italian thriller based on or inspired by early twentieth-century mystery novels, which in Italy were often published with yellow covers) go deeper than genre affiliations and superficial plot points. In several of his films, Hitchcock popularized a transformation of psychoanalytic commonplaces into elaborate plot devices that render aberrant human minds as mysteries to be solved, mysteries that can supplement or even supplant the "whodunit?" question that usually supplies form and interest for the mystery genre. This transformation propels *Psycho*, bringing all the strands of the story together, and it offers a touchstone for Argento's departures from the Hitchcock tradition.

Psycho ends with a psychiatrist explaining the pathological process that has led the multiple murderer Norman Bates to dress up as his mother and kill people with a butcher knife. Today, many viewers come to *Psycho* already knowing whodunit—knowing about the cross-dressing psycho-killer's adoption of his mother as a split personality's darker, dominant side. When the film was new, viewers mostly came to it unaware of its surprise ending. Nevertheless, the surprise is not that of a typical whodunit because offscreen dialogue and even a womanly shadow with a knife indicate from the start that Norman's mother is the killer. Thus the primary mystery of the film is never *who* is behind the grisly slayings but *why* they occur and *which* character is next. The film climaxes when Lila Crane, the surviving sister of the woman Norman/Mother famously murders in the shower, discovers that the seated Mother figure the film has offered as the culprit is actually a corpse. Upon the discovery, Norman/Mother quickly leaps out in his womanly costume to menace Lila with the butcher knife, and almost as quickly, Lila's savior grabs him/her from behind and, in a brief struggle, removes much of the costume. The camera follows Norman/Mother's wig to the floor, and the shot of the wig fades to an exterior shot of a crowd in front of a police station.

This quick twist—if viewers thought Mother is whodunit, they were wrong because Norman did—is even more quickly dampened by a line claiming that the new answer to whodunit is still not the final answer. After a cut from the police station's exterior to a detective's office, the first line spoken is, "If anyone gets any answers, it'll be the psychiatrist." The psychiatrist, Dr. Richman, will supply the real answer. When asked whether Norman killed Lila's sister, Dr. Richman says, "Yes and no," taking away the twist's whodunit answer and leaving both diegetic and nondiegetic audiences completely dependent on his explanation of the yes-and-no paradox. Dr. Richman works to maintain this dependency: when a member of his small police-station audience interrupts him to answer, "Why was [Norman] dressed like that?" with, "He's a transvestite," the psychiatrist silences the interrupter with, "Not exactly." Thus Dr. Richman establishes total authority: *no one* but the psychiatrist can provide answers in this film.

Dr. Richman's yes-and-no answer to whodunit shifts the mystery's emphasis from a simple question of *who* to more complex questions of *why,* and the doctor's authority frames psychoanalysis as the only means of making the whys appear. Why is Norman both innocent and guilty of murdering Lila's sister? The psychoanalytic response casts him as an improper version of one of Sigmund Freud's favorite characters, Oedipus. In part because "his mother was a clinging, demanding woman" who lived with her son after his father's death "as if there was no one else in the world," when she met a new man, "it seemed to Norman that she threw him over for this man, and that pushed him over the line, and he killed them both." Mother clung to her son too much, so he went through a perverse version of what Freud calls the Oedipus complex, in which a normal boy at first identifies his father with himself and his mother with the object of desires, and eventually "the little boy notices that his father stands in his way with his mother, [so] his identification with his father then takes on a hostile colouring and becomes identical with the wish to replace his father in regard to his mother" (Freud, *Group*). In Norman's abnormal case, his identification with the role of his father became so hostile that he killed his father-surrogate in order to replace him. In the process, he happened to kill his mother, too, so, as Dr. Richman explains, "he had to erase the crime, at least in his own mind . . . he began to think and speak for her, give her half his life, so to speak." In a psycho version of marriage, the joining of two lives into one, Norman joined with his mother, giving his uber-Freudian Oedipal tale a sinister finish.

Hitchcock's camera stays on the psychiatrist and his diegetic audience throughout the scene, and when Dr. Richman finishes explaining how Norman's mother-half has won complete control of his psyche, the real mystery of *Psycho* is solved. One of the detectives in the diegetic audience foolishly holds on to another mystery, asking what happened to the forty thousand dollars that Norman's victim Marion Crane had stolen at the beginning of the movie. Dr. Richman barely has time to belittle the question, saying, "These were crimes of passion, not profit," before a uniformed policeman interrupts to ask whether he can give Norman/Mother a blanket, which, when the policeman leaves, gives Hitchcock's camera an excuse to abandon the irrelevant conversation about money and find its way to Norman/Mother and his/her chilling final monologue that substantiates everything the psychiatrist has explained.

The Bird with the Crystal Plumage

The ending of *The Bird with the Crystal Plumage* is what the DVD commentator Alan Jones calls the film's "most obvious homage to *Psycho*." That the scene echoes *Psycho*'s ending is obvious, but the significance of that echo might not be. The scene evokes Hitchcock's transformation of psychoanalytic inquiry into a popular plot device, but by contrast, in *Bird*, the transformation appears only to be dismissed, echoing *Psycho* only to contradict it. Thus while his first film established Argento's fame as the Italian Hitchcock, it also began a project that worked against Hitchcock's apparent elevation of psychoanalytic interpretation.

At the end of *Bird*, Sam Dalmas, the protagonist, confronts the killer, who turns out not to be a man as everyone has suspected but a woman,

Monica Ranieri. The confrontation almost costs Sam his life, but the police arrive in time to save him. The film cuts from this quick resolution to a TV news show. Turning to the police detective who has led the investigation throughout the film, the anchorman says, "Inspector Morosini, can you explain what moved this woman to commit such horrible murders?" Morosini humbly replies, "I believe that the most qualified person to answer these questions is Dr. Renoldi, the well-known psychiatrist, our consultant during the investigation." Thus he cedes the authority to psychiatry that *Psycho*'s Dr. Richman claims through his mysterious answers to the whodunit question.

Like Dr. Richman, Dr. Renoldi provides an expository monologue that replaces whodunit, which the film has already revealed, with a psychological resolution to the higher mystery of *why*dunit. He begins with a reference to the killer's traumatic experience with a sexual assault:

> For the time being we can only say this: Ten years ago, Monica Ranieri, who was born with paranoid tendencies, was the victim of an aggression, which traumatized her severely. Her mental disturbance remained dormant for ten years, until she came across a painting that depicted the horrible scene of which she had been the protagonist. Her latent madness came to life, violent and irresistible. Strangely, she did not identify herself with the victim but with the aggressor, maybe to rid herself of fear.

This explanation relies on psychoanalytic theory about identification, giving the same power to psychoanalysis as *Psycho*.

However, the film's presentation undermines the authority of this explanation. As the psychiatrist speaks his first explanatory line, his voice continues on the audio while the image transitions into a shot of an airplane on a runway, preparing for takeoff. A series of quick cuts shows the airplane in multiple positions from multiple angles; the ostentatious editing pulls focus from the sound track, which gets diluted by rising music from Ennio Morricone's score. Sam Dalmas and his girlfriend Julia appear, boarding the plane, getting settled, and looking relieved after their harrowing experiences with the killer. The camera's abandonment of Dr. Renoldi before he finishes his explanation contrasts sharply with Hitchcock's treatment of Dr. Richman. Although Frank Burke and others have read *Psycho*'s ending as ironic, any irony in the ending is subtle, and Hitchcock's camera grants Dr. Richman an image of authority, not leaving him until after he finishes solving the psycho-mystery and exits the room to emphasize the irrelevance of the money-mystery to which one foolish detective still clings. Argento's camera leaves his psychiatrist before the psycho-mystery is resolved. *Psycho* dismisses the money-mystery, the type of mystery most common to the thrillers of its time, and *The Bird with the Crystal Plumage* dismisses the psycho-mystery, the type of mystery that *Psycho*'s influence had made common during the decade between the two films.

Argento's visual abandonment of the psychoanalytic explanation ultimately frames psychoanalysis, as well as the films that rely on it as machinery to propel and resolve their plots, with ridicule. When Dr. Renoldi finishes his diluted audio-only monologue with an explanation of why Monica's husband Alberto assisted with the slayings ("he was influenced by his paranoid wife to the point of becoming homicidally psychotic himself"), Sam, an American, refers musingly to a friend who had encouraged his murder-harried trip to Italy: "I can hear him saying it now: 'Go to Italy. It's a peaceful country. Nothing ever happens there.'" For Sam, this line is a joke about an American's experience abroad, but for the audience who has just finished listening to Dr. Renoldi, it is a terse, risible coda for the very serious psychoanalyst's revelation of truth. In its position as the psychoanalytic revelation's punctuation, and also as the film's final statement, the line undercuts the revelation's serious-ness and recasts the entire explanation with levity. Just as the camera dismisses the psychiatrist's image, Sam's line dismisses the psychiatrist's words. The final impression of this film is not that of a psychological mystery thrillingly unveiled or of a psycho-killer giving credence to a psychoanalyst's darkest revelations; it is a joke that frames the entire film as *nothing happening*. The explanation replaces psychoanalysis as the key to a mystery's meaning with a suggestion, perhaps more serious than it sounds, that the mystery lacks meaning altogether.

Argento forecasts his turn away from psychoanalysis in the title *The Bird with the Crystal Plumage*. The title *Psycho* takes part in the trans-formation of psychoanalytic theory into a meaningful plot mechanism; if a title indicates important content, then the important content in Hitchcock's film is not "the mystery of the motel murders," which might be a true-to-genre title based on the weak whodunit aspect of the plot, but the *psycho*-logical story hidden within the murderer's mind. *The Bird with the Crystal Plumage* is far more enigmatic: it refers to the clue that finally leads Sam and the police to discover the killer's whereabouts and identity. The clue is central to whodunit, but since whodunit is not central to the film, it merits fewer than five minutes of onscreen discussion. It appears thanks to Monica Ranieri's unfortunate habit of telephoning Sam and the police to taunt them with whispers about her murderous plans. Sam and the police record some of the phone calls, and the police analyze the recordings with their sophisticated (for the late 1960s) lab equipment. In typical *giallo* fashion, the resources of Sam the amateur detective succeed where the police's equipment fails.[2] At a point when the recordings seem almost forgotten, Professor Carlo Dover, Sam's acquaintance, comes to Sam having figured out the source of strange noises they had heard in one recording's background: the call of *hornitus nevalis,* a rare bird found in the Siberian wild. Conveniently, only one bird of this type exists in Italy, in a zoo just below the Ranieris' apartment. As soon as they piece the bird puzzle together, the camera cuts to Sam, Carlo, and Julia rushing through the zoo with police in tow. The camera pans across the titular caged bird, lingering only for a moment on its exotic white plumage, before following the detective team to the apartment. As quickly as it appears, the titular phenomenon is gone. While Hitchcock's title refers to the psychological interest that defines his film, Argento's refers to something beautiful but ephemeral, only significant enough to interest the camera for an instant.

Giving the ephemeral bird the status of title (which it has in both Italian and English versions, although a French-language version, *Le sadique aux gants noirs,* translates as *The Sadist with Black Gloves*) does not necessarily make the avian creature itself important. It does, however, foreground the film's values or, more precisely, what the film *does not* value. Just as psychoanalytic interpretation appears at the end only to be dismissed as a valueless nothing, Sam follows psychological threads throughout the film, expecting them to lead to the solution, only to have his expectations dashed by the bird noise that actually leads to the film's final revelations. These threads, and the entire psychology-driven investigation that they constitute, are finally as unimportant as "the mystery of the motel murders" in *Psycho.*

The thread in which Sam invests the most energy stems from what he witnesses at the beginning of the film. In *Bird's* most celebrated sequence, Sam walks down a dark city street and notices, through the brightly lit glass façade of an art gallery, a struggle between two figures. One of them, apparently male and dressed in the black jacket, hat, and gloves that the previous Italian generation's *maestro* of terror, Mario Bava, made the signature costume of the *giallo's* killers, seems to be attacking a woman in an all-white outfit. As Sam rushes through the gallery's first set of glass doors to intervene, he becomes trapped in a glass cage, a vantage from which he can only watch the violence unfold (figure 2). Sam's helpless position prefigures that of Betty in *Opera*: since he cannot enter the scene he is witnessing, he becomes, like the moviegoing audience, a passive voyeur.

Sam watches the black-clad figure flee the scene, leaving the wounded woman to writhe in agony. Surrounded by bizarre metallic sculptures, she sees Sam and extends a hand toward him, blood dripping bright red drops from her fingers to the stark white floor, but all he can do is press against the glass and assure her that the police are on their way. When the police arrive and question him, Inspector Morosini demands, "What

Figure 2. In *The Bird with the Crystal Plumage*, Sam (Tony Musante) becomes trapped in a glass cage, where he takes the position of voyeur that becomes an integral feature of virtually all of Argento's major works.

happened? I want to know everything you saw and heard." The stakes are high: the attack Sam has witnessed, in which the victim has appeared to be the beautiful Monica Ranieri, seems to be connected to the recent murders of several other beautiful women. After a few interruptions, Sam tells the inspector, "There was something wrong with that scene. Something odd. I can't pin it down, but I have a definite feeling that something didn't fit." This unproductively indefinite "definite feeling" that he has seen or heard something wrong and therefore remembers something wrongly launches him on two quests. One is the typical quest of the mystery/thriller, a journey outward through the dark world of an unfamiliar city to follow clues toward the identity of the killer. The police goad him onto this quest, agreeing that he has seen something important and even giving him the address of the Ranieris as encouragement for him to share in the detective work. The other quest, less typical of the genre but archetypal for Argento, is a journey inward, toward the reconstruction of Sam's unconscious memory, which he believes could hold the solution. At several key moments in the film, the scene in the gallery replays as Sam remembers it. The camera zooms in when Sam focuses on a detail, and in freeze-frame he contemplates what might be a critical observation.

The reconstruction of unconscious memories plays a central role in psychoanalytic practice, as Freud explains in *Beyond the Pleasure Principle* (1922):

> At first the endeavours of the analytic physician were confined to divining the unconscious of which his patient was unaware, effecting a synthesis of its various components and communicating it at the right time. Psychoanalysis was above all an art of interpretation. Since the therapeutic task was not thereby accomplished, the next aim was to compel the patient to confirm the reconstruction through his own memory. In this endeavour the chief emphasis was on the resistances of the patient; the art now lay in unveiling these as soon as possible, in calling the patient's attention to them, and by human influence—here came in suggestion acting as "transference"—teaching him to abandon the resistances.

Sam's quest makes him both patient and analyst in a psychoanalytic process. He must uncover whatever his memory needs to seem right, and he must confirm what he uncovers by unveiling the resistances that made his memory wrong in the first place.

Each time Sam (and the film) replays his memory of the apparent attack on Monica Ranieri, he sees a little bit more and seems to get a little bit closer to some kind of revelation. Before he gets there, Professor Carlo Dover cracks the mystery of the strange noises in the telephone recording, and the pursuit of the rare bird, which owes nothing to Sam's introspection, leads to the killer. After Sam, Carlo, Julia, and the police race from the zoo to the Ranieris' apartment, Sam and the police burst in on a struggle for a knife between Alberto Ranieri (Umberto Raho, who looks a little like Anthony Perkins playing Norman Bates) and his wife Monica, Alberto wins the struggle and brandishes the knife at the intruders. A brief scuffle pushes Alberto through a high window, where he dangles from a ledge. Sam and a detective fail to pull him back up, and a spectacular effect that cost Argento a camera allows the audience to take Alberto's point of view all the way down to the bounce and thump of his body on the pavement. Dying, Alberto confesses to the murders and begs Sam and Morosini to take care of his wife.

The film gestures toward closure, but just when the credits might have started rolling, Sam notices that Julia is missing. In fact, she and Carlo have not appeared since the race to the Ranieris' apartment. Sam's search leads him to the back entrance of the Ranieris' building. He is concerned enough to enter the building, go upstairs, and prowl through the Ranieris' darkened apartment, but whatever suspicions he entertains during the search do not trigger further reconstruction of his memory. He does not seem to doubt Alberto's guilt at all until he sees Carlo seated in a chair holding a knife. No flash of memory helps him to notice that Carlo is a corpse; only the man's dead weight flopping on top of him when Sam tries to grab the knife stops him from blaming Carlo for the crimes. On the floor, trying to push away the corpse, Sam sees Julia bound and gagged, and he hears laughter from across the room. The source of the laughter emerges from the darkness, and only then, with Monica Ranieri standing in front of him in *giallo*-killer regalia, does his reconstructed memory kick in. The scene cuts quickly back and forth between Monica's laughing face and Sam's memory of the gallery where she was apparently attacked, and this time, the clarified shot reveals something new: as Monica struggles with the black-clad figure, Alberto, *she* is the one holding the knife and attacking *him*. "You were trying to kill your husband, not the other way around," Sam says, having a delayed eureka moment that is absolutely useless.

The nature of the mental blocks, which Freud calls "resistances," that had been keeping Sam from remembering all the details of the attack in the gallery become clear at the moment the memory does. When Sam saw a man struggling with a woman, his expectations related to gender and aggression (and to people who wear black versus white) made him see wrongly, misidentifying and then misremembering the roles in the conflict. Even though the reverse was true, Sam's prejudices functioned as resistances, making him identify the man as the aggressor and the woman as the victim. In an interview on the Blue Underground DVD of *The Bird with the Crystal Plumage*, Argento explains his thinking behind this scenario:

> It is a theme and one of my obsessions, psychoanalysis . . . and memory becomes the theme. . . . It's the memory that's faulty. In addition, we only remember the things that we want to remember, in every case. We remember things that our culture wants us to remember. The rest we remember in a different way or we don't remember at all. This is the theme on which I based the film.

Argento slides easily from a claim about psychoanalysis, to an idea about what *we* want, to an idea about what *our culture* wants, suggesting a deterministic relationship not only between culture and memory but also between culture and identity, who *we* are. *The Bird with the Crystal Plumage* examines memory and identity through Sam's misremembering and misidentification of actors in a scene of violence. Sam's errors expose the power of gender norms as so strong that they shape what people perceive and recall, but behind this critique of normative gender codes lies another part of the critique of psychoanalysis inherent to the dismissal of Dr. Renoldi at the end of the film. By having the psychoanalytic thread lead Sam to a gender-bending revelation that is too late to do any good, the film paints psychoanalysis as an obsession-worthy intellectual pastime that is nevertheless devoid of functional utility.

Sam follows another psychoanalytic thread related to memory, gender, and identity that turns out to be equally useless. It begins when he visits an antique shop where Monica Ranieri's first victim worked. He learns that the victim sold a painting on the night she died; the man who runs the shop describes the painting as "primitive, very macabre, too." It depicts a man in black clothes and a black hat attacking a woman who lies in a bright red pool of blood that contrasts starkly with the large snowy landscape around them. The antique dealer, whom a DVD commentator rightly describes as a "gay caricature," at first refuses to give Sam a black-and-white copy of it, but when Sam turns on the charm and says "please," the scene cuts to Sam pinning the copy on his wall at home. When Julia comments on the image, Sam describes it as "a photo of a painting that is somehow mixed up in all these murders." He has a feeling that *somehow* he will find a vital connection between the painting and the mystery. Confirming Sam's feeling, the camera moves in on the portion of the painting that features the attack and then tracks backward as the image becomes color, finally revealing that the original painting hangs in the killer's lair. Although he lacks the audience's confirmation of the painting's relevance, Sam fixates on it as crucial evidence, gazing at it on one occasion and saying to himself, "This damned thing is turning into an obsession," and on another occasion saying, "Damned painting, there's got to be a lead there somewhere." Later, when Sam's search for Julia leads him back into the Ranieris' apartment building, a shot of the painting on the wall confirms that Sam has found his target.

As Dr. Renoldi explains in his audio-only monologue, the painting is a representation of an assault that Monica Ranieri suffered ten years prior to the film's action. The painter knew about the attack because she was "a girl I knew," and he found it inspiring. The painting, in turn, inspires Monica to kill, reopening the wounds of her traumatic experience and sending her spiraling into psychosis. Dr. Renoldi notes that in reaction to the painting, "Strangely, she did not identify herself with the victim but with the aggressor, maybe to rid herself of fear." Like Sam, Monica has a problem with identification, but their problems pull in two different directions. Sam misidentifies the gender roles in his memory because he remembers what his culture wants him to remember. Monica, by contrast, misidentifies *with* the gender roles in the painting, refusing to identify herself with the victim, a member of her own sex who in fact *is* a representation of herself, and identifying instead with the aggressor, a member of the opposite sex.

This misidentification works contrary to cultural expectations and contrary to the process of identification that Freud associates with the female version of Oedipus complex ("Psychogenesis"), which reverses the gender roles in the following explanation of male Oedipal identifications:

> It is easy to state in a formula the distinction between an identification with the father and the choice of the father as an object. In the first case one's father is what one would like to *be,* and in the second he is what one would like to *have.* The distinction, that is, depends upon whether the tie attaches to the subject or to the object of the ego. (Freud, *Group*)

Oedipal identifications, which are the prototype of all identifications, rely on distinctions between who a person wants to *be,* which in normal (according to Freud) identification is someone who shares the person's gender, and whom a person wants to *have* (sexually), which in normal (according to Freud) identification is someone of the opposite gender. Monica's identification with the representation of her male attacker, which leads her to assume his role and attack other women as she was attacked, is, then, the result of what psychoanalysts would call an abnormal psychosexual process, a perversion. Considering psychoanalysis as a cultural force, psychological processes that are normal or abnormal according to Freud become normative and counternormative, cultural models that dictate how a person should or should not behave and thus inculcate certain behaviors. When Sam misidentifies roles in the struggle between Monica and Alberto, he is only behaving in accordance with cultural norms. When Monica misidentifies *with* roles in the struggle between attacker and victim in the painting, with a representation of her own victimization, she becomes a pervert. Sam and Monica thus become rhetorical figures that reflect critically on Freudian notions of gender and perversity.

Throughout the film, the presumably male killer's attacks on women are perversely sexualized, and the killer's knife looks like a standard visual representation (or displacement) of phallic aggression. The knife's status as a phallic symbol becomes graphic during the attack on the killer's fourth victim, the first murder the movie depicts on screen. The phallic blade rips through the female victim's translucent nightie, partially exposing her breasts. It slides along her flesh and hovers over her panties, which the killer's hand rips off. The next shot shows the killer's hand lift the knife upward, and then the film cuts to a splash of blood accompanied by a scream. The attack with the knife thus becomes simultaneous rape and murder, a figurative association that recurs during several of the killer's attacks.

Reviewing such scenes of phallic aggression in light of the ending's revelation of Monica as the killer recasts the killer as a phallic woman, a conventional representation of lesbianism in gothic and horror fiction (Cooper, *Gothic*, 72–73). The movie does not explicitly characterize Monica as someone who identifies with lesbianism or seeks out sexual relationships with women and *not* men. The Ranieris are gallery-owning, swinging artist-types, but their marriage seems sound enough for Alberto to kill and die to protect his insane wife. In addition, the *giallo* costume obscures the killer's identity, and the figure in the dark coat, hat, and gloves is not necessarily that of Eva Renzi, the actress who plays Monica. Creating a visual signature comparable to Hitchcock's cameos, Argento uses his own hands in close-up shots of the killer manipulating knives and other frightening symbols, which means that the manliness of the killer going incognito should not be overread. Nevertheless, Monica's identification with her male attacker transforms her appearance, prompting her to don a masculine suit during her final confrontation with Sam, which features the costume in full view of her pretty face and long, feminine hair. Although Monica may not actually *be* a lesbian, her appearance during this confrontation and her sexualized attacks on other women make her a mannish woman, which is consistent with what Freudians would classify as a classic case of female inversion, a common type of perversion in the annals of Freudian psychoanalysis.

Classification and examination of perverts are central activities in many of Argento's films, and they are crucial aspects of his early mystery narratives. His work thus engages with Freud's proclivities in the essay on "The Sexual Aberrations" in his *Three Essays on the Theory of Sexuality*. In *Bird*, classification and examination combine when the police attempt to have Sam pick the killer out of a lineup that Petrini, a detective subordinate to Morosini, introduces as if he were reading from a psychoanalyst's catalog of sexual abnormalities:

PETRINI: Bring in the perverts. Take a good look, Mr. Dalmas. . . .
We can't rule out the possibility that he is a pervert. Aldo Sarti, forty-two
years old, eight convictions, sadomasochist. Sandro Lorrani, thirty-one
years old, exhibitionist, eight convictions. Mario Zandri, sixty-six years
old, sodomite. Giacomo Rossi, fifty years old, three sentences for cor-
rupting the morals of minors. Rubatelli, Luigi, alias Ursula Andress,
twenty-six years old . . .
MOROSINI: No! Petrini! . . . What's he doing here? How many times
do I have to tell you? Ursula Andress belongs with the transvestites, not
the perverts.

The men take their places in the lineup as the detective calls their names.
When Ursula Andress appears, Morosini corrects Petrini's misclassification. Ultimately, the scene plays for laughs, and not only because of the
jibes at the perverts (even though the depiction, like the caricatured depiction of the gay antique dealer, is tinged with the homophobia that pervades
the thriller and horror genres, as Harry M. Benshoff has demonstrated).
Because the lineup has no relationship with the crimes whatsoever, the
entire process of parading those whom psychoanalysts call aberrations as
criminals ends up being a farce, a sign of the police's ineptitude consistent
with Sam as amateur detective being more capable of tracking the killer
than the men who are actually trained to fight crime. Furthermore, the
misclassification of a cross-dresser as a pervert resonates with Monica's
cross-dressing and Dr. Renoldi's dismissed diagnosis of her problems
with identification: identifying with the attacker in the painting may very
well be part of Monica's sickness, but to explain her behavior in terms
of psychoanalytic perversion is as misguided as putting Ursula Andress
in the lineup. The lineup leads nowhere, and so does following the psychoanalytic thread suggested by the painting. Far from sharing Freudian
proclivities, *Bird* actually lampoons them.

The Cat o' Nine Tails

Psychoanalysis is not the only (supposed) science that falls inside the
critical frames of *The Bird with the Crystal Plumage*. Sam's amateur
sleuthing (with help from Professor Dover) beats out the sound analysis
that the police demonstrate with their lab's fancy equipment and the
forensic analysis indicated in the aftermath of the gallery attack at the

film's beginning, during which Argento's camera carefully notes police dusting for fingerprints and gathering samples of blood. Science's failure to reveal or establish the truth becomes even more pronounced in Argento's second directorial feature, *The Cat o' Nine Tails* (1971). In an interview included on the Blue Underground DVD of the film, Argento's cowriter Dardano Sacchetti explains the basis for a central concept in the story:

> It had a scientific angle. In *Scientific American* magazine there was an article about [men with] XYY [sex chromosomes]. It seemed that in an American study, a sample of prison inmates displayed a very high percentage of people with an extra chromosome. It seemed that this extra chromosome was indicative of a violent nature.

The DVD cuts to Argento, who explains, "The media was talking about it, so I made it the focus of the movie. Of course it's not true, but it made a good story." As in *Bird*, sexual abnormality takes center stage. While he views the genetic theory as interesting enough to provide the basis for a movie, Argento ultimately dismisses this development in genetics as a falsehood. For Argento, science does not have to be true to be the subject of film narrative. In the move from *Bird* to *Cat*, he moves from one truth-challenged science to another.

The Bird with the Crystal Plumage, The Cat o' Nine Tails, and Argento's third film, *Four Flies on Grey Velvet* (1971), are commonly known as "The Animal Trilogy." "Since the first movie was successful," Argento claims in the same DVD interview, "I thought of making a trilogy, always putting the name of an animal in the title." This naming convention spawned a host of imitators exemplified in the titles of *gialli* such as Paolo Cavara's *Black Belly of the Tarantula* (1971) and Lucio Fulci's *Lizard in a Woman's Skin* (1971). In each of these films the title has thematic or narrative relevance that is not immediately obvious, but the titles' significance is not always the same. Unlike *The Bird with the Crystal Plumage, The Cat o' Nine Tails* does not refer to the clue that thwarts the film's psychological threads; instead it refers to all the film's threads taken together. It derives from a conversation about the film's mystery between the protagonists Franco Arno, a blind former journalist who is now a puzzle maker, and Carlo Giordani, a journalist:

GIORDANI: Nine leads to follow. It's a cat with nine tails.
ARNO: A cat of nine tails, like the old naval whip. If we could just latch on to one of those nine tails, we'd be on our way to solving the puzzle.
GIORDANI: Yeah, but which one?

The mystery begins with Arno and his niece Lori overhearing a snippet of conversation about blackmail. Arno uses Lori as his eyes, telling her to observe the people they overhear. The scene transitions to a robbery at the Terzi Institute for Genetic Research. Not long after, a scientist from the institute is pushed in front of a train, and a photographer takes a picture just as it happens, providing a clue that gets him killed. The investigation ends up involving five scientists, one daughter of the top scientist, one fiancée of another scientist, one set of missing photographs, and one robbery—5 + 1 + 1 + 1 + 1 = 9—which somehow reminds Giordani of a severely deformed feline, which makes Arno think of a whip common in naval history as well as in contemporary fetish clubs.

Arno probably does not intend to evoke the sexual connotations of a cat o' nine tails, and since the titular phenomenon never reappears, the connotation is never explored. However, the whip's connection to illicit sexuality makes its name more apt as a title than the bird from Argento's previous effort because the majority of the mystery's nine threads involve some sort of sexual aberration. Significantly, one thread expands on an interest that appears briefly in *The Bird with the Crystal Plumage*. On his *Bird* DVD commentary, Alan Jones notes that "Dario always said he would make a complete thriller with just nothing but homosexual characters in it." *Bird* only goes as far as the pervert lineup, the gay antique dealer, and the killer's first victim, about whom the antique dealer in passing mentions, "It was said that she preferred women." *Cat* goes further into the gay world, leading Giordani into a gay nightclub so that he can meet with one of the five scientists, Professor Braun. For the handsome straitlaced hero, the meeting is quite awkward. The camera follows his slow journey through the club, capturing drag queens, a man applying face makeup, gay friends casually touching one another, and other spectacles that seem like part of the setting's quotidian reality despite their extreme rarity in mainstream society—especially mainstream cinema—in 1971.

Giordani exhibits unflappable poise as he delves into the world that his (and the camera's) lingering gaze marks as alien. He seems only mildly uncomfortable when Professor Braun flirts with him: "You know you have very beautiful eyes." An instant before Giordani tenders his gracious reply, "You really think so?" a cut leaps over the scene's axis of action, changing the camera angle by 180 degrees and reversing the positions of the two men on screen. One moment has Giordani in control, pursuing a potential suspect, and then a compliment reverses the relationship, putting Braun in the position of aggressor as he says, "Blue with a touch of red. Very rare." When Giordani identifies himself as a reporter, another cut restores the men to their previous positions, and Braun rises to leave. The context makes Braun's impulse to flee a reporter implicitly understandable: a gay scientist would not want public attention focused on his nightlife, which could damage his career. (Lest there be any doubt about gay men's fear of exposure, a later scene involves a man telling Giordani how to relocate Braun; the man says, "And for reasons that I won't trouble you with but which you can probably imagine, I prefer not to have dealings with the police," and then he explains that his young male lover left him for Braun.) Giordani tries to stop Braun's flight by grabbing his arm. A cut reverses positions again, and a young man rushes to Braun's aid, reminding Giordani that he is not in a place where he can assume control. Giordani backs off, Braun dismisses the young man, and the rest of the conversation unfolds in a standard shot/reverse pattern featuring one empowered speaker at a time. This sequence's editing calls attention to a minute drama of sexuality and power that resonates with the larger drama surrounding the mystery of the robbery and the murders that follow.

Braun's line about Giordani's eyes relates directly to the heart of that drama: as a scientist in the Terzi Institute for Genetic Research, Braun trades in genetic rarities, blue-with-red eyes and especially the aberrant XYY chromosomes that motivate the robbery and the murders. But Braun does not mention XYY—his connection to it only appears through his work at the Terzi Institute and through Giordani and Arnò's bundling of nine clues. The film's exposition of the (untrue, according to Argento) XYY phenomenon falls primarily to two characters, the as-yet-unrevealed killer, Dr. Casoni, and top-scientist Dr. Terzi's adopted daughter, Anna. Anna provides one of the first dead-end threads for the hero-team of Arno and Giordani to follow. Giordani goes to visit Dr. Terzi, and when he meets Anna, flirting begins immediately. They drive to a bar, where Anna starts giving her new beau information:

> ANNA: [Father has] taken on four research assistants, specialists in genetics. They're working on two parallel projects. One deals with a very revolutionary drug, and the other is a research program for the government. It's a highly confidential investigation into the chromosomal alteration known as XYY, which apparently indicates a criminal tendency in the individual. . . . It's already been brought into several criminal trials as an extenuating circumstance.

The drug, which later supplies the main topic of conversation for Giordani and Braun, is a red herring, but the "chromosomal alteration" relates to the killer.

But Anna does not establish that relationship. Instead she serves as both love interest and suspect, exciting the most suspicion when Giordani learns that she is in a sexual relationship with her adoptive father. The lack of consanguinity makes the incest only figurative, but the taboo nevertheless weighs heavily in Giordani's investigative ratiocination. The combination of incriminating sexuality and incriminating circumstantial evidence—Anna cuts herself on a broken vase, so she appears with blood literally on her hands just after Giordani wounds the killer, whom he of course does not see—prompts him to accuse her. She responds, "You petty, narrow-minded little reporter. You figured it all out, didn't you? A neat equation, Italian style: whore equals liar equals murderer. I thought I'd finally run into somebody reasonably civilized, but I was wrong." Anna's rebuke spells out for Giordani and the audience why this sexual prejudice is a dead end. Like Sam in *Bird*, Giordani makes a mistake because of his knowledge of "Italian-style" social conventions, and this time, the conventions are more than misleading: they are condemnable, "uncivilized."

The second source of exposition about the XYY phenomenon is Dr. Casoni, who is eventually revealed as the killer. During the robbery at the film's beginning, Dr. Casoni steals the files that would reveal his genetic abnormality, and to keep his secret he first pushes Dr. Calabresi, the scientist spotted by Arno and Lori at the beginning, under a train, and then kills a chain of others connected to the institute or to the photographer's unlucky capture of the Calabresi murder on film. When Arno gets too close to the truth, Casoni kidnaps Lori. Arno finally confronts Casoni after a chase that leads them to a tall building's rooftop. Casoni explains himself with James Bond–villain flair:

> CASONI: I had to do it. It wasn't my fault. Calabresi was the only one who knew I had the XYY triad. Me of all people! After all these years of research, I would have been ruined!
> ARNO: What have you done with my little girl? Huh? Speak up!
> CASONI: I broke into the lab and replaced my report sheet with a negative one. No one would ever have found out, but Calabresi knew, he knew, and he tried to blackmail me. I had to kill him, don't you see?
> ARNO: Never mind about that.
> CASONI: And then the others . . .
> ARNO: Never mind all that! Now tell me. What did you do with Lori?
> CASONI: I killed her.

Arno tells the killer and the audience to never mind about this last bit of XYY exposition—like the psychiatrist's diagnosis at the end of *Bird*, Casoni's explanation of his psychological motivation is irrelevant, and that irrelevance results in the dismissal of the entire XYY plotline. What finally leads Arno to the killer is Lori's kidnapping, not some convoluted plot about aberrant sexual characteristics, and his niece is all Arno and the audience should care about. Infuriated by Casoni's taunting claim about killing Lori, Arno pushes him down an elevator shaft. After Casoni's graphic death, the sound track plays Lori's voice shouting her nickname for Arno, "Cookie, Cookie!"

In the DVD interview, Argento comments on the ending: "The murderer that still wants to inflict pain and lies about killing the little girl. . . . I like this final ambiguity." The ambiguity of the ending is manifold. First, killing the killer, who at that point would be easily captured by police, thrusts Arno into moral ambiguity, which he shares with the alleged heroes of Argento's next three *gialli*, *Four Flies on Grey Velvet*, *Deep Red*, and *Tenebre*, as well as with the victim-turned-killer Anna Manni in *The Stendhal Syndrome*. Second, hearing Lori but not seeing her puts viewers in the same position as the blind puzzle maker, and the film's final line, "Cookie, Cookie!" could be an editorial amelioration of Arno's crime, a summoning of a dead girl's voice from Arno's memory to make the vigilante slaying seem just. Argento's reference to Casoni's statement as a lie disowns this possibility, which Maitland McDonagh calls "breathtaking and sadistic," but the film does not (69).

Neither does the film overtly disown the theory that XYY chromosomes "indicate a criminal tendency," as Anna Terzi claims. In fact, its storyline seems to support the link between XYY and criminality: Casoni is working on a project that demonstrates the link, he learns that he has the extra Y chromosome, and he resorts to criminal behavior to conceal his condition, ironically proving his own theory. The irony is more meaningful than tragic coincidence. Casoni's fear of what his own theory says about him leads him to kill. Having XYY does not necessarily *cause* criminality—correlation does not prove causality, so finding a correlation between XYY chromosomes and imprisonment for crimes does not really mean that the chromosomes *indicate* criminality—but the theory leads to the fear, and the fear leads to the crimes. While theories about sexual aberration lead nowhere in *The Bird with the Crystal Plumage*, they lead somewhere far worse in *The Cat o' Nine Tails*. The film does not argue that the genetic theory is incorrect (even though Argento says it is), but it does argue that the theory has bad results.

Four Flies on Grey Velvet

Bad science suggests the storyline for Argento's next *giallo* as well. Like *The Bird with the Crystal Plumage*, the title *Four Flies on Grey Velvet* refers to the clue that leads to the discovery of the killer. A detective explains:

> It's been recently discovered that the last image seen by the victim before death is retained for several hours on the retina. It's a very difficult procedure, but it is possible to photograph this image. Experiments carried out in Germany, the United States, and more recently Italy have had surprisingly good results. In some cases it's even possible to distinguish the murderer's face at the very moment he committed the crime.

The image retrieved from one of the film's final victims looks like four flies on a velvet background, and when the protagonist, Roberto, notices that his wife, Nina, wears a very strange necklace that contains a fake fly, he solves the mystery. Onscreen visual reasoning leads him to conclude that the victim's eye captured one fly on a dangling necklace four times, like a piece of film exposed four times to a single moving object. Nina is therefore the killer.

Pseudoscience thus provides a baroque clue to one of Argento's most baroque, convoluted mysteries. *Four Flies* opens with a sequence that contains intercut images of Roberto playing the drums with his rock band and being spied on by an unknown stalker, Carlo. Along with these images appear the credits and one of Argento's most bizarre stylistic flourishes: an image of a beating heart that first appears next to the title, then against a black screen, and then beside more credits. Juxtapositions suggest that the realistic-looking heart represents Roberto's mounting anger at the stalker; rapid drumming underscores the pounding tension. In a shot of the band rehearsal, a fly lands on the rim of a drum, and Roberto almost squashes it with a drumstick. Next the fly crawls between Roberto's cymbals (figure 3), and the scene cuts to Roberto eyeing the stalker, who is tailing him, in his car's rearview mirror (figure 4). Editing and cinematography create a metaphoric relationship between Roberto's connection to the fly and his connection to Carlo. In the shot of the band rehearsal, the fly appears between the cymbals in the foreground, a potential victim of Roberto in the background. In the shot of the car's interior, Roberto is in the foreground, a potential victim of out-of-focus Carlo, whom the mirror places in the background. The camera tracks in toward the mirror, and then it decisively racks focus so that Carlo is now in the foreground of the image (figure 5). The scene cuts back to the rehearsal, where Roberto crushes the foregrounded fly and smiles (figure 6).

The fly shifts from being a metaphor for Roberto as a potential victim to being a metaphor for Carlo as a potential victim, and the shift reflects Roberto's desire to turn the tables on his pursuer, which he does in the next scene. He follows Carlo to a seemingly empty music hall, confronts him, and in a brief struggle, seems to kill him. The killing of the fly represents the fulfillment of Roberto's wish to slay his stalker, a wish that he seems to fulfill in reality.

During the struggle with Carlo, a person in a strange mask, later revealed as Nina, takes photographs from a high position in the music

3

4

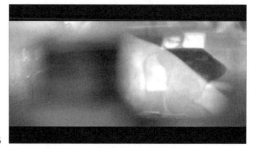

5

Figures 3–6. In
*Four Flies on Grey
Velvet,* intercut
scenes reverse the
relationship between
stalker (Carlo, played
by Calisto Calisiti,
visible in figure 5) and
prey (Roberto, played
by Michael Brandon,
visible in the other
three images).

6

hall. Nina's voyeurism prefigures Inspector Santini's in *Opera*, but her motivation is anything but erotic desire for the object of her murderous gaze. Nina uses the photos not to blackmail Roberto, as their appearance in the apartment he shares with her suggests, but to make him *think* he might be blackmailed; the singular aim of her scheming is to torment and destroy him. Twists and turns eventually reveal that Carlo did not die at Roberto's hand; Nina set up the encounter to make Roberto feel the torments of believing he has killed a man. To cover up her scheme, she eventually kills her maid Amelia, her accomplice Carlo, and a private investigator, Gianni Arrosio. The power struggle and wish fulfillment dramatized in the intercut scenes of drumming and stalking turn out to be shams, as irrelevant to what is really going on as any of the thwarted threads in Argento's previous films.

Four Flies' blackmail-and-cover-up scenario is a red herring, and it keeps Roberto from recognizing that he, like Sam Dalmas, is dealing with someone who exhibits what a psychoanalyst might describe as classic signs of perverse identification and sexuality. During the film's final confrontation between killer and hero, Nina shares Casoni's inclination for villainous exposition, but Roberto does not share Arno's disinterest. He hangs on every word as he struggles to understand his psychotic wife's desire to torment him:

> NINA: I want so badly to see you die slowly, painfully.
> ROBERTO: Why?
> NINA: Why? Because you're so much like him . . . my pig father. . . . Did you know he brought me up as a boy? He felt cheated because he had a girl, so he treated me like a boy. And he beat me, he beat me! *For years. He was capable of everything. But I let him down. I didn't react like a man.* He said I was crazy. My mother, she died in an asylum. He put me there too. Three whole years. *Do you know what the doctors said? They said I was insane. That I was a poor crazy. A maniac. How could they know all I had suffered? I didn't have time to get revenge because he died before . . . he died before I could get out. Before I could kill him. I had to find someone else who could pay for him. For everything he had done to me. I have to revenge myself. And I found him.* When I met you, I couldn't believe it. It was like a miracle. You were just like him. I knew I'd kill you.

Interestingly, the English sound track of the Mya/Ryko DVD switches to subtitled Italian for the lines italicized above, indicating that those lines were cut from the original English-language release, so an English track was either never recorded or not preserved. Such language switching is even more prominent in the Blue Underground DVD of *Deep Red,* which restores more than twenty minutes of footage from the Italian- to the English-language release. In *Four Flies,* these omissions suggest that the original distributors doubted the English-speaking public's appetite for psychological elaboration, which only delays Nina's just deserts.

What they omitted, however, is an efflorescence of the dark humor that runs throughout the film. Like Casoni's confession, Nina's confession foregrounds a terrible irony: she acts like a maniac because people treated her like a maniac. The moment does not necessarily play for laughs, but when Nina says, "How could they know?" about the doctors claiming she was a maniac, the audience has a golden opportunity to think something along the lines of, *By paying attention to the things you say and do.* At a distance, the reasoning behind her elaborate scheme—since she missed out on killing her father, she planned to marry a man who resembled him, torment her husband with the guilt and paranoia of murder and blackmail, and then kill him—is absurd enough to be laughable.

Argento's sense of humor in *Four Flies,* which does not appear again so pronouncedly until his two contributions to the *Masters of Horror* television series, *Jenifer* (2005) and *Pelts* (2006), finds its greatest outlet in the character of Godfrey, a.k.a. God, who serves as Roberto's adviser for dealing with his murder-and-blackmail conundrum. When Roberto first goes looking for him, he finds a man, nicknamed the Professor, lying in a hammock, and the puns begin:

> ROBERTO: Do you know where God is?
> PROFESSOR: You surprise me, brother. God is here, he's there, he's everywhere. And he's fishing down by the river. Hey, buddy, you got a hundred lira to spare?
> ROBERTO: I got fifty. [Calls toward the river] God! [Cue music: "Hallelujah!"]
> GOD: Godfrey . . . if you're gonna call me God, call me God Almighty.

Luigi Cozzi, one of Argento's longtime collaborators and the author of *Giallo Argento*, cleverly sums up the outcome of Roberto's relationship with God: "It's God who will eventually save him" (40). Taking the pun to the level of structure, God bursts in on Roberto and Nina's final confrontation *ex machina*, mere seconds after she refers to finding someone else to pay for her father's crimes. He shouts "Stop!" and gives Roberto an opportunity to knock the gun from Nina's hand.

Unlike God and the risible potential for allegory that he injects into the story, Nina's transgendered identification—forced on her by her father, as repeated flashbacks to childhood trauma show from the then-unidentified killer's perspective—is only solemnly ridiculous, even as her boy-short hairdo and masculine attire belie her refusal to accept her father's will. Nevertheless, the sexual confusion and boundary crossing that Nina inherits from Monica Ranieri refract through other aspects of the film that are far less serious. At a party that Nina and Roberto host, the sober concern the hosts express over their missing maid is completely undercut by a nearby friend telling an off-color joke:

> Come and listen to this story. "The Rape of Frankenstein." This Austrian psychiatrist is giving the baron the lowdown on why his monster is so bloodthirsty. It's because he's got no sex life. Libido frustration accounts for the homicidal impulse. The baron figures this headshrinker knows what he's talking about, so back to the lab. This time his monster's gonna have sex appeal. Unfortunately, the baron overdoes it, and the first thing the monster does is try to rape him. The baron escapes in the nick of time, but he's bugged by the thought, "Maybe his monster's queer." No way! Down in the village, the word is out. The Frankenstein monster will rape anything in sight. The local farmers scour the countryside. And so does the local schoolmarm. Not a day over seventy, she rips off her bra and panties and rushes out, more willing than able to sacrifice herself for the sake of science.

A cut back to Roberto engaging in a separate conversation denies the audience the punchline, but not before the jokester has summoned a host of resonant allusions. *Frankenstein*, of course, is the horror genre's most hallowed critique of scientific ambition. Significantly, the science targeted for critique in this reworking of the classic is that of the "head-shrinker," the psychiatrist, who, along with other purported experts on things sexual, is condemned to irrelevance in the first two films of Argento's Animal Trilogy. On top of the *Frankenstein* allusion, the story of "The Rape of Frankenstein" comes from the novel *Toi, Ma Nuit*, by Jacques Sternberg, which expresses the author's "disgust with *all* cinema" while offering a "mass-elite critique of popular culture" (Sconce 274). Thus the joke and its teller also reflect on the clash between Argento's art-house sensibilities and the sensibilities of the *giallo*'s primary audience. As Mikel Koven claims, "This genre was never intended for the art house, but for the grind house" (19).

The titular rape of Frankenstein would be a homosexual encounter, making Frankenstein think—until he discovers what Freudians might call his monster's polymorphous perversity—"Maybe his monster's queer." The specter of queerness raised in this joke appears throughout the film. A review posted by S. J. Sondergaard on both Amazon .com and the Internet Movie Database claims that Argento originally intended for Roberto to be gay; if that is the case, then the only visible scrap of that intention is Roberto's somewhat androgynous appearance, which matches well with the early-seventies androgyne chic of most of the leading characters (McDonagh 81).

The film does not offer a gay lead, but it does feature the most prominent gay character in the unusually large population of gay people who appear in Argento's films. Gianni Arrosio, the private detective Roberto hires to help him figure out who is persecuting him, is neither shy about his sexuality nor hesitant to correct the prejudices Roberto draws from social conventions. When Roberto first enters Gianni's office, he sees Gianni wearing an apron and painting the room, broadcasting effeminacy. Roberto mentions that he had come in search of a detective to help him with a problem, and then he tries to back out:

> ROBERTO: It's a bit risky, and I don't . . .
> GIANNI: And you're thinking this fairy is going to jump up on a chair and scream bloody murder if he sees a mouse, huh, right?
> ROBERTO: Yes, that's what I thought.
> GIANNI: [Flapping a limp wrist at Roberto] Oh, you heterosexuals! I don't suppose you've ever had a homosexual experience?
> ROBERTO: Let's forget it, man.
> GIANNI: Yes, we are men too, you know, just a little different.
> ROBERTO: That's very comforting.

Gianni's first line in this part of the exchange describes the conventional prejudice, which Roberto confirms. In a move that echoes the power struggle between the journalist and the scientist in *The Cat o' Nine Tails*, Gianni turns the tables on psychoanalytically supported heterosexism, first by referring to heterosexuals as a pathetically wrongheaded class of people ("Oh, you heterosexuals!") and then by pointing to a conventional prejudice that gay men have about straight men: very few people in the straight category live their entire lives without going crooked at least once. Roberto does not deny this prejudice, and Gianni graciously lets the subject go, creating equilibrium between them by restoring the "little" difference that separates gay from straight, the difference that the gay man's prejudice would erode. Gianni's behavior is funny, but his sexuality is not. Ultimately, what is most funny about Gianni is his failure to solve any of the eighty-four cases he has worked as a detective. He does solve Roberto's case, but Nina kills him before he can report his triumph.

Through Gianni, *Four Flies* continues a rhetorical response to the psychoanalytic (mis)classification of perverts that runs through the queer characters of Argento's first two *gialli*. Like the earlier films, *Four Flies* compounds this critique with another shot at scientific reasoning, this time aimed at what is arguably psychoanalysis's most revered area of authority: dream interpretation. In *The Interpretation of Dreams*, Freud famously asserts that the heart of every dream is the fulfillment of a wish. Roberto has a dream that recurs several times in the film; it visualizes a story he overhears about an execution by decapitation of a criminal in Saudi Arabia. At this point in the film, Roberto still thinks he is guilty of murdering Carlo, so the dream seems to be at once an expression of his anxiety about getting caught and a fulfillment of his wish to receive just punishment as an end to the guilt he feels over his crime. The psychoanalytically inflected dream adds depth to Roberto's character, but like Sam's flashbacks in *The Bird with the Crystal Plumage,* and like Roberto's own wish fulfillment dramatized in the opening sequence's intercut power struggle of drumming and stalking, the wish at the dream's core has no substantial connection to the mystery's solution: the titular four flies, like the titular bird, render the dream irrelevant as they lead to the revelation that Roberto has no real guilt to punish. Furthermore, as several other critics have noted, the dream's greatest significance stems from its foreshadowing of the film's final violent death, Nina's decapitation in a car accident. Ironically, then, the dream does not reflect punishment for Roberto's guilt but for soon-to-be-revealed Nina's. The great truth of the dream is prediction, not psychoanalytic interpretation.

The dream's premonitory quality goes against Freud's rejection—articulated at great length in *The Interpretation of Dreams*—of superstitious dream theories that preceded his own, and it sets up the film's most elaborate visual moment. Nina's decapitation occurs in slow motion; Argento used a special camera to capture the effect at one thousand frames per second. The spectacle begins when Nina slams into the back of a truck, and as the car continues forward, the truck's high bed shears off the car's top. The windshield explodes, and in Nina's point of view the truck looms closer. Her head gets severed and rolls out onto the street. The car explodes, and the frame freezes, abruptly ending the film. Spectacle, not psychoanalysis, gets the final word in *Four Flies on Grey Velvet*, and the closing emphasis on spectacle underscores the title's significance. In one sense, the title refers to the theory that leads to Nina's discovery, the theory that has the human eye capturing images on the retina like a camera captures images on film. Because the eye/camera captures Nina's swinging fly necklace through multiple exposures of the same retinal film, the image that police get from one of Nina's victims looks like four flies on grey velvet. The titular velvet could also refer to the use of velvet in photography more generally, noted in the synonym for camera that provides the title for the film journal *The Velvet Light Trap*. Argento's title, then, not only refers to the eye-provided clue that solves the mystery but also to the camera's eye, aligning his work with the self-referential tradition of horror noted by Carol Clover and others.

The significance of the dream, which foreshadows the film's most elaborate visual moment, and the significance of the title, which casts *Four Flies* as a reflection on film as an ocular medium, combine. Together they make the act of viewing, rather than the act of psychoanalytic interpretation, the most significant—and perhaps the only—source of truth in the film. *Four Flies* thus solidifies the dismissal of psychoanalysis begun in *Bird* and anticipates the turn away from psychoanalysis as the key to filmic meaning that David Bordwell, Noel Carroll, and other film theorists took more than two decades later. It also begins to articulate what *Deep Red*, generally acknowledged as one of Argento's two greatest masterpieces, demonstrates in full: aesthetic experience, not psychoanalysis, genetics, forensics, or any other science, is the authoritative source of meaning in film and in life. Spectatorship, which Argento's later films save from accusations of sadistic voyeurism, replaces psychoanalysis as the ne plus ultra of cinematic interpretation. In a sense, *Bird*'s Sam Dalmas does the right thing when he revels in repeatedly replaying the memory of his voyeuristic experience at the Ranieris' art gallery, but since he does it to uncover a repressed memory, he does it for the wrong reason. Similarly, the decapitation in Roberto's dream is not to be psychoanalytically interpreted but enjoyed as a companion to *Four Flies'* ultimate spectacle, the decapitation of Roberto's wife.

Deep Red

Deep Red develops this emphasis on aesthetics and spectacle through all of the film's elements, including the identities of its actors. Although Argento supposedly holds actors in low regard—several of his critics and collaborators suggest that ego issues arose between Argento and Tony Musante, who plays Sam in *The Bird with the Crystal Plumage*, which gave Argento's view of actors a negative tint ever after—Argento's choice of the actor to play *Deep Red*'s amateur detective, Marcus Daly, is highly significant. In fact, David Hemmings playing Marcus Daly is one of the most significant uses of casting in Argento's oeuvre, perhaps second only to his use of his daughter Asia in *Trauma* (1993) and *The Stendhal Syndrome*. In 1975, the year of *Deep Red*'s release, Hemmings was best known for playing Thomas in Michelangelo Antonioni's *Blow-Up* (1966), one of the most successful films by one of Italy's most revered auteurs. *Blow-Up* set the stage generally for Argento's subversion of narrative conventions, discussed at length in the next section, and specifically for his meditation on spectacle and spectatorship in *Deep Red*. *Blow-Up*'s Thomas is an affluent photographer who spends his time exploiting women on film and in the bedroom, living a lifestyle that exposes the decadence of London's art scene as well as the corruption of camera-enabled voyeurism. Taking pictures in a park on a sunny day, Thomas accidentally captures details of what he thinks might be a murder. He becomes an amateur detective like the artist-detectives in Argento's *gialli*, blowing up his pictures larger and larger to determine whether strange blobs on the film reveal in one instance a gun-wielding assassin and in another a dead body. Thomas's efforts lead nowhere, leaving the mystery unsolved and the status of perception, both the human eye's and the camera's, in a mire of subjective uncertainty.

The uncertainty surrounding what Thomas really sees in *Blow-Up* directly parallels the uncertainty surrounding what Marcus really sees in *Deep Red*. Like Sam in *Bird*, Marcus walks down a Roman street at night and witnesses an act of bloody violence. The victim is Helga Ulmann, a psychic already shown detecting the presence of a murderer in an audience come to observe her abilities. As Marcus passes her apartment, she presses her face against the glass of a high window, screaming for help. From behind, someone strikes her with a meat cleaver, and she crashes through the glass, which slices her throat in gory close-up. Marcus runs to her rescue and arrives too late to save her, but like Sam, he later thinks he has seen something that could be crucial to the investigation. His fixation on the memory prompts his amateur sleuthing, and like Sam's, Marcus's memory finally does no good, as he recalls what he has seen—the killer's face reflected in a mirror, which he mistook for one of Helga's bizarre paintings of faces that evoke Edvard Munch's *The Scream*—just in time for the killer to reveal herself and attack.

Deep Red's use of the memory motif from *Bird* stands alongside yet another Freudian problem with gender, sexuality, and identification that surrounds the hunt for the killer. These and other repetitions of elements from earlier Argento films—painting again takes a central role in the mystery, as well as another flashback to a childhood trauma—help to situate *Deep Red* within the *giallo* tradition and to ossify Argento's contributions to *giallo* conventions. They also mark *Deep Red* as the culmination of the filmmaker's responses to a set of problems with the authority of psychoanalysis and of science more generally. By repeating plot points and character types as well as various visual strategies, such as the editing of the scene at the gay club in *The Cat o' Nine Tails* and the intercut scenes of drumming and stalking in *Four Flies on Grey Velvet*, Argento's films present, deploy, and improve rhetorical methods for exposing the weaknesses of psychoanalytic and other scientific claims. His aesthetic patterns ultimately suggest aesthetics themselves as the authority to replace the authorities critiqued; they become a rhetoric that is ready to be adapted and redeployed in other films.

Argento does not deny his films' rhetorical repetitiveness. In fact, he emphasizes his use of repetition, explaining in an interview on the Blue Underground DVD of *Deep Red* that contrary to the beliefs of many, the film does not introduce new dimensions to the *giallo* tradition. "*Deep Red* may appear to be a more violent and bloodier film," he says, but "this is not true because the film was a nightmare, so all the facts were exaggerated; all these facts were present in my other films." One could quibble about whether calling violent elements "exaggerated" amounts to admitting that the film is, in fact, more violent and bloodier, but more important here is noting Argento's self-consciousness about repetition, repetition with the significant difference of exaggeration. *Deep Red* is not *new*; it is simply *more*.

The exaggerated, nightmarish quality of *Deep Red's* violent set pieces stems from their extended lengths and their magnification of everyday incidents into life-ending mutilations. Helga's death scene begins when she hears faint, strange notes of children singing "la-la-la," and it escalates through rapid splices of quick tracking and asymmetrical still shots of her flamboyantly decorated apartment (in which the Munch-like images join a gargantuan menorah and Star of David that emphasize her Jewish identity). The scene hits a high when the killer bursts through the front door, which leads to multiple close-ups of the killer's cleaver rending Helga's flesh. The brutality is interrupted by a cut to Marcus and his friend Carlo conversing in the street, picks up again when Marcus sees Helga through the window, and finally ends when Marcus lifts Helga's body from the shards of the window where she is impaled. The sequence takes about seven minutes from the first notes of the creepy la-la-la children's music that announces the killer's arrival to the final shot of blood dripping from the mouth of Helga's corpse.

The most gruesome aspect of Helga's murder is not the flesh-rending cleaver, which somehow transformed into a hatchet and spawned the title for the film's American release, *The Deep Red Hatchet Murders,* but the skin-slicing glass of the broken window. While few people are familiar with the sensation of being hacked by a meat cleaver, many have been cut by sharp glass, so what finally dispatches Helga is an exaggerated form of a relatable experience. Similarly, when Professor Giordani, Helga's colleague and Marcus's sleuthing partner, meets his bloody end during four grueling minutes of violence, the most squirm-inducing moment is likely not the blade that stabs him in the neck but the repeated slamming of his mouth into the sharp corners of his fireplace mantle and his hard wooden desk. Argento's cowriter, Bernardino Zapponi, explains in an interview on Blue Underground's *Deep Red* DVD:

> We started to write the story, looking for all the essential elements that would be scary. For example, if someone gets shot by a gun, there are very few people that can relate to that sensation or experience. But if we stick someone's head in the middle of boiling water, it's a sensation that everyone's had—almost everyone's burnt themselves with hot water. For example, when someone bumps into a sharp corner, it's a sensation that everyone's experienced.

The film's status as nightmare dilates familiar dangers of broken glass and bumpable objects into specters of gruesome death.

Gruesome violence is not the only source of *Deep Red*'s nightmarish exaggeration. As in *Four Flies,* Argento begins *Deep Red*'s onslaught during the credits, which appear slowly on a black screen accompanied by major themes from the sound track by Goblin, the band Argento assembled and used for this film and a few others. After Argento and Bernardino Zapponi's writing credit disappears, Goblin's music fades out, and the creepy la-la-la children's music fades in along with a floor-level shot of a bright room decorated with a Christmas tree. A scream resounds as a shadow on a wall stabs another shadow repeatedly with a butcher knife. The bloody knife falls in front of the camera, and the kneesock-clad legs of a child (sex indeterminate) step into the frame, stopping just beside the knife. The scene fades out, and the credits and Goblin score fade back in as if the interruption has not occurred. Since this scene is a childhood trauma that plays an integral role in *Deep Red*'s convoluted mystery narrative, it is not truly random; the interruption of the credits suggests the force with which the past trauma is reasserting itself in present events. The interruption makes an argument: if the trauma the scene depicts is powerful enough to disrupt the credits, it is certainly powerful enough to motivate murder. Nevertheless, the scene's initial appearance lacks all context, so on a first, uninformed viewing, it plays as a random violation of the convention of opening credits, a convention that has seldom, if ever, been so violated.

Read within the context of the rest of the film, the interrupting scene makes sense as the return of a repressed childhood trauma, a notion Freud explains in his essay "The Uncanny." Another bit of creepiness that Freud addresses in that essay is the uncanny feeling associated with dolls and automatons, which he claims stems from a child's fear that the inanimate will come to life, a child's wish that the inanimate will come to life, or both. Such creepiness appears when Amanda Righetti, a writer who knows too much about the killer's murderous history, finds a child's doll hanged in her apartment just before the killer murders her via submersion in boiling bathwater, and when Professor Giordani is accosted by a cackling automaton (which inspired the puppet used by the killer in the *Saw* series of American horror films) before his encounters with sharp corners and a knife. Similar creepiness appears just before Helga is attacked as well. Before the sequence begins, the camera slowly scans along a row of childlike objects that includes an ornate figurine, some colorful rope, some marbles, a miniature devil, and a miniature baby, the latter of which is selected from the array by *giallo*-gloved fingers. The camera then reveals the final items, knives, and cuts to an extreme close-up of eyeliner being applied beneath what context suggests is the killer's wide, staring eye.

The row of objects also includes crude hand-drawings of murder. Unlike the other items, which serve no narrative function beyond Freudian creepiness and therefore appear random, these drawings relate to revelations crucial both to the plot and to the psychological make-up of the killer, who, like Monica Ranieri, has aspects of her history revealed by art. Marcus becomes too interested in finding out who murdered Helga, so the killer goes after him, playing the creepy la-la-la children's music before whispering menaces of death. For the musician, the children's music provides an irresistible clue, so he tracks down the song and learns from a book by Amanda Righetti that it is associated with a house some people think is haunted. He finds the house, in which he discovers a wall with a chip in its paint that reveals a child's drawing underneath. After using some nearby broken glass to chip away more paint, he sees what looks like a depiction of the scene of childhood trauma: in front of a Christmas tree, a child holds up a bloody knife, and a man nearby gushes blood from a gaping wound. When Marcus leaves, more paint falls from the wall, revealing more of the drawing—a third person in the scene—and showing that Marcus literally does not have the whole picture (figure 7).

Marcus returns to the house later and finds a secret room hiding a man's decomposed corpse, but he never sees the third person in the drawing, so he never gets the clue indicating that the long-ago murder involved more than the child and the victim. He has enough clues, however, to react when he sees a similar drawing in the possession of the creepy daughter (she likes putting lizards on pins and watching them squirm) of the house's caretaker. The creepy girl admits that she took the drawing from the archives of her nearby school, which Marcus and his love interest and partner-in-sleuthing, the journalist Gianna Brezzi (played by Daria Nicolodi), soon visit. There Marcus finds another drawing, and it bears his friend Carlo's name. Carlo drew the pictures, so the trauma depicted must be his. Marcus concludes that Carlo is the killer.

The drawings that represent Carlo's traumatic childhood are not the only clue that point toward Carlo as the murderer. The drawings are compelling because they show that he has a trauma worth repressing that could very well return as a murderous impulse, and thus they compound another according-to-Freud problem that Marcus discovers earlier in the film: Carlo is homosexual, and as Robin Wood and Harry Benshoff demon-

Figure 7. In *Deep Red,* Marcus discovers a hidden drawing that depicts the childhood trauma shown during the film's opening credits.

strate, cinematic history suggests that homosexuals are monsters (and vice versa). The conclusive revelation of Carlo's sexuality occurs after Marcus visits the house Carlo shares with his mother, who tells him that Carlo has gone out with "someone called Ricci." Ricci turns out to be a man in drag (played, however, by a woman, Geraldine Hooper), and drunken Carlo is more than a little distressed to be found out: "Good old Carlo," Carlo says, "he's not only a drunk but a faggot as well. Surprise, surprise!" Although he displays a discomfort level comparable to that of the valiant journalist having a tête-à-tête with Dr. Braun in *The Cat o' Nine Tails,* Marcus looks neither surprised nor upset. The strong feelings lie completely on the side of Carlo, who in his drunken depression suggests that he wants to die. As *Bird* and *Cat* demonstrate, being gay is enough to incite suspicion of murder, and the line between suicidal and homicidal is as thin as the line between homosexual and homicidal. Add to the combination of suicidal with homosexual tendencies a childhood trauma as significant as murder, and the recipe for a killer queer is enough to seem as complete as Marcus takes it to be when he finds Carlo's drawing.

Deep Red does not directly address Carlo's sexuality until he calls himself a "faggot," but it begins his characterization as a homosexual prior to his self-hating rant. The signs accumulate when Carlo's mother, Marta, answers the door for Marcus, and the exchange that follows is not unlike one boy asking another's parents whether a friend can come out to play. Marcus asks for Carlo, and Marta calls upstairs before she realizes, "What was I thinking—my boy's gone out!" She then prattles on about her glory days as a movie star. Referring to Carlo as a "boy" infantilizes him only slightly less than the pronoun "my." Not only does Carlo, a grown man, live with his mother, but she still thinks of and treats him as a boy, *hers,* and of course she knows that he has gone out and even has the address for where he has gone. The relationship recalls Norman Bates's proclamation, "A boy's best friend is his mother"; the two are close, perhaps problematically close, and in casually revealing this closeness, Marta seems to reveal plenty of what a Freudian psychoanalyst would recognize as causal factors for homosexuality. Freud explains the etiology in his book *Leonardo da Vinci*:

> In all our male homosexuals there was a very intensive erotic attachment to a feminine person, as a rule to the mother, which was manifest

in the very first period of childhood and later entirely forgotten by the individual. This attachment was produced or favored by too much love from the mother herself, but was also furthered by the retirement or absence of the father during the childhood period. . . . Deeper psychological discussions justify the assertion that the person who becomes homosexual in this manner remains fixed in his unconscious on the memory picture of his mother. By repressing the love for his mother he conserves the same in his unconscious and henceforth remains faithful to her. When as a lover he seems to pursue boys, he really thus runs away from women who could cause him to become faithless to his mother.

For Freud, a mother loving her son too much, or vice versa, can make a boy gay, and that seems to be precisely what has happened with Marta and Carlo. Just like Monica Ranieri, Carlo fits a classic Freudian profile, and thus he fits perfectly with preconceptions for a killer in the Norman Bates vein.

Except that Carlo is not the killer. Shortly after Marcus discovers the drawing with Carlo's name on it, Carlo arrives with a gun and says he will kill Marcus, who should not have "meddled." Police crash into the room, guns blazing, before any meaningful exposition can occur, and Carlo flees. He runs into the street, gets his leg caught on the back of a truck, is dragged screaming and bouncing off curbs for several blocks, and then, when the truck stops, his head is crushed by a speeding car. The case seems to be closed until Marcus realizes that he was having a conversation with Carlo at the very moment when the original attack on Helga occurred: Carlo *cannot* be the killer. Marcus goes back to Helga's apartment and has his memory of seeing the face of the killer—of Marta, Carlo's mother—replay just in time for Marta to confront him in a rage over the death of her son: "He was only trying to protect me! Carlo never murdered anybody. It all began such a long time ago." Instead of beginning an elaborate explanation like the ones provided by the killers in *Bird, Cat,* and *Four Flies,* Marta's "long time ago" line cues a flashback to the scene that interrupted the credits, this time from Marta's rather than Carlo's perspective. Carlo's father explains that Marta will be fine, he will take her back to the hospital, but she refuses to go and murders the father in front of his son, who looks on in shock as the knife falls at his feet.

Suddenly, Marta's prattle about her glory days becomes more significant. After referring to Carlo as "my boy," she explains, "When I first married Carlo's father, he made me give up acting, at the height of my career. Now it's all gone." This loss apparently destabilized her enough to require hospitalization, and although the film never directly states a causal relationship, it implies that the loss of her acting career combined with Marta's unwanted hospitalization to motivate murder. The mother/son relationship, like Monica and Nina's cross-gender identifications in *Cat* and *Four Flies,* may or may not have something to do with what her son has turned out to be. Freudian speculation about what causes perversion is more irrelevant than ever because Carlo's sexuality and Carlo himself have no direct connection with the murders. As Marta states, Carlo never murdered anybody: his mother did, and her insanity lacks other characters' elaborate Freudian justifications.

The flashback to Marta's perspective on the film's primal scene of murder is as close to explanation as *Deep Red* comes. Whereas Argento's earlier films provide verbal answers undermined by images, *Deep Red* provides only images, and the total abandonment of the verbal in favor of the visual completes Argento's transition to a rhetoric of aesthetic authority. After the flashback, Marta attacks Marcus, and their brief battle culminates in Marta's necklace getting stuck in the metal cage around an elevator shaft. The elevator car catches the necklace and pulls until Marta, like Nina before her, is decapitated, and as in *Four Flies, Deep Red* ends with a freeze-frame on a spectacle: a pool of Marta's blood in which Marcus sees his own reflection (figure 8). Credits roll over the image, beginning with a note to the audience, "You have been watching DEEP RED, directed by Dario Argento," a closing self-reference that is a hallmark of some of Argento's greatest films. The note reflects the audience's activity in the same way that the pool of blood, a metaphor for the entire film as a bloody spectacle, reflects Marcus. *Psycho* ends with a psychoanalytic explanation of what viewers have just seen, *Bird* ends with an explanation that mocks such explanation, and *Deep Red* foregoes end-of-film explanation entirely, emphasizing instead what for Argento is far more important than sense-making: the act of looking at a spectacle of violence.

This final replacement of psychoanalytic and other rationally grounded sources of explanation with an assertion of aesthetic engagement with spectacle as film's most important source of interest—its most *meaningful*

Figure 8. *Deep Red*'s final image shows Marcus
Daly (David Hemmings) staring at his own
reflection in a puddle of blood.

element, if "meaningful" can be divorced from the clarity or truth commonly associated with "meaning"—becomes *Deep Red*'s fulfillment of the mystery story's promise of revelation. Whereas *Psycho* replaces detectives with psychoanalysts as revelators, Argento's first four *gialli* take steps toward replacing psychoanalysts and other scientists with art and artists as revelators. *Bird* and *Cat* provide scientific revelations about their killers in their endings in order to dismiss them, *Four Flies* provides a scientific revelation of its killer's identity in order to overshadow the revelation's importance with a final fiery spectacle, and *Deep Red* provides no scientific revelation about its killer at all, closing instead with the spectacle of blood as the final message and the only viable means of understanding the film as a whole. Viewers have often complained that *Deep Red* and some of Argento's later films are hard to follow, that they do not make sense. These viewers are correct if they insist on looking for a detective, psychoanalyst, or other source of rational authority to appear at the end and explain how all the film's pieces fit into a meaningful interpretation. Such viewers would get their best answers from Argento's assertion that *Deep Red* is a dream, not in the Freudian way that would have dreams' excessive nonsense reduced to kernels of wish-fulfilling, interpretable sense, but in a way that would view a dream as a series of exaggerated images that may or may not be connected to one another according to consistent chains of cause and effect.

Continuing his exploration of films as dreams that do not need rational, interpretable motivation, Argento left the *giallo* after *Deep Red* to create supernatural tales of witchcraft in *Suspiria* and *Inferno,* his most visually sumptuous films. The next section of this essay takes up Argento's use of the supernatural to create irrational narratives that make his case for the primacy of aesthetic experience in the hierarchy of filmic meanings. These films go further toward this end than the *gialli* because the *giallo* is still a type of mystery, and thus it requires its detectives and revelations, however different those detectives and revelations might be from their traditional counterparts. Without these conventional elements, a film simply is not a *giallo,* so Argento's convention-defying trajectory naturally took him away from the genre that made him famous.

Tenebre

He did not stay away, however. Many of Argento's post-*Inferno* works qualify as *gialli,* but none better than *Tenebre,*[3] hailed as his return to form after the wild excursions of *Suspiria* and *Inferno.* Like *Bird, Cat, Four Flies,* and *Deep Red, Tenebre* features an amateur detective—another artist, this time a novelist. Self-reflexive elements run throughout Argento's oeuvre, making artists such as Sam Dalmas in *Bird* and Marcus Daly in *Deep Red* (with whom Argento has said he particularly identifies) potential stand-ins for the director. Michael Brandon, the actor who plays Roberto in *Four Flies,* even resembles Argento. Nevertheless, *Tenebre* is Argento's first film to feature a clear stand-in not only for artists in general but specifically for an artist known for creating violent art. This connection makes Peter Neal a cipher for Argento in ways that add layers of significance to dialogue, images, and events.

At *Tenebre*'s start, the successful novelist Peter Neal has written a *giallo*-style novel called *Tenebre,* just as the successful filmmaker Dario Argento has created a *giallo*-style film called *Tenebre.* As an Argento-like creator of violent fiction, Peter gets to respond to his genre's critics in a manner that anticipates, in a much gentler manner, the response Argento delivers via *Opera.* Meeting with reporters shortly after his arrival in Rome, Peter is ambushed by Tilde, a feminist reporter:

TILDE: *Tenebre* is a sexist novel! Why do you despise women so much?
PETER: Sexist? No, I don't think it's sexist.
TILDE: Women as victims . . . the male heroes with their hairy macho bullshit. How can you say it isn't?
PETER: What's the matter with you? You've known me for ten years, ever since you studied in New York. You know very well that I . . .
TILDE: Look, I'm talking about your work.
PETER: Well, I don't know, uh . . . would you like me to tell you I supported the Equal Rights Amendment?
TILDE: Okay, so then explain the books. Do you write to a fixed pattern, or do your publishers tell you that this kind of sexism sells copies?

At this point Peter's agent, Bullmer, interrupts, heading off what could be a public embarrassment by offering Tilde a separate interview. After Bullmer and Peter stand to leave, Tilde smiles, tugs at Peter's jacket, and says, "Hey, my mother was hoping you'd call." Peter responds with similar pleasantry, even complimenting Tilde on the interview's toughness. These two phases of Peter and Tilde's interaction, the first adversarial and the second congenial, suggest a layered response to those who call Argento's work sexist, misogynist, homophobic, and otherwise hateful: first, Argento disagrees with them, and second, he respects and even appreciates the sharp interest they take in his work.

Tenebre's rhetorical response to those who read Argento's work as hateful toward disempowered sexual groups is not always so gentle. Like Argento's first four *gialli*, the two *Tenebres*—the film and the novel within the film—focus a great deal of attention on perverts and perversion, and the film's critique of assumptions about perversion embeds a critique of simple-minded film critics. During the film's first murder sequence, the killer hisses "Pervert!" before using a straight razor to slash a woman first shown shoplifting a copy of the novel *Tenebre*. Because she offers sex to the store manager who catches her shoplifting to avoid being reported to the police, her perversion is figural if not literal prostitution. Literal prostitution gets caught up with Argento's favorite so-called perversion, homosexuality, when the film reveals trouble in the relationship between Tilde and her female lover Marion, who has sex with male clients in the home the two women share. The couple's deaths soon follow the revelation of their troubled romance, and just before he slashes Tilde with a razor, the killer again hisses, "Pervert, filthy, slimy pervert!"

This killer's concern with perversion echoes the concerns of killers from Argento's earlier films, and when *Tenebre*'s pervert-killer is revealed as Christiano Berti, another reporter who interviews Peter about his book *Tenebre,* it becomes part of the film's critique of Argento's simple-minded interpreters. Although Christiano presents himself as an ardent admirer of Peter's work, their conversation is just as adversarial as Peter's conversation with Tilde:

> CHRISTIANO: *Tenebre* is about human perversion and its effects on society, and I'd like to know how *you* see the effects of deviant behavior on our lives.
> PETER: Well first of all, it isn't just about that.
> CHRISTIANO: Two of the victims are deviants. The killer is try—
> PETER: Now wait a minute, who says they're deviants? One of them is gay, but so what? He's portrayed as perfectly happy. In fact, his relationship with . . .
> CHRISTIANO: The killer's motivation is to eliminate what he calls corruption.
> PETER: Now the killer is insane. What I mean by that is that the only aberrant behavior . . .
> CHRISTIANO: But what is aberrant behavior? [laughs] I was brought up a very strict Catholic, were you?
> PETER: Yeah, I guess so.
> CHRISTIANO: But I believe in abortion, I believe in divorce. That makes me aberrant from a strictly Catholic standpoint.
> PETER: I see. I thought this was an afternoon show. You really want us to get this heavy?
> CHRISTIANO: I guess not. It's just that I'm very interested myself.

This exchange makes Peter a mouthpiece for the critique of sexual norms that begins in *The Bird with the Crystal Plumage.* In Peter's view, gay people can be "perfectly happy," so homosexuality is not deviant, which sets up a definition of deviance and perversion that differs sharply from the definitions offered by psychoanalysts and also, as Christiano points out, by the Catholic church.[4] Disagreement over the definitions of perversion, aberration, and deviance foregrounds the cultural contingency of the broad category of "human perversion" and positions Peter, and through him Argento, as interested in dismantling cultural assumptions.

When Christiano points out that the killer in Peter's book targets "corruption," a word treated as a synonym for perversion, Peter's sensible response is that the killer is insane. At that moment Peter might not know that Christiano is the killer, but his characterization of his own book's killer applies equally well to the man interviewing him: Christiano has assumed the killer's motive from Peter's novel, and in doing so he has also assumed the killer's insanity. According to Peter/Argento, targeting homosexuals and others outside the cultural norm and regarding them as perverts are part of the same insanity as killing women with a straight razor. Christiano's assumption that Peter agrees with murdering so-called perverts is idiotic, just another part of his insanity, and thus Argento's film argues that equating the makers of violent art with the violent criminals that their art depicts is simply crazy.

Tenebre critiques simple equations of artists with the killers in their art, but it does not critique or dismiss *all* associations between artists and killers. Reading Peter as a diegetic stand-in for Argento becomes problematic at the film's end, when Peter is revealed as the murderer behind some of the film's most gruesome slayings. About two-thirds of the way through the film, Peter and his sidekick Gianni's pursuit of the razor-killer leads them to Christiano's house. Peter and Gianni separate, and Gianni witnesses Christiano being murdered with an axe. Since Christiano has destroyed the evidence of his guilt, including the straight razor he has used to kill, the police see him as just another victim. The murders that follow—of Gianni, Peter's agent Bullmer, and Peter's fiancée Jane—have a modus operandi that differs from the razor killings: Gianni is strangled in a car, Bullmer is stabbed on a bright city street, and Jane is axed in her apartment. The motives behind these murders, at least on the surface, are as different from Christiano's motives as the weapons used. Gianni dies because, like Sam Dalmas and Marcus Daly, he has witnessed something important that he cannot quite recall; this detail turns out to be Christiano telling Peter, who is about to murder him, that he is the razor-killer, so Peter's motive is self-protection. Bullmer and Jane are having an affair, so Peter's motive for killing them is jealousy. Peter's motives are revealed when Detective Germani, the lead investigator on the razor-killer case, finally catches up to him:

PETER: [Laughing maniacally] When I realized Christiano Berti was the killer, and it didn't take me long to realize that . . . the rest, Mr. Germani, was like writing a book. A book!

GERMANI: The perfect revenge. The razor-killer was dead, but you wanted him to live on long enough to be blamed for the murder of your fiancée and her lover. The two people you hated most.

Unlike Christiano's story, which is a tale of horror and madness, Peter's story is classic *noir*: he kills his fiancée and her lover for revenge, and he kills Gianni before the young man can remember enough to ruin the elaborate cover-up that Peter has plotted. The author might be like a killer in a book, but in light of these motives, he is not like the killer in the book *Tenebre*. If Peter is Argento's stand-in throughout the film, through him Argento seems to say teasingly that he might indeed kill people, just not because of the insane motives of the sexist, homophobic killers in his art.

This teasing refusal to exculpate artists completely becomes even more convoluted in light of flashbacks scattered throughout the film to a bizarre scene of a circle of teenaged boys on a beach engaging in sex play with a seductive woman (the scene recalls a similar moment in Fellini's $8\frac{1}{2}$). One of the boys slaps her, and she and the other boys punish him: the other boys hold him down while she violates his mouth with the high heel of a red shoe. Like those in *Bird, Four Flies,* and *Deep Red,* this flashback repeats with a little more information each time. The final, crucial piece of flashback information appears after Jane receives a pair of red shoes as an anonymous gift and, while wearing them, meets a spectacularly gory end. A shot of her body jolted by a blow from the axe to her off-camera midsection fades to an extreme close-up of an eye, which fades to a first-person sequence in which the woman from the beach scene is stabbed to death, violated by a knife in her midsection as an answer for the boy's violation by her shoe in his mouth. After he kills her, the boy takes her shoes, and the shot fades back to the eye close-up, which fades back to Jane's corpse, which apparently wears the very same shoes.

The phallic shoe/knife violations have heavy overtones of Freudian sexual trauma leading to fetishism, an aberration Freud describes as "the normal sexual object [being] replaced by another which bears some relation to it, but is entirely unsuited to serve the normal sexual aim" (*Three* 19). First a shoe, then a knife: in the flashbacks, both penetrate areas of the body associated with sexual activity, but neither is normal. When Detective Germani reveals that as a youth Peter was accused of killing a woman, intercut images of the woman from the beach confirm that the flashbacks have been scenes from Peter's past, experiences that suggest the psychological impetus behind Peter's present-day revenge plot. As a boy, he was traumatized by a fetishistic violation, so he took revenge on the woman who violated him with a fetishized form of murder. As a man, Peter is traumatized by the violation of his agent and friend Bullmer having an affair with his fiancée Jane. His first response is to violate Bullmer in a first-person sequence involving a knife to the midsection that directly mirrors the knife to the midsection received by the woman on the beach. His second response is to violate Jane, whose wearing of the red shoes equates her with the traumatizing woman from his past, with an axe to her midsection (and just about everywhere else). Perversely violated, Peter becomes a perverse violator. If Jane and Bullmer's infidelity is a type of perversion, his revenge makes him a perverse punisher of perverts. Perhaps Christiano was right about Peter's attitude toward perversion all along?

Maybe. The idea that Peter is ultimately a punisher of people outside of sexual norms gains support from Argento's casting of Eva Robins, who was born a male but developed female sexual characteristics in puberty, as the woman on the beach. When Detective Germani confronts Peter with his crimes, he calls him "completely mad" despite the apparently rational plotting of the "perfect revenge," so if Germani is right, Peter has even more in common with Christiano. *Tenebre* suggests this possibility but does not confirm it. As a result, the film provides both the exculpating claim that only idiots like Christiano think artists necessarily share the views of the killers in their art and the condemning possibility that *this* artist, Peter, who is at least sometimes a stand-in for Argento, does indeed share such views. If Peter might be Argento, and Peter might be a punisher of perverts, then Argento might be a punisher of perverts, too. The exculpation and the condemnation appear in suspension, contradicting without cancelling one another. Peter's psychoanalytically overdetermined backstory is so perfectly and heavy-handedly

Freudian that it verges on self-parody, but its status as the film's truth is as indeterminate as the film's ultimate position on the character of violent artists. Argento cannot be pinned down; no position in this film can be trusted.

Tenebre's ending graphically demonstrates the untrustworthiness of the artist and of art. After Peter kills Jane and a female detective, Detective Germani corners him and engages him in discussion of the backstory and revenge plot. Peter starts to cooperate with Germani's order to surrender, but he breaks away, brandishes a straight razor, and cuts his own throat. Germani and Anne, Peter's assistant (played by Daria Nicolodi), leave Peter's presumably dead body behind so they can call for police backup. Germani returns to the scene and finds Peter gone. On the floor where Peter's body has been lies the straight razor, which turns out to be fake, a prop that squirts blood from the blade. Shortly after the discovery that Peter has used a bit of cinema magic to deceive Germani and the audience, Argento's camera performs a similar trick (figures 9–11). In one moment, Germani's body, shown in medium close-up, fills the frame. When he bends down, Peter appears in the exact space he has occupied. Peter has been standing behind Germani, but the camera's angle has kept him hidden from the audience, so his appearance seems sudden, and a silence-interrupting chord reinforces the jolt that this suddenness delivers. When Germani stands back up, he hides Peter again until another camera angle shows Peter raise his axe and slam it into Germani's back. Different camera placement would have made the surprise of Peter's attack impossible from the audience's perspective, but the camera colludes with Peter, tricking the audience into sharing Germani's false sense of security. Ultimately, Argento's often-imitated visual trickery allies him with Peter the murderer, just as Argento's violent art allies him with Peter the novelist.

The deceptiveness that forms another bond between Argento and his onscreen stand-in suggests that finding meaning in art, especially in images, is always dangerous because of the way images frame truth, both literally and figuratively. This reflection on the dangerousness of art continues as the struggle between Peter and Germani knocks over a large sculpture that looks like a pillar of silver spikes. The sculpture falls against the apartment's front door, setting up the film's final link

Figure 9–11. In *Tenebre,* a shot demonstrates that Argento's camera cannot be trusted to show a complete picture: the angle helps a murderer (Anthony Franciosa) hide behind a detective (Giuliano Gemma).

of the problematic association between Peter and Argento to Argento's larger concerns about aesthetics. At this point in the film, both detectives have fallen; indeed, all but two of the film's notable characters are dead. Only Peter and Anne remain, and Anne is on her way back into the apartment where Peter waits, still holding the axe. As she tries to open the front door, which the sculpture blocks, Peter raises the axe, ready to kill her when she enters. Finally, she pushes the door hard enough to move the sculpture, which falls in the opposite direction, toward

Peter. It smashes into him, and one of its spikes breaks off and impales him against a wall, killing him slowly as Anne looks on, screaming. Her screaming continues so long that she seems to have gone mad. All that remains in *Tenebre* is screaming, which carries over a fade to black and into the scrolling credits.

Deep Red ends with its survivor staring into a pool of blood, figuring the *significance* of violent spectacle. In similar metaphoric form, *Tenebre* ends with its killer being killed by art while its survivor screams insanely, figuring the *dangers* of violent spectacle. As in Argento's earlier films, the psychoanalytically overdetermined backstory of *Tenebre*'s killer is irrelevant to the story's resolution, which instead emphasizes art, this time suggesting not only that aesthetic experience is meaningful for a violent spectacle's audience but also that it has the potential to push onlookers toward the madness of endless screaming. While on one level *Tenebre* defends violent art from the accusations of sexism and homophobia hurled by simple-minded critics like Tilde and Christiano, on a more fundamental level it depicts art as anything but safe, anything but a politically correct vehicle for good intentions or for consistent, interpretable critiques. The value of the aesthetic is the pleasure of looking at spectacle, but it is also respect for spectacle's power to present and critique meanings without any commitment to reliable or even accessible interpretation. Art is tricky, so it demands attention, and if viewers take anything for granted—such as the sole appearance of Germani in the frame signifying that he is the only thing of importance in the space that the frame represents, or Anne approaching the front door signifying that she is the only obstacle against the killer's escape—they risk a fatal error. Death by art actually bookends this film: the opening murder of the shoplifter stealing a copy of the novel *Tenebre* begins with the killer shoving pages of the book down her throat before he starts slicing her with the razor. If the aesthetic experience of spectatorship is the ne plus ultra, the truth that Argento's films offer to replace the truths of psychoanalysis, science, and reason, it is a truth that is untrustworthy, unpredictable, and, as *Tenebre* was titled for its diminished U.S. release, *Unsane*.

Unsane is not a bad title, but *Tenebre,* translated as darkness or shadows, fits better with the film's uncertainties and ambiguities as well as its emphasis on imagery, on the art that the title of Chris Gallant's 2000 book on Argento correctly names *Art of Darkness*. Argento's visual flair permeates *Tenebre*, perhaps most notably in a long tracking crane shot that precedes the murders of Tilde and Marion. The camera captures the lovers' quarrel and then tracks backward from Tilde, through a window, to the exterior of their massive asymmetrical home, a Brutalist design by the prominent Italian architect Sandro Petti (Cozzi 79) that looks like a collection of concrete slabs piled asymmetrically into a postmodern structure. From the window near Tilde, the camera climbs upward and to the left, along the concrete, past several shuttered windows, until it finds an unshuttered window with a clear view on Marion. Lingering on the furniture and other details of Marion's room, the camera seems to be on its way through the window and back into the house, but then it retreats to the exterior and climbs further up, to the roof. It goes over the roof, back alongside the building, then downward, past more windows, back to the ground floor.

Suddenly a pair of clippers appears, and the camera assumes the killer's point of view as he cuts his way through the shutters to attack Tilde. The fluid movement prior to this perspective, movement up and around the walls of a tall building, could not have been human—they were the camera's alone—but the camera enters the killer's perspective as easily as it glides through a window. After the clippers make way for the killer to enter, the long take (about three minutes, not long by "long take" standards, but since nothing happens during those minutes, they feel longer than 180 seconds) ends with a cut to Tilde standing in front of the window where the take has started. The killer ends up coming at her from the opposite direction, so while the long take has involved marvelous, acrobatic, and expensive continuity, the cut from the part of the long take motivated by the killer's perspective to the shot of Tilde by the window defies continuity. The *cut* returns to the point in space, the window, where the long take started, suggesting that the long take has formed a complete circle, but since the killer comes at Tilde from a different direction, the long take must have actually ended at a different point, a different window, which means the cut must actually have been spatially discontinuous. Taken together, the long take and the cut that ends it form a sequence of camera movements and perspectives that are both motivated and unmotivated, spatially connected and spatially disjoined. It is pure style, calling attention to the camera as an independent entity that requires no rationale beyond an appetite for images.

This self-consciously virtuosic sequence is one of many elements in *Tenebre* that continue Argento's career-spanning interest in film that calls attention to itself as film, an interest marked by the representations of voyeurism that run from *Bird* to *Opera* and by the artist-protagonists who fumble through almost all of his early films. Peter's fiction writing not only allows him to function as a layered cipher for Argento; it also allows him to discuss the plot of *Tenebre*, the movie he is in, as a work of fiction. He does not quite fit the postmodern mold of fictional characters who know they are fictional characters, but Peter does refer to the murders he commits as "like writing a book," and prior to this artsy confession, he discusses his own and Germani's investigations in terms of plotting a mystery. A conversation between Peter and Gianni provides the film's most noticeable wink at the audience: during their surveillance of Christiano's house, Gianni comments, "This is boring," and Peter answers, "All detection is boring. If you cut out the boring bits and keep the rest, you've got a bestseller." In addition to conveying a pithy formula for the entire mystery/thriller genre, Peter's answer describes what Argento has just done: the scene begins with Peter and Gianni climbing the fence and positioning themselves in Christiano's yard, cuts to Christiano destroying evidence, and cuts back to Gianni's complaint about boredom, which immediately precedes the two men getting what they are waiting for. Peter is talking about detection in print fiction, but his discussion of cutting makes his formula a fine gloss on how editing creates the successful *giallo* film.

While conversations that compare diegetic reality to diegetic and real-world fictions match the self-conscious dimension of the long take that builds up to Tilde and Marion's murders, two other scenes significantly share the long take's surrender of rational motivation in favor of an appetite for images. The first involves a vagrant who menaces the shoplifter and chases her home, where she breathes a sigh of relief just before the razor-killer strikes. The second involves a dog who menaces Maria, Gianni's girlfriend and an assistant at Peter's hotel in Rome, through a long chase that ends up at Christiano's house, where Christiano catches and murders her. Both of these scenes involve random threats from the outside world from which women flee to the insides of homes, where even greater threats await. The link between these scenes and the long take that precedes Tilde and Marion's murders is randomness—narrative and cinematographic elements disconnected from the context of the story that nevertheless climax in deaths that contribute to the story's core. Although McDonagh and others have remarked that *Tenebre* makes a lot more sense than many of Argento's films (164), these moments of nonsense are crucial to the film's atmosphere of terror, an atmosphere suggesting that the film's threats come not from specific murderers but from an innately and ubiquitously horrifying world (Koven 74). This suggestion is perhaps *Tenebre*'s clearest inheritance from Argento's previous two films, *Suspiria* and *Inferno,* which confound explanation in terms of conventional storytelling. Whereas Argento's first five *gialli* attack psychoanalysis, science, and other sources of reason as means of interpreting narrative, the Three Mothers trilogy—*Suspiria, Inferno,* and *Mother of Tears*—as well as *Phenomena* attack narrative itself, tearing apart the bones and sinew that conventionally allow storytelling to stand.

Against Narrative:
The Three Mothers Trilogy and *Phenomena*

Argento's early *gialli* are set in Rome, which appears not as the ancient city of the Colosseum, St. Peter's Square (the Vatican), and dozens of other landmarks recognized around the world, but as a modern city of tall buildings, concrete, and asphalt. It is recognizably Roman to people who know the city well but sufficiently nondescript for Argento's international audience to feel like it could be anyplace. As a result, American and British characters such as Sam Dalmas, Marcus Daly, and Peter Neal fit their surroundings as well as anyone, which is to say sometimes well and sometimes not at all, for the faceless crowds and endless concrete are as welcoming and alienating as any other modern metropolis (Koven 47). Indeed, one of the most recognizable places in the Rome of *Deep Red* is not Roman at all. Several scenes, including the scenes on the street that allow Marcus to witness and to solve Helga's murder, occur in and around the Blue Bar, which Argento fashioned as a near-replica of the bar in the American painter Edward Hopper's masterwork *Nighthawks.* The painting's loneliness and isolation reflect the situations of Italians and foreigners alike in *Deep Red*'s Rome, and the integration of this American work on a street that also features classical statuary highlights Argento's setting as a mélange of places and traditions as well as people.

This depiction transforms Rome from a city of precious antiquity to a city of aggressive modernity, so Rome becomes functionally placeless.

After citing an interview in which Argento describes *Tenebre*'s stark setting as a Rome of the near future, McDonagh observes that the film takes this erasure of place even further:

> It undeniably takes place in a Rome that has no past: there are no shots of the Colosseum, the Trevi fountain, classical statuary, Renaissance paintings or churches, or any of the architecture of centuries past that define "Rome." *Tenebrae* takes place in a city of dazzling white concrete, high-rise apartment buildings, malls, airports, television studios, and modern private homes; no baroque or rococo influence is permitted to sully the *mise-en-scène*, no superfluous ornament clutters its clean planes. It's all cool, stark, and slightly remote. (162–63)

Eschewing the architecture of centuries past does not equate to disinterest in architecture. *Tenebre*'s long take around the postmodern, Brutalist home of Tilde and Marion savors every inch of the bizarre structure, evoking comparisons of the building's incongruities with the distorted minds of the film's madmen.

Argento's camera may avoid locations easily recognizable as Roman, but from *The Bird with the Crystal Plumage* forward, it savors the shapes and patterns that architecture lends to the films' cinematic tapestries. In addition to the glass cage of *Bird*'s most famous set piece, Argento's directorial debut picks up many interiors and exteriors that enrich suspense and characterization. In the moments leading up to one of the razor-killer's most gruesome slayings, the camera shows the same stairway from both bottom and top, which creates a dizzying effect comparable to stairway shots in Hitchcock's *Vertigo* (1958) but also a striking geometric pattern that evokes the abstract expressionism of the painter Wassily Kandinsky as well as compositions by the classic film directors Robert Wiene and Fritz Lang, the latter of whom Argento has often cited as an important influence. *The Cat o' Nine Tails* offers a similar shot of a stairway, using a spiral instead of triangles as the geometric motif (figures 12–13).

The dizzying sublimity of such images provides a complement to the grotesque sublimity of the murders in the *gialli*. When in *Deep Red*

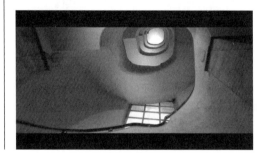

Figure 12–13. Shots of staircases in *The Bird with the Crystal Plumage* (top) and *The Cat o' Nine Tails* (bottom) demonstrate Argento's early interest in using architecture as a source of imagery that is geometric, abstract, and expressionistic.

Helga's expressions of agony join the paintings on her walls that evoke Munch's *The Scream,* and when in *Tenebre* Jane's severed arm sprays blood on the wall in a spatter that evokes Jackson Pollock's action painting, these images, too, are art, and they rely on setting to create their colorful effects. Stripping Rome of conventional Roman-ness allows Argento to use his city as a blank canvas for compositions that are allusive, elusive, and distinctly his.

Suspiria

Visual strategies that involve the camera picking apart architecture in ways that resonate with killers picking apart bodies reach their pinnacle in *Suspiria,* which is universally regarded as one of Argento's greatest accomplishments and which, largely because of its stunning imagery, appears again and again on critics' lists of the most frightening films of all time. While on the one hand *Suspiria* leaves the reality of specific places behind, creating a colorful, oneiric, fairy-tale world that contrasts sharply with the cold metropolitan spaces of the *gialli,* on the other hand it makes its specific location central to its plot and to its layers of visual and auditory significance. The film begins with credits made of elongated white letters against a black background; like the credits of Argento's previous film, *Deep Red*, the sparseness of this opening emphasizes the creepy score composed by the Argento-assisted band Goblin. Instead of interrupting the sparse credits with a scene of primal trauma à la *Deep Red*, *Suspiria* has a voiceover that begins just after the title appears:

> Suzy Banyon decided to perfect her ballet studies in the most famous school of dance in Europe; she chose the celebrated dance academy of Freiburg. One day, at nine in the morning, she left Kennedy Airport in New York and arrived in Germany at 10:40 P.M. local time.

This voiceover, the only overt narration in the film, not only identifies the upcoming setting as Freiburg, Germany, but it also specifies the city and the airport Suzy has left as well as the times of departure and arrival.

When the final credit disappears, a sound like the slam of a hammer brings with it the first shot: a sign in English and German that lists flights arriving from London, Rome, Rio, and New York. This list picks up where the voiceover left off, specifying places where the action is *not* while showing where the heroine is, the German airport. Then, when the camera tracks toward the door through which Suzy, played by the American actress Jessica Harper, will soon emerge, a subtle clue indicates the film's primary setting: a poster showing tall dark trees labeled "Black Forest." Another copy of this poster appears by the doors through which Suzy exits the airport and enters a dark and stormy night. She gets into a taxi and asks to go to Escher Strasse, a street named for yet another abstract artist who has influenced Argento's visual style. The cabdriver either has or pretends to have difficulty understanding Suzy's American accent, so the two repeat "Escher Strasse" several times, making the name difficult to miss. Although it does not appear right away, a wall in the dance academy features a painting very similar to the abstract work of M. C. Escher, contributing to the place's otherworldliness and reinforcing the allusion built into the academy's address. Place names overwhelm this film's first few minutes, highlighting the importance of place that is absent in Argento's early *gialli*. Argento's only film prior to *Suspiria* that puts so much emphasis on place is *Le Cinque Giornate*

(1973; a.k.a. *The Five Days of Milan*), a dark political comedy set during the 1848 revolt of the Milanese against Austrian control. Argento's only feature film outside the *giallo* and supernatural-horror genres, *Le Cinque Giornate* marked a retreat from the internationalism of the *gialli*, allowing Argento to speak directly to the Italian people about their own political history.

As an Italian film with an American lead actress and a German setting, *Suspiria* combines the internationalism of the early *gialli* with the national specificity of *Le Cinque Giornate* in a way that, according to Linda Schulte-Sasse, allows the film to reflect on the history of fascism that Germany and Italy share. This reflection on European political history, more or less absent in the early *gialli*, appears most pervasively in depictions of power.[5] The evil in *Suspiria* is the classic evil of the supernatural fairy tale: the female-dominated group of people who run the dance academy is really a coven of witches, and as such they represent what Barbara Creed calls the "monstrous-feminine," the threat of abjected female power to the patriarchal symbolic order (77). Helena Marcos, the superannuated Greek immigrant who is secretly the school's "Directress" and the coven's leader, is bent on victimizing the young, presumably because doing so somehow increases her power. The spells that she and the other witches cast work most often through implication rather than direct representation; two scenes in particular provide vivid demonstrations.

In the setup for the first of these scenes, Suzy refuses an offer of a room in the academy from Vice Directress Madame Blanc—played by the veteran actress Joan Bennett, known for her roles in Fritz Lang's *Scarlet Street* (1945) and the TV show *Dark Shadows* (1966–71). Suzy has already settled off campus with another student, and she prefers to stay there. Miss Tanner, Madame Blanc's right hand, remarks about Suzy's refusal, "I had no idea that you were so strong-willed. I see that when you make up your mind, nothing will change it for you." This line soon becomes ironic because the witches change Suzy's mind for her. In the next scene, Suzy walks through a hallway in the academy, and Goblin's creepy score announces the presence of evil as an ominous shot/reverse editing pattern connects her to a Gypsy-like servant. The servant stands with an evil-looking little boy, Madame's Blanc's nephew

Albert, and holds a piece of glass like a talisman. When the glass reflects a glaring light, the score's nondiegetic, rumbling, and barely comprehensible shout of "Witch!" suggests a spell being cast. Suzy grasps her head and neck as if she feels stifled, and in the following scene, she tries to dance but finds herself weak, unable to keep up with her fellow dancers' steps. Instead, she lolls about the rehearsal room like a puppet suspended from invisible strings. She collapses, and the witches take her into their care—into the very room Suzy has refused. The witches' invisible power thus carries out their will.

In the second of these scenes, a combination of sound and editing again makes invisible agency, in a sense, visible. The scene is set up when the blind pianist who accompanies the dancers' rehearsals, Daniel, crosses his demonic employers. His guide dog bites Albert, presumably because the dog has detected something amiss through the special sense that dogs often possess in tales of the supernatural (Cooper, *Gothic,* 158). Daniel defends his dog from accusations of viciousness, arguing that the boy must have done something to disturb the dog's gentle nature. In a fury, Miss Tanner fires him. Later, Daniel and his dog walk through a square composed of neoclassical structures. Schulte-Sasse explains that these buildings, which seem out of place "in the quaint, medieval crampedness of Freiburg," evoke the "neo-classical architecture Nazism privileged," and she argues the point through a convincing comparison of Argento's set with famous images from the Third Reich. The significance of her argument lies in a comparison of the witches' reign of terror, which consists of omnipresent surveillance implied by the camera's suggestions of invisible agency as well as elimination of anyone who deviates from the witches' opinions and worldview, with the Nazis' "systematic reign of surveillance and paranoia, a disciplining of the body and social behaviour (those punished in *Suspiria* are the ones with a 'strong will'), a process of selecting who belongs to the 'we' and elimination of who does not." Suzy's strong will makes her a target, and so does Daniel's. His walk through the fascism-evoking square leads to his death.

Sensing something amiss, Daniel and his dog come to a halt in the square, and sound cues the invisible agency's presence: the creepy score plays, the dog starts barking, Daniel shouts "Who's there?" and the score provides the nondiegetic, garbled answer, "Witch!" An editing pattern that juxtaposes extreme low-angle and high-angle shots of Daniel and the dog emphasizes the pair's terror while implying a presence on the rooftops of the neoclassical buildings (figures 14–15).

In one of the film's most intricate and expensive sequences, a statue of a giant, vicious-looking bird appears perched atop one of the square's buildings. The camera shows the building where the statue perches from a greater distance, and shadows moving along its walls and columns look

Figure 14–15. In *Suspiria,* the juxtaposition of extreme high- and low-angle shots suggests the presence of an invisible agency as Daniel (Flavio Bucci) and his guide dog walk through a square flanked with neoclassical architecture.

vaguely like witches flying by on broomsticks. A reverse shot from the statue's position suggests the statue's perspective, and with sounds of flapping wings, the camera swoops down from the statue's perch, flying along a line of attack, but it zooms past Daniel, and nothing happens immediately. The score switches from soft jingling to frantic drumming, and shots of Daniel, the dog, and the building from various angles express increasing danger, confusion, and fear. When the music fades, the climax erupts: the dog, presumably under the witches' influence, jumps up and rips out his master's throat, giving Miss Tanner and her associates the last word in the argument about whether the dog is gentle or vicious.

Interpreting the mystical weakness that changes Suzy's mind and the mystical influence that controls Daniel's dog as the results of witchcraft's invisible agency relies utterly on inference. The repetition above of words such as "presumably" and "suggests" marks key points in this argument where inference is necessary to support the logic behind the interpretation. Without such inferences, these scenes are just jumbles of weird music and quick cuts; they provide no direct, unquestionable evidence that establishes witchcraft as the causal agent behind the sequences' outcomes. Clinging to such inferences, viewers might develop the same sort of paranoia as Suzy and the others who suspect witchcraft. *Any* shot could be a representation of invisible agency; the only way to know is if a shot or shots culminate in an outcome worthy of witchery. Thus the inference of witchcraft occurs upon retrospection, a review of moments prior to an event occasioned *by* the event. If Suzy went from the weird moment with the servant in the hallway to a perfectly adequate performance, or if Daniel left the neoclassical square to spend a quiet evening at home, there would be no reason to suspect that the sound and editing were anything more than irrational atmosphere.

This kind of retrospection helps many other scenes in the film to make sense as well. The buildup to the first murder sequence provides a great example. Suzy's taxi ride to Escher Strasse brings her face to face with Pat, a young woman fleeing the academy as Suzy tries to enter. Pat says something that Suzy cannot hear clearly over the torrent of rain and thunder, and she sprints away. Suzy fails to gain admittance to the academy, and as her taxi departs, a shot through a window follows Pat's flight through the woods. The camera then abandons Suzy to observe Pat's arrival at a friend's apartment building, which shares the bizarre, art nouveau décor of the dance academy's interior. Pat tries to explain why she is so upset, but she gives up, saying, "It's useless to try and explain it to you. . . . You wouldn't understand. . . . It all seems so absurd, so fantastic. . . . All I can do is get away from here as soon as possible." The friend leaves her alone to dry off, and Pat eyes her surroundings warily. A gust of wind blows open a window, startling her. The friend rushes in to close the window, saying, "It was just the wind." Alone again, Pat paces the room. An exterior long shot of the too-high-to-be-an-entrance window moves in toward her, and the creepy music rises. A cut to the interior shows Pat slowly approaching the window from the other direction. She looks outside, turns away, looks over her shoulder, turns away again, looks over her shoulder again, and steps back toward the window. The film provides no diegetic explanation for Pat's behavior, no reason to share her suspicion of the window. Bringing her face close to the glass, Pat gazes outside. She grabs a lamp to shine some light through the window, but the glare only makes seeing harder. After two long minutes of this back-and-forth, unexplained window gazing, something finally happens to justify it: a pair of eyes suddenly glows, returns Pat's gaze, and fades out. A moment later, an inhumanly hairy arm bursts through the glass, and the film's most (in)famous murder begins in earnest.

In retrospect, all the fuss over the window can be explained by the presence, invisible until the glowing eyes appear, that materializes as the hairy arm. Just as the nondiegetic music and editing cue the audience to something sinister outside the window, a special sense, likely the "being watched" feeling that does not require evidence from the five normal senses, lets Pat know that an invisible danger lurks outside. Until the attack of the hairy arm, however, this sequence, like the sequences in the hallway and the neoclassical square, involves nothing but unmotivated, unexplained cuts and sounds. It uses style, not a logical reason to be afraid, to build suspense. Although the killer's appearance retroactively justifies the buildup, it lacks any other explanation. Who or what is the killer with the hairy arm? He or it uses a knife for the murder, so despite the hair, it seems human, but a human would not be able to come through the too-high-to-be-an-entrance window, and a human's eyes would not suddenly glow and fade out. The film never reveals who or what the killer is, and he or it is never discussed beyond the friend's eventual screams about "a murderer" attacking Pat. The only explanation, like the explanation for the sequences in the hallway and neoclassical square, is that witchcraft is at work. The explanation for all of these sequences and their outcomes is that the supernatural, the unexplained, provides causality.

The explanation of the strange events in *Suspiria* is that they are unexplained. As Pat says, they are "so absurd, so fantastic" that they exceed explanation. A universe in which the supernatural is possible implicitly admits unexplainable phenomena. Where the laws of nature do not apply, a too-high-to-be-an-entrance window can be an entrance anyway. Nevertheless, the explanation "it's unexplainable" is not entirely satisfying. Desperate to understand the strange events at the dance academy, Suzy becomes a *giallo*-like amateur detective, and she eventually seeks out the help of her psychiatrist friend Dr. Frank Mandel (Udo Kier, who also has a role in *Mother of Tears*). Suzy meets Dr. Mandel in the middle of a bright urban area that contrasts sharply with every other setting in the film: instead of the neoclassical stateliness of the square where Daniel dies, and instead of the sharp-angled, primary-colored strangeness of the dance academy and the apartment building where Pat is murdered, this scene features rounded skyscrapers and concrete in soft whites and silvers. The contrast in settings emphasizes the difference of the scene's calm, rational conversation about what might really be happening at the dance academy. As the camera moves from an establishing shot of a skyscraper to the place where Suzy and Dr. Mandel sit for their conversation, it passes a sign for the "Sixth Meeting on New Studies in Psychiatry and Psychology," which explains the presence of Dr. Mandel and his colleague Professor Milius. The sign also summons a bogey familiar from Argento's earlier films: psychoanalysis.

Suzy's most immediate motivation for seeking Dr. Mandel's help is concern for her dance-academy roommate, Sara, who has gone missing (and has already died in one of the film's grisliest sequences—fleeing from a razor-wielding figure, she tries to escape a room in the academy through a small window and tumbles on the other side not to the ground but to a room full of razor wire, in which she becomes entangled until the figure arrives to slash her throat). Dr. Mandel says that he knows Sara well because she was a patient of his, and without regard to patient confidentiality, he reveals that she once had a nervous breakdown and that she had "wild ideas" about the dance academy. In recounting these ideas, Dr. Mandel provides crucial exposition about Helena Marcos. After Helena Marcos founded the dance academy in 1895, "[t]he local people believed her to be a witch." The psychiatrist's story becomes wilder as he speculates that Madame Marcos "had something about her" that incited persecution from religious people, and it becomes wilder and more fanciful still when he notes her nickname, "The Black Queen." He casually refers to the academy as "a school of dance and occult sciences," as if the combination were natural, and explains that after Madame Marcos's (presumably faked) death by fire, the occult part of the combination fell away. Dr. Mandel claims that "the current spread of belief in magic and the occult is part of mental illness; bad luck isn't brought by broken mirrors, but by broken minds," and in doing so he not only provides McDonagh with the excellent title *Broken Mirrors/Broken Minds*; he also frames everything in the film as madness.

At this point, the film's accumulated weirdness is enough to cue skepticism about the psychiatrist's diagnosis, which does not explain the glowing eyes, suddenly deranged dog, and other phenomena that have appeared independent from any one perspective that could be discredited as insane. In addition, the first, longer part of his exposition—about the mysteries of the Black Queen—overshadows his moment of diagnostic simplicity, which contradicts the evidence he has presented *for* Madame Marcos's witchery without presenting any evidence *against* it. Furthermore, immediately after his exposition, Dr. Mandel introduces Professor Milius, whom he grants authority greater than his own. Author of the (fictional) book *Paranoia or Magic?* Professor Milius says that he has known real witches. Despite referring to witchcraft as "an appendage of contemporary psychiatry," he completely upends the "broken minds" hypothesis with his description of magic's practitioners:

> They are malefic, negative, and destructive; their knowledge of the art of the occult gives them tremendous powers. They can change the course of events and people's lives, but only to do harm. . . . Their goal is to accumulate great personal wealth, but that can only be achieved by injury to others. They can cause suffering, sickness, and even the death of those who, for whatever reason, offend them. . . . [Helena Marcos was] a powerful witch with a tremendous talent for doing evil, a real

> mistress of magic. . . . A woman becomes queen if her magic is a hundred
> times more powerful than the rest of the coven, which is like a circle.
> Its strength rests with its leader, its head. A coven deprived of its leader
> is like a headless cobra, harmless. Skepticism is the natural reaction of
> people nowadays, but magic is ever present . . . magic is everywhere,
> and all over the world, it's a recognized fact, always.

Professor Milius's transportation of witchcraft from the realm of broken minds to the realm of "recognized fact" trumps any skepticism that Dr. Mandel's flimsy argument has not already discarded. Once and for all, Suzy's amateur sleuthing leaves the quasi-realistic territory of the *giallo*. In *Tenebre*, Detective Germani explains that he has figured out Peter Neal's guilt with a quotation, used by Neal earlier in the film, from Arthur Conan Doyle's Sherlock Holmes: "'When you eliminate the impossible, whatever remains, however improbable, must be the truth.'" This line succinctly sums up the improbabilities of the *giallo* while distinguishing them clearly from the impossibilities of supernatural horror. Impossibility is the essence of *Suspiria*'s world. By letting someone at a psychiatric conference speak truth rather than some dismissable, irrelevant theory, *Suspiria* is kinder to science than Argento's earlier films. In fact, Dr. Milius's comment about cutting off the head of the coven sets up the film's ending, in which Suzy kills Helena Marcos and thereby destroys the coven and the dance-academy building. Whereas the science of *The Bird with the Crystal Plumage, The Cat o' Nine Tails*, and *Deep Red* has nothing to do with the downfalls of their killers, Dr. Milius's science is the key to the triumph of *Suspiria*'s heroine. The scientist's belief in witchcraft provides the film's impossibilities their most sensible support as well as their practical resolution, but instead of making the impossibilities seem rational, this successful science ultimately allies itself with irrationality.

This argument has so far explained *Suspiria*'s irrational moments— the too-high-to-be-an-entrance entrance, the dancer's weakness that begins with a look from a stranger holding a talisman, the gentle guide dog that suddenly kills its master—as motivated by an invisible, magical agency that the film represents through sound and editing. Instead of the drugged mous(s)e used by the witches in *Rosemary's Baby* (1968), or the poisoned apple used by the witch in Disney's *Snow White* (1937), which

Argento has often said inspired *Suspiria*'s colorful fairy-tale aesthetic, invisible agency represents the inexplicable workings of Argento's witches. For many of *Suspiria*'s viewers, the result of using stylized sound and editing to show something invisible instead of props to show something visible is total confusion. Gary Arnold's 1977 review in the *Washington Post*, "*Suspiria*: Upstaged Terror Gone Wild," provides one perspective on what this confusion does to the film:

> Argento's latest thriller, a ridiculously self-indulgent spree of satanic bogeymannerisms entitled "Suspiria," virtually self-destructs in the opening sequence. Eager to menace the audience from every sensory direction, Argento doesn't so much create and sustain an illusion of terror as invite you to marvel at his garish ingenuity, at the spectacle of a filmmaker who can't resist overstylizing and upstaging his material.

According to Arnold, the film "self-destructs" because it is "self-indulgent"; the excess of style causes a nonsensical sensory overload. Continuing to lambast Argento's work, Arnold notes of Suzy's consent to stay at the dance academy, "There's no reason beyond sheer plot necessity for the heroine to expose herself to this particular milieu." From this unflattering perspective, contrivance, not reason, propels Argento's plot.

Arnold's negative perspective is not the only way of understanding the film, but it successfully captures *Suspiria*'s emphasis on style. In a review of *Suspiria* on DVD and Blu-ray in the January 9, 2010, issue of *The Guardian*, Phelim O'Neill calls the film "classic horror" and puts Arnold's point in a prettier light: "Film is a visual medium. . . . *Suspiria* takes things to such extremes visually, it often pushes away such trifles as dialogue and logic to blow the mind and assault the eyes and ears." Although these two reviews differ on whether Argento's hyperstylization of the horror film is a good thing, they agree that he forsakes the sensible for the sensory, subjugating rational narrative to press the cinema's two sensory modalities, sight and sound, to their limits.[6]

One strategy for reaching these limits is Goblin's score, which juxtaposes soft chimes, pounding drums, and barely comprehensible vocals to such an eerie effect that David Gordon Green, who is slated to direct a *Suspiria* remake, is planning to reuse it (Moore). The sharp contrasts of the score combine with the sharp angles that Argento's camera highlights in his settings. The angular, colorful decors of the dance academy, which Arnold rightly compares to the madhouse in *The Cabinet of Dr. Caligari* (1920), and of the art nouveau apartment building where Pat meets her doom provide geometric, expressionistic surroundings that match the bewildering violence of the witches' impossible world (figures 16–17).

To achieve extremes of color, Argento and the cinematographer Luciano Tovoli used Eastman Color Kodak film and an outdated Technicolor printing process, which James Gracey explains:

> This film would also be the last ever to be "dio-transferred": the negative was given to Technicolor who split it into three separate black-and-white negatives—one for red, one for blue, and one for green. These were then printed one on top of the other to create the vibrant look of the finished film. Argento insisted that Technicolor also use the highest possible contrast to increase the presence of primary colours. (70–71)

Jarring sounds, jagged shapes, and jolting colors come together in compositions that suggest madness and horror. Their exquisite workmanship makes the film both sublime and beautiful, repellant and hypnotic. It telegraphs the unreality of the diegetic world.

Suspiria's exquisitely wrought, unreal compositions reach their pinnacle in murder scenes. Pat's death, accompanied by frantic drumming and dissonant synthesizers, is the most elaborate. In a move that echoes Helga's murder in *Deep Red,* the hairy arm bursts through the too-high-to-be-an-entrance window, grabs Pat's head, and pushes her face through shattering glass. A medium shot shows Pat with her back to a wall as the arm enters the right side of the frame and stabs her. She clutches the wound, screams in agony, slides down the wall, and is stabbed again and again. Cuts to her friend running through the building, screaming for help, interrupt the violence and stretch it out. Pat's prolonged suffering continues as the knife rends her flesh and as the killer prepares a rope for her neck. Lying on top of the stained-glass ceiling of the building's vast lobby, she screams and gasps at further stabbings. An extreme close-up shows her beating heart through a gaping hole in her chest, and the knife enters the frame once more to penetrate the exposed organ. Her head presses backward, breaking glass, and finally her body falls through the high ceiling. A shot from the lobby floor, where Pat's friend watches in terror, shows the stained

Figure 16–17. In *Suspiria,* Pat (Eva Axén, top left) is eclipsed by her art nouveau surroundings, which create a hyperstylized aesthetic context for the hyperstylized violence that is to come.

glass and its metal support beams explode. Hanged, Pat's body dangles in midair. The camera tilts downward to follow streams of blood flowing from her wounds, down her legs, toward the distant floor, where the shot tracks across blood puddles on black, red, and white tiles until it settles on Pat's friend, who has been killed by falling shards of glass and fragments of support beams.

The violent chaos of this sequence ends on a still composition that the camera savors as the music calms (figure 18). This shot captures the combination of the friend's death with the strange geometric patterns of the floor. Her blood is a red closer to that of the floor's tiles than that of real human blood; her splayed arms and bent legs form angles comparable to angles in the floor's pattern, as do the angular shards and beams sticking out of her body. The corpse becomes an extension of the aesthetically wrought setting, the central figure in a violent work of art. That the blood is unrealistic or that the corpse's position is at least improbable, perhaps impossible, does not matter in a context where style and aesthetic impact take precedence over everything.

Aesthetic experience is arguably the ultimate source of "meaning" in all of Argento's films, but *Suspiria* and the other films of the Three Mothers trilogy, *Inferno* and *Mother of Tears,* take their emphasis on aesthetics further by self-consciously connecting their irrational worlds to nineteenth-century romanticism and the aestheticism that grew out of it. As McDonagh and others have noted, the connection begins in *Suspiria*'s title, which means "sighs" and is a reference to Mater Suspiriorum, the Mother of Sighs, one of the three "Ladies of Sorrow" discussed by Thomas De Quincey in his work *Suspiria de Profundis.*

Figure 18. In *Suspiria,* a corpse is an extension of the aesthetically wrought setting, the central figure in a violent work of art.

Although no one in *Suspiria* refers to Helena Marcos as the Mother of Sighs or makes any direct reference to De Quincey, the titular reference suffices to make *Suspiria* the first of a trilogy in which the other two films involve the other two Mothers.

While De Quincey's descriptions of the Three Mothers' personalities and depredations in *Suspiria de Profundis* inform the Mothers' depictions in Argento's films, another work by De Quincey has even stronger resonance because it informs Argento's aesthetic sensibilities. "On Murder, Considered as One of the Fine Arts," published in 1827, explains how murder becomes art:

> Everything in this world has two handles. Murder, for instance, may be laid hold of by its moral handle . . . or it may also be treated *aesthetically,* as the Germans call it, that is, in relation to good taste. . . . [B]oth a thief and an ulcer may have infinite degrees of merit. They are both imperfections, it is true; but to be imperfect being their essence, the very greatness of their imperfection becomes their perfection. . . . [A]s it is impossible to hammer anything out of [murder] for moral purposes, let us treat it aesthetically . . . a transaction, which, morally considered, was shocking, and without a leg to stand upon, when tried by principles of Taste, turns out to be a very meritorious performance.

De Quincey's argument about murder as art provides an inverted scale for judging horrific spectacles. From an aesthetic standpoint, a horrific spectacle is not supposed to be beautiful in the same way that a calm pastoral vista can be beautiful. Horror's nature is to be imperfect, to be horrific, so the more horrific the horror, the more perfect it might be. Judging *Suspiria* by De Quincey's inverted scale, the deaths of Pat and her friend are meritorious indeed, and their contexts, particularly the colors and geometric patterns of the stained-glass ceiling and the irregularly tiled floor, invite spectators to consider them as just the sort of art to which the inverted scale applies.[7]

The difference between Arnold's and O'Neill's reviews of *Suspiria* may reflect the fact that in the thirty-three years (and a torrent of films visually enhanced by digital technology) between them, audiences for horror films have come around to De Quincey's way of thinking. Arnold assumes that a filmmaker in the horror genre has an obligation to "create and sustain an illusion of terror" and to "resist overstylizing and upstaging his material," but O'Neill's first principle is that "film is a visual medium," and in horror, "visual extremes" are far more important than "such trifles as dialogue and logic." If what distinguishes film narrative from a random sequence of images is the presence of logic, a chain of moments displayed in a manner that conveys significant relationships rooted, however indirectly, in cause and effect, Argento's hyperstylized violence makes narrative far less relevant to horror than the presence of visual excess. Sequences like the deaths of Pat and her friend work against narrative because they demonstrate that horror's effectiveness, what De Quincey would call its perfection, relies on narrative very little, if at all. Thus Argento invests his energies in capturing the patterns of his elaborate set designs and in subjecting his film to outdated printing processes rather than in crafting narratives that come together into a tapestry of perfect, comforting sense.

Decades of fans' responses to Argento's work tend to share the elevating perspective in O'Neill's review, avoiding the paracinematic and camp approaches that Janet Staiger associates with fans' embrace of what they regard as low culture. Instead, fans often approach Argento's films according to conventions for consuming avant-garde productions, for which a fan typically identifies the film's "subject matter and then searches for aesthetic patterns complementing or creating the supposed subject" (Staiger 137). Peter Hutchings notes that fans exhibit "unashamed auterism" as they rail against Argento's mainstream-critical detractors and attempt "to raise the cultural status of Argento's work," wondering why critics fail to "'recognise talent when they see it'" (134). The fans see talent where Arnold's review sees overstylization, and they implicitly seek to raise Argento, and with him the horror genre, higher within cultural/aesthetic hierarchies. Where viewers perceive horror's perfection as its imperfection, perfect sense is anything but perfect, and narrative needs to be beaten down to a place in the aesthetic hierarchy far below image. Fans and reviewers who would elevate Argento's imagery join his works in arguing that film is a visual medium, and visual excess is what film does best. Argento's works call attention to and valorize their narrative shortcomings by beautifying horror, and in displaying such excess they suggest not only what horror film is but also what film as a medium has the potential to be. Like the fans', the films' appreciation of horror depreciates narrative, raising the possibility that a film that subjugates image to narrative ignores the essence of its medium.

Aesthetic appreciation for the horrible is not the explicit subject of De Quincey's *Suspiria de Profundis,* but it has a noteworthy presence, especially in De Quincey's descriptions of the three Ladies of Sorrow as incarnations of "all individual sufferings of man's heart" (149). These descriptions interrupt De Quincey's fragmentary, hallucinatory narrative with poetic elaboration comparable to the visual elaboration of Argento's violent set pieces. Argento does not translate De Quincey's descriptions of the Three Mothers fully into film, but he does use some of them. For example, De Quincey's comment that the Mother of Sighs "sighs inaudibly at intervals. . . . Murmur she may, but it is in her sleep" becomes a moment in *Suspiria* when Suzy and Sara, sleeping in the rehearsal studio after a rain of maggots has infested the dancers' bedrooms, identify the silhouetted sleeper next to them as Helena Marcos because of her sigh-like snoring (150–51). Similarly, the terrible, stormy presence of De Quincey's Mater Tenebrarum, the Mother of Darkness, appears in Argento's portrayal of her in *Inferno,* and the gliding, regal ways of De Quincey's Mater Lachrymarum, the Mother of Tears, appears in *Mother of Tears.* The adaptation of De Quincey's Three Mothers makes *Suspiria de Profundis* as well as De Quincey's larger aesthetic philosophy a source and a frame for Argento's trilogy.

More important to understanding Argento's project in the Three Mothers trilogy than the descriptions of the Three Mothers, however, is what the Mother of Tears says about De Quincey at the end of his vision:

> "Lo! here is he, whom in childhood I dedicated to my altars. This is he that once I made my darling. Him I led astray, him I beguiled, and from heaven I stole away his young heart to mine. Through me did he become idolatrous; and through me it was, by languishing desires, that he worshipped the worm and prayed to the wormy grave. Holy was the grave to him; lovely was its darkness; saintly its corruption. Him, this young idolater, I have seasoned for thee, dear gentle Sister of Sighs! Do thou take him now to *thy* heart, and season him for our dreadful sister. And thou"—turning to the *Mater Tenebrarum,* she said—"wicked sister, that temptest and hatest, do thou take him from *her.* . . . So shall he be

accomplished in the furnace—so shall he see the things that ought *not* to be seen—sights that are abominable, and secrets that are unutterable. . . . And so all our commission be accomplished which from God we had—to plague his heart until we had unfolded the capacities of his spirit." (152–53)

The Mother of Tears credits herself with giving De Quincey his fascination with "the wormy grave," with gruesome death and decay, and she abjures the Mother of Darkness to show him "sights . . . abominable," horrible visions. The Mothers, then, are responsible for De Quincey's aesthetic appreciation of horror, the loveliness he finds in darkness. Their "commission," their purpose, is to serve up as much horror as is necessary to make De Quincey's poetic nature unfold. They make him an artist of the ugly, a master of horror, a product of the mold that also shaped Argento. The Three Mothers that Argento inherits from De Quincey produce the macabre spirit that motivates the best of the horror genre.

A similar spirit informs the writings of Edgar Allan Poe, whom Argento has often cited as a lifelong influence. In an interview included in Luigi Cozzi's documentary *Dario Argento: Master of Horror* (1991), Argento reflects, "My films are very Poe-ish, but with a difference in time and ambience." The difference in time and ambience is critical in the adaptation of Poe's short story "The Black Cat" that forms Argento's half of the film *Two Evil Eyes* (1990), on which he collaborated with George A. Romero (a colleague since the two of them worked together on Romero's 1978 film *Dawn of the Dead*). Argento's "The Black Cat" takes extensive liberties with the Poe original, modernizing it and making its central character, Roderick Usher (Harvey Keitel), a photographer whose work centers on murder victims. The protagonist's name, a reference to Poe's "The Fall of the House of Usher," and his photographs, which include images of murder directly from Poe's "The Pit and the Pendulum" and other stories, make Argento's "The Black Cat" a broad homage to the macabre master of American romanticism. Making Usher a photographer, of course, also makes him yet another cipher for Argento: Usher shares Argento, Poe, and De Quincey's fascination with making art out of the wormy grave. The artists' media may differ—De Quincey and Poe use the printed page, while Usher and Argento use photographic images—but their purpose is the same.

Poe's writings reflect De Quincey's predilections for turning murder into art, and they provide a foundation for Argento's aestheticism. In his essay "The Poetic Principle" (1850), Poe writes, "[U]nder the sun there neither exists nor *can* exist any work more thoroughly dignified—more supremely noble—than this very poem—this poem *per se*—this poem which is a poem and nothing more—this poem written solely for the poem's sake" (417). This idea of the poem for the poem's sake prefigures the imperative "art for art's sake" from British aestheticism, whose best-known spokesmen are Walter Pater and Oscar Wilde. In the conclusion to *The Renaissance*, published in 1873, Pater provides a kind of manifesto:

> Some spend [the short interval of life] in listlessness, some in high passions, the wisest, at least among "the children of this world," in art and song. For our one chance lies in expanding that interval, in getting as many pulsations as possible into the given time. Great passions may give us this quickened sense of life, ecstasy and sorrow of love, the various forms of enthusiastic activity, disinterested or otherwise, which come naturally to many of us. Only be sure it is passion—that it does yield you this fruit of a quickened, multiplied consciousness. Of this wisdom, the poetic passion, the desire of beauty, the love of art for art's sake, has most; for art comes to you professing frankly to give nothing but the highest quality to your moments as they pass, and simply for those moments' sake.

Pater justifies his valuation of art for its own sake as the surest and best way to make the most of life. Refracted through the dark lens of De Quincey's vision of murder as art, Argento's films seize this justification, showing grotesque death for the sake of showing grotesque death. The images do not need narrative logic because they are valuable in themselves; their value lies in the fulfillment of the Three Mothers' purpose of unfolding the artist's spirit as well as in the excitement of passions that make the most of life's short interval. While on the surface the worship of the grave that Argento inherits from De Quincey may seem nihilistic, an affirmation of nothingness, it is in fact a means of enrichment, an affirmation of life.[8]

Inferno

Abandonment of narrative logic in favor of powerful, macabre imagery that excites the passions and unfolds the capacity of an artist's spirit may be what makes *Inferno*, the second installment of the Three Mothers trilogy, not only Argento's most difficult film to follow but also a film he discusses in terms of superlative personal impact. In an interview excerpted as an introduction to the 2000 Anchor Bay VHS release of *Inferno*, Argento seems to confide in his audience:

> Remember that this was one of the most difficult films for me. It was a movie that took a lot of my energy and imagination. I hope you will enjoy it. It is one of my most sincere and purest films.

Argento's language—translated from Italian as "for *me*," "*my* energy," "*my* most sincere"—emphasizes his own role in the film with a recognizably auteurist bent. Indeed, during his early days as a film critic or at any point in his pan-European career, Argento might have become familiar with the *Cahiers du Cinema* or Andrew Sarris's articulation of auteur theory as an approach to film that considers "the distinguishable personality of the director as a criterion of value" and "interior meaning" as the quality of a film that earns a director the mantle of auteur (452–53). The repeated elements of Argento's films—artist-detectives, his own hands as the gloved killer's, faces smashing through glass, and more—could very well be deliberate attempts to create the sort of artistic signature that auteur critics seek.

Whether or not they are evidence of auteurism, the presence of such elements as well as the film's oneiric qualities, which are even more pronounced than *Suspiria*'s, invite comparison with Federico Fellini's dreamlike, autobiographical masterpieces, particularly *8½*, which is about the experiences and dreams of a film director trying to make a film. Since Argento once again uses an artist, a musician, as a protagonist, and since he once again casts his longtime girlfriend and cowriter Daria Nicolodi in a major role, an autobiographical, Felliniesque reading might be possible. A reading of the film in terms of dream logic is certainly possible, and Jodey Castricano has done just that in "For the Love of Smoke and Mirrors: Dario Argento's *Inferno*," which calls attention to the film's surreal uses of color, the languid movements of the character Rose during an underwater scene, and "an overwhelming sense of strangeness" in awkward dialogue, all of which add up to the feeling of being in a dream. Nevertheless, arguing that *Inferno* is an autobiographical dreamwork in the Fellini tradition only suggests, rightly, that Argento's work deserves to be considered as both art film and genre film and that it can be read in very personal terms. Acknowledging Argento's place in the Fellini tradition does not help his dreamwork's convolutions to make any more sense.

Excerpts from an interview with Argento included on the Blue Underground DVD of *Inferno* provide additional perspective on the film's difficulty:

> I had no idea it would be so difficult. It was very hard, even from the writing. It was very complex, because I did not want to enter the world of witches, as in *Suspiria,* but the world of alchemy, the magic science, the meanings of designs of buildings. . . . The alchemists were scientists who studied all kinds of physic[al] phenomen[a], as well as the human psyche.

McDonagh uses an alchemical metaphor to describe the difficult narratives of Argento's films in general when she claims that their "internal logic" is "metaphoric rather than metonymic," so "images proceed from one to another not in the service of linear narrative, but by way of poetic connections, a kind of alchemical reasoning" (18). Alchemical reasoning, in contrast to linear reasoning, is the transformation, even the transcendence, of image into personal experience rather than the sort of sense that derives from a signifying chain. It does not have to make sense as long as it creates poetic feeling.

For the success of this rationale for the irrational, Argento's mention of "magic science" is key: if *Suspiria* reconciles with science to a point where a scientist within the film is willing to admit the irrational into science's realm, *Inferno* reconciles still further through alchemy, a science that *is* the irrational and the impossible. Instead of being at odds, magic and science become one. The consequences for writing through this sort of irrational scientific reasoning are, as Argento claims, "very complex." One consequence is that Argento's interest in psychoanalysis, skeptical and even adversarial in earlier films, manifests in an affirmative move toward psychoanalysis's more mystical side. As McDonagh and others have pointed out, *Inferno*'s elemental images of fire and water relate to Jungian archetypes:

> Archetypes are images that aren't derived from the specific psychological processes of the individual dreamer, but rather drawn from the vast reserve of images that inform all cultural phenomena, from religious symbolism to the world of legends and fairy tales. The image of water—particularly bodies of water: oceans, pools, lakes—is consistently associated with the first of Jung's major archetypes, that of the Great Mother who embodies the conflicting aspects of the feminine principle, simultaneously nurturing and devouring. The Great Mother can also be personified in dreams by houses, a particularly evocative association in light of the entire notion of the houses of the Three Mothers. (McDonagh 146)

McDonagh's argument shows how archetypal imagery brings one type of (arguably) magic science, Jungian psychoanalysis, together with another that is not immediately apparent, alchemy. Argento approaches alchemy not by representing it immediately in the story—which has nothing to do with the philosopher's stone, the elixir vitae, or other typical signs of alchemy—but by entering it on the level of narrative form. His form combines the magic science of the psyche with the art of filmmaking, and the result is a film that is irrational because it is itself irrationality, madness incorporated as art.

The figure of the house, which relates to the Jungian Mother, becomes *Inferno*'s rhetorical means of uniting alchemy with psychology and irrationality with film. Indeed, Argento's mention of "the meanings of designs of buildings" in the *Inferno* DVD interview points toward the master metaphor through which the film asks to be read. *Inferno* begins with close shots of something that looks like a dagger (a cutter for the pages of an uncut book), a set of keys, and a book, *The Three Mothers* by E. Varelli. This book makes the Three Mothers trilogy's connection to De Quincey, which appears only in *Suspiria*'s title, overt. As the camera shows the book's cover, soft piano music, a sharp contrast with the frantic drums and synthesizers of *Suspiria*, establishes a sleepy, dreamlike atmosphere. A title on the screen reads "New York ~ April," picking up *Suspiria*'s emphasis on place, which a voiceover reading from *The Three Mothers* soon gives a new explanation:

I, Varelli, an architect living in London, met the Three Mothers and designed and built for them three dwelling places, one in Rome, one in New York, and a third in Freiburg, Germany. I failed to discover until too late that from those three locations, the Three Mothers ruled the world with sorrow, tears, and darkness. Mater Suspiriorum, the Mother of Sighs and oldest of the three, lives in Freiburg. Mater Lachrymarum, the Mother of Tears, and the most beautiful of the sisters, holds rule in Rome. Mater Tenebrarum, the Mother of Darkness, who is the youngest and cruelest of the three, controls New York. And I built their horrible houses, the repositories of all their filthy secrets. Those so-called mothers are actually wicked stepmothers, incapable of creating life, in . . .

With a burst of horns on the score, the title *Inferno* takes over the screen and interrupts the voiceover. After the title, the voiceover goes on, combining paraphrases of De Quincey with original text. It continues:

The land upon which the three houses are constructed will eventually become deathly and plague-ridden, so much so that the area all around will reek horribly, and that is the first key to the mothers' secret, truly the primary key. The second key to the poisonous secret of the three sisters is hidden in the cellar under their houses. There you can find both the sister and the name of the sister living in that house. This is the location of the second key. The third key can be found under the soles of your shoes. There is the third key.

The voiceover is masculine, presumably representing the author Varelli, and the person we see reading the book is a woman, Rose, the film's first candidate for a protagonist. She finishes reading and begins a letter to her brother Mark, who lives in Rome, setting in motion the multiple storylines that will converge in the New York house of Mater Tenebrarum. This convergence makes the house, the meaning and design of Varelli's building, central to the meaning and design of the film.

The houses' meaning begins with the cities and countries where they lie. The introductory voiceover's emphasis on the Three Mothers' cities as places from which they rule extends *Suspiria*'s use of Germany to summon notions of the imperial Third Reich with references to other empires, the ancient Roman but also the (relatively) new American empire. Putting De Quincey's youngest of the three Ladies of Sorrow in New York resonates pointedly with the United States' status as the youngest of the three empires, and Varelli's home in London evokes the British Empire as well, which resisted imperial Germany, positioned itself as the heir to ancient Rome, and gave birth to the United States. Thus *Inferno* makes the witches' motivation by world domination, given only the weakest of implications in *Suspiria,* explicit.

The voiceover goes further into place-specificity with discussions of the houses that Varelli has designed. The house in *Suspiria* provides an abundance of weird backdrops for the film's weird goings-on; Varelli's book makes that weirdness a plot point, and it does the same for the weirdness *Inferno* shows within the New York home of Mater Tenebrarum. Varelli's lamentation over building the houses suggests that through their weird designs, they somehow enable the witches' evil. By giving his readers three "keys" to determining the locations of the houses, he directs Rose and any other potential opposition toward confrontation with the evil, providing an impetus for the storyline. Varelli's discussion of his houses' weird designs also explains the storyline's end, which echoes *Suspiria*'s ending. *Suspiria* concludes with a confrontation between Suzy and Mater Suspiriorum. When Suzy stabs the ghastly looking old witch, the dance-academy building crumbles around her like the House of Usher in Poe's tale. *Inferno* concludes with a confrontation between Mark and Mater Tenebrarum. By coincidence, the house has been set on fire by an unwitting inhabitant, so all Mark needs to do is flee, leaving Mater Tenebrarum and the house to be destroyed together. Varelli's discussion of the witches' connections to his architectural designs supports these endings, which show a connection so strong that neither house nor witch can exist without the other.

To call the voiceover an explanation for *Inferno*'s ending is, admittedly, a stretch. By prompting Rose to identify Mater Tenebrarum's house and providing a wisp of reasoning to explain the spectacle of destruction that Mark flees at the end, Varelli's writing becomes the vaguest of maps not only to the locations of the houses but to the events in the film. Without it, the incoherence that McDonagh and others note would be total (149), but with it, *Inferno* is still difficult, or perhaps preposterous, to follow. In the first sequence, Rose reads from *The Three Mothers,* writes to her brother Mark, and leaves her apartment to mail the letter. A series of shots—one of a sketch of the house in Varelli's book, one of a picture of the house on Rose's wall, and one of the façade of Rose's apartment building—identifies Rose's building as Mater Tenebrarum's home. As she returns from the mailbox, Rose starts to figure out what the series of shots has already told viewers. She looks at the metal plate that covers the exterior entrance to her building's basement, and Varelli's voice in her memory replays, "The second key is hidden in the cellar." She goes to Kazanian's Antiques, the shop on the first floor of her building where she originally acquired *The Three Mothers* from the mysterious owner, Kazanian. When she asks him about the book, he replies dismissively, "Lots of books have been written about houses of the damned." Not dissuaded, Rose points out that the book mentions a strange odor (key number one), and just such an odor permeates the area where she and Kazanian are standing. He dismisses her ideas again. Rose leaves the shop, the voice in her mind repeats the fact about the second key, and passing by a group of cats, she lifts the plate and begins her descent into the building's basement.

This descent quickly takes Rose into a surreal and confusing world. She passes through a room stuffed with junk, random papers, and cob-webs, all normal enough for a building's basement. She comes upon a staircase, inexplicably filled with blue light, leading further beneath the city. Down she goes, reaching a level marked by broken pipes and dangling wires that suggest architectural chaos, which might be at least marginally believable were the creepy blue light from the stairs not complemented with creepier purple light from the room beyond. Water trickles down along a vertical pipe until it spills onto the concrete floor, providing both Jungian imagery and a trail that Rose follows to a hole in the concrete. Yet another level awaits beneath Rose's feet, but it is completely flooded. Leaning over to peer into the water, Rose drops her keychain, which falls in and gets caught on a floating piece of furniture just barely out of reach. Even though the flooded level seems to glow blue from within, Rose finds an old lamp to help light her pursuit of her keys (in both senses—the literal keys she has dropped, and the keys Varelli provides in *The Three Mothers*). Exhibiting extraordinary (perhaps unbelievable) bravery, Rose lowers herself into the water and explores.

The effects for the underwater sequence were beautifully conceived and executed by (uncredited) Mario Bava; *Inferno* was the last film Bava worked on before his death in 1980. The sequence's otherworldly, under-water aesthetic amplifies the surreality established by the lighting and other bizarre details of the building's surprisingly vast, deep basement. Able to hold her breath for a very long time (a prerequisite for the character that was an important factor in casting Irene Miracle in the role), Rose moves slowly into the underwater realm. Taking her perspective, the camera shows a room with ballroom décor amidst which lies a portrait labeled "Mater Tenebrarum," the second of Varelli's keys. When she tries to retrieve her keychain, Rose accidentally knocks it further down, all the way to the distant floor. A quick trip up for air precedes another descent, and point-of-view shots from her slowly moving position closely capture the rococo designs on the mantle of the underwater fireplace, similarly ornate chandeliers, throbbing orange drapery, the floral pattern on the rug beneath her keys, and finally the ridges of decay on a corpse that suddenly floats toward her as if attacking. Panicked, she swims up, kicking at the rotting corpse as it continues to drift toward her. She escapes.

Not many houses have underwater sub-sub-basements with telltale corpses detailed in eerie blue light, but Mater Tenebrarum's house is exceptional. Mark, the second candidate for protagonist after his sister is murdered, gets another experience of the house's exceptionality as he unknowingly heads for his confrontation with the evil Mother. He begins in the same room where the film begins, the place where Rose reads *The Three Mothers*, and starts following Varelli's threads. Staring at the picture of the house that the earlier series of images places between Varelli's sketch and an exterior shot of the house's facade, Mark recalls Varelli's third key, which is "under the soles of your shoes." He notices an abundance of ants (an evocation of Luis Buñuel and Salvador Dali's surrealist film *Un chien andalou* [1929]) on the wall and floor, some of which are emerging from between boards of the hardwood floor. Using a length of wire, he discovers a narrow passage beneath the boards. Pulling up boards leads to a hole big enough to enter, and like his sister before him, he travels downward.

Mark's search of the cobweb-lined, scrap-covered, blue-glowing area beneath the floorboards leads him to a small sliding door, which opens on a stairway that goes further down. Down one level is another sliding door to another space like the one Mark has crawled through, and down another level is a door, which leads to more rooms and hallways, a short flight of steps up, and finally another door that opens on a corridor that looks part cave, part building (figure 19). The only way Mark's

Figure 19. In *Inferno,* Mark (Leigh McCloskey)
discovers Mater Tenebrarum's lair within a house
that has a completely irrational structure.

path through the house and the spaces he encounters makes sense, the
only way the structure itself makes sense, is to see it as deliberately
convoluted and obfuscated. Whether such a structure would be able
to stand is a reasonable question, but even with disbelief suspended on
that question, the house is irrational, full of weirdness for the sake of
weirdness, architectural art for the sake of architectural art.

While the utilitarian potential for such a house is minimal, the metaphoric potential is huge. Metaphorically, the film's title is far more relevant to its content than *Suspiria*'s, and the house realizes that relevance.
Rose and Mark's journeys through the house take them continually
downward, deeper and deeper into its dark places, toward the terrible
Mother of Darkness. In Dante Alighieri's *Inferno,* the poet and his
guide's journey takes them continually downward, deeper and deeper
into hell, toward the terrible Prince of Darkness. The connection of the
house to Dante's hell gets stronger as the house starts burning at the
end; during Mark's downward journey through areas not yet aflame,
cuts to burning places emphasize that he is going deeper into a fiery
pit. If the house stands for Dante's hell, all the film's gory moments
within the house might be readable as part of a larger allegory in which
characters' violent deaths relate to the tortures of the damned. Such a

reading works in places. Two of the goriest deaths have a kind of poetic justice in them. Kazanian, the antiques dealer, tries to drown a bag of cats and in the effort gets eaten alive by rats and hacked to death by a deranged cook. John, a butler, conspires with Carol, a housekeeper (Alida Valli, who plays Miss Tanner in *Suspiria*), to rob their rich but ailing mistress Elise (Daria Nicolodi); John gets his eyes ripped out, and Carol, startled by seeing his body, drops a candle, sets herself as well as the house on fire, and falls through a window to her death. Poetic justice is absent, however, in the deaths of Mark's friend Sarah, who makes the mistake of reading Rose's letter to Mark; Sarah's neighbor Carlo, who makes the mistake of trying to help Sarah; Rose, who makes the mistake of trying to solve the mystery of the Three Mothers; and Elise, who makes the mistake of trying to help Mark do the same. The allegorical *Inferno* connection is fragmentary at best; it does not provide a coherent way of understanding the film.

The architect Varelli provides another metaphoric understanding of the house. After Mark crawls through the space beneath the floorboards, he finds a red-lit passage that offers vantages on a room with gold wallpaper inhabited by a nurse with a man in a wheelchair, house residents whom Mark has previously encountered. The nurse leaves, the man wheels himself out of the room, and Mark pursues the man, who turns out to be Varelli himself. "You found the way down, I see," the architect says. Relying on a voicebox in his throat connected by a wire to a sound board, the old man tells Mark about building the Mothers' houses, which "became their eyes and ears." He elaborates, "This building has become my body, its bricks my cells, its passageways my veins, and its horror my very heart," suggesting that the building is a metaphor for its creator. This suggestion is tempting—particularly since it opens the door to questions about whether the film *Inferno*, itself a convoluted structure, might be a metaphor for its creator, Dario Argento, and these questions circle back toward the film's Fellini-like, autobiographical dimensions—but it does not hold up simply because the only evidence to support it is Varelli's claim. The house is far too chaotic to sustain comparison to an organic system, and Varelli, who inadvertently strangles himself on the wire connecting his voicebox to the soundboard after a botched attempt to poison Mark with a syringe, is not nearly important enough in the Three Mothers mythology to have something as important as Mater Tenebrarum's house be a metaphor for *his* body.

The suggestion that the house is like a human body is not altogether without merit. In his attempt to glorify himself through an equation of the house with his body, Varelli leaves out the part of the body that has the most metaphoric potential when applied to the house: the head. In *Suspiria,* Professor Milius tells Suzy, "A coven deprived of its leader is like a headless cobra, harmless," and when Suzy kills Mater Suspiriorum, she figuratively cuts off the coven's head, and both the coven and the dance-academy building are destroyed. Each of the Three Mothers is the head of her own house; cut off the head, and the body, the rest of the house, dies. Taken in this direction, Varelli's body metaphor applied to Mater Tenebrarum instead of to Varelli connects to the metaphor of the body politic that traditionally casts royalty as the political body's head and various subjects in other parts. This body approach is not entirely satisfying either, though, because Mater Tenebrarum, unlike her older sister, has no coven. She may be the head of her house, but she heads no state. Other than Varelli, who is more her prisoner than her polis, Mater Tenebrarum lacks solid connections to her house's tenants, who are occasionally wicked but not clearly witches. She seems to work alone.

The relationship between the body and the house in *Inferno* only works in terms of destruction: the house does nothing bodylike when its head is still on, but it dies like a body when the head is cut off. That the body metaphor only really applies when the body is mutilated seems apt, however, in a film that features mutilations as its most outstanding qualities. Nina Darnton's *New York Times* review of *Inferno* from 1986 remarks that the film deserves the "highest rating" in the "slice-and-dice" category of movies, but she also notes that "[t]he movie's distinguishing feature is not the number or variety of horrible murders, but the length of time it takes for the victims to die." Like the *gialli* and *Suspiria,* *Inferno* strings together violent, drawn-out set pieces, and for at least some of the target audience, everything else in the film is subordinate to delivering the gory goods (Koven 33). The goods in *Inferno* are notable for their extremity (Kazanian and John's deaths, already mentioned, are particularly nasty) as well as for their improbability. Elise's death, for example, is so unlikely that it straddles the line between funny and frightening: after she runs through the building, pursued by an unseen force (and with a lot of wind in her hair), she finds a quiet spot where some of the film's ubiquitous cats start flying into the frame from all sides, scratching her and bringing her helpless to the ground, where a gloved killer finishes her with a knife.

Elise's death is arguably the strangest, but the death sequence that comes closest to being a microcosm of the film's approach to spectacles of death is the first, which culminates with the murder of Mark's friend Sarah. Mark and Sarah study music in the same class in Rome. When Mark leaves Rose's letter behind in class, Sarah picks it up and takes it with her during her journey home through a dark and stormy night. She reads it while riding in a taxi driven by the same man (or at least the same actor) who drives Suzy's taxi in *Suspiria*. The letter's contents inspire her to tell the driver to take her to a library, and when she gets out of the taxi, she pricks her finger on a needle sticking out of the door. The pricked finger has fairy-tale resonance (see Sleeping Beauty), and an extreme close-up emphasizes it with foreboding. After nabbing a copy of *The Three Mothers,* she gets lost trying to find her way out of the library. She soon finds herself in a strange room, lit with the same primary colors that signal bad places in *Suspiria,* filled with open flames and a cauldron of bubbling goo. A figure tending the cauldron sees that Sarah carries Varelli's book, and he attacks her, his monstrous hands almost thrusting her face into the goo. She flees for home, where she runs into her neighbor Carlo (Gabriele Lavia, who plays a different Carlo in *Deep Red* and Mr. Betti in Argento's 2001 film *Sleepless*). Carlo agrees to stay with her until she feels less afraid, and when she asks whether he has heard of the Three Sisters (a.k.a. the Three Mothers), he fatefully replies that he only believes in what he can see and touch. Sarah puts on music by Verdi, which provides the sound track to the coming violence. When she goes to phone Mark about the letter (she gets his answering machine), the scene cuts to black-gloved hands unfolding four attached paper dolls. As a hand begins to use scissors to decapitate one of the dolls, the scene cuts to a lizard eating a moth, a random insert that corresponds with an image that appears later in the film when Mark, crawling under the floorboards on his way to meet Mater Tenebrarum, sees a cat eating a rat (figures 20–22). These moments' randomness underscores the randomness set in motion by the black-gloved hands mutilating the paper dolls. After the first doll decapitation, the scene cuts to a woman being hanged

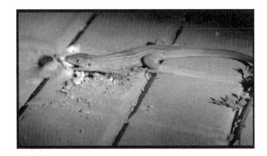

Figure 20–22. In *Inferno,* images of random violence—such as a lizard eating a moth, a woman being hanged, and a cat eating a rat—underscore the randomness of the murders.

(figure 21). After the second doll decapitation, the scene cuts back to the exterior of Sarah's building, wherein Sarah is about to meet her doom.

As in *Suspiria,* the editing in this scene suggests the workings of magic, with the editorial cuts from the scissor-cut dolls, to the mysteriously hanged woman, back to the dolls, and then to Sarah's death sequence, signifying a voodoo-like equation between the dolls' mutilations and the characters'. This connection is not necessarily obvious, however, and the surprisingly decontextualized hanged woman contributes to the aura of randomness surrounding the scenes that follow (commenting on the hanged woman in an interview by Francesco Locane on the fan Web site Dark Dreams, Argento says, "The city is in chaos; it is an image of death"). As Sarah begins to realize the extent of her danger, the lights go out, and Carlo goes to fix the fuse box. He stumbles back into Sarah's view, a knife buried in his neck, and falls on top of her, choking and spitting blood, grasping at her, pinning her, until finally a black-gloved hand removes the knife and plunges it into Sarah's back. Carlo's gruesome demise increases the film's abiding sense of randomness by having the ratio of his death scene to his total screen time be painfully skewed toward death. The chain of dolls, rather than clearly signifying a chain of mystical deaths, works as a metaphor for the chain of random violence, and the chain of random violence works as a metaphor for the movie as a whole. The chain of dolls reflects on the film as a sequence of bizarre happenings held together more by style and editing, aspects of the medium, than by coherent story. Just as the paper is the medium and linkage of the dolls, celluloid is the medium and linkage of the deaths.

The medium, then, replaces narrative as the film's central focus. The paper-doll series of deaths dramatizes this replacement, giving the Marshall McLuhan saw "the medium is the message" a new, darker shade of meaning. After Mark comes to Sarah's apartment and finds her stabbed to death, the action switches from Rome to New York, where a monstrous hand uses a window like a guillotine to dispatch Rose and create another link in the chain of randomness. Up to this point, Rose has been a protagonist from the same mold as *Suspiria*'s Suzy Banyon, a strong-willed woman stirring up trouble by asking too many questions, so her death is a blow to audience expectations as well as to genre conventions, à la the blow delivered to audiences by the genre-changing murder of Marion Crane (shower-dying Janet Leigh) after *Psycho* spends its first third developing her as the lead. In killing off Rose, *Inferno* goes to an even greater extreme, again throwing off a common screentime ratio, that of time given to a victim versus time given to a survivor. Unaware of his sister's death, Mark arrives at Mater Tenebrarum's house in New York and picks up the *giallo*-like amateur sleuthing for the film's second half, with the result that the audience either has to transfer identification from one lead to another, or (as is often the case with *Inferno*) the audience feels lost, abandoned by a narrative that eschews the convention of unfolding a story by consistently following an individual or group, a convention so widespread that it seems a defining element of film narrative itself.

Because it has a chain of two protagonists instead of horror's typical sole survivor,[9] *Inferno* provides only one consistent focus from beginning to end: Mater Tenebrarum's house. While many tales of haunted houses treat their settings as characters, *Inferno* is one of the few that use stylized representation of a setting *instead* of characters as a source of (arguably insufficient) coherence. Whether this replacement of character with hyperstylized mise-en-scène and editing succeeds in creating a good film is debatable, but successful or not, it follows *Suspiria* in downgrading narrative and affirming spectacle as the defining element of film experience. Furthermore, even the house, whose architectural impossibility doubles the impossibility of the storyline, dies in the end, and since Mark does not so much triumph over the evil of Mater Tenebrarum as run away from it, the final conflagration produces no real hero, tragic, antiheroic, or otherwise. *Inferno*'s opposition to narrative is stronger than *Suspiria*'s because out of all Argento's films, it comes closest to being pure spectacle. Freedom from narrative may or may not be the purity that Argento invokes when he calls *Inferno* one of his "purest" films, but it is the purity that marks the film's greatest feat.

Mother of Tears

Almost everything about *Inferno* is unconventional, but it does make one move that is very conventional for the second film in a horror series: it paves the way for part three. During the early scenes that show Mark and Sarah in the music conservatory in Rome, Mark twice encounters a beautiful woman whose presence coincides with strange happenings. First, she appears in the conservatory, and Argento's editorial representations of magic indicate that she is preventing Mark from reading Rose's letter. Second, she appears in a car driving past Sarah's building just after Sarah's brutal death, which suggests that her power has caused the brutality. These coincidences combine with Varelli's voiceover from the beginning of the film, which notes that Mater Lachrymarum is the most beautiful of the three sisters and located in Rome, to suggest that this woman is the third Mother herself. *Inferno* did not achieve *Suspiria*'s mainstream success, but both films garnered enough of a cult following for these glimpses of the third Mother to create fervor for the third film. Stories circulated widely that a script was ready soon after *Inferno*'s release, and to explain a growing delay, speculations grew about Argento's trouble with Fox, *Inferno*'s distributor, as well as about his troubled relationship with Daria Nicolodi. Argento's explanation, in an interview on BloodyDisgusting.com, is that after five years working on the series, he "was a little tired of telling the story" (Argento, "Interview with *Mother*"). The whole truth is likely a combination of reasons. In any case, thirty years passed between the release of *Suspiria* (1977) and *Mother of Tears: The Third Mother* (2007), and during that time, Argento's work had transformed in ways that the final section of this essay explores. As a result, *Mother of Tears* hardly looks like it belongs with the previous two films. Among Argento's devotees, reactions have been polarized, but the poles have not been the extremes of total garbage and pure genius that marked *Suspiria*'s reception: while many hate it, few are willing to rate *Mother of Tears* more highly than "acceptable" or "pretty good." Even McDonagh describes it as "sadly unconvincing" (xxv).

In their time, *Suspiria* and *Inferno* were revolutionary. Although their colorful palettes can be traced back to films such as Mario Bava's *Blood and Black Lace* (1964) and even to the tinted frames of *The Cabinet of Dr. Caligari* (1920), their combinations of wild visuals with storylines that challenge storytelling itself were unlike anything the world had ever seen. During the years since *Inferno*, horror cinema has produced many visually stunning films, and the best-known of such works often acknowledge Argento—for example, the makers of the American *Saw* series (2004–10) tag his works visually through their signature puppet's resemblance to the puppet in *Deep Red* as a cornerstone of contemporary horror. A film that merely duplicated the by-2007 familiar aesthetics of *Suspiria* and *Inferno* would not be worthy of the series; *Mother of Tears* had to be different, rooted in its own moment as much as in its predecessors, to pose the sort of challenges that define the Three Mothers trilogy. The differences of *Mother of Tears* achieve just that sort of challenge, and like most films that are shockingly different, it has often been misunderstood.

While summarizing the stories of *Suspiria* and *Inferno* is difficult to do without lapsing into misrepresentation, summarizing *Mother of Tears* is easy. It begins with the Catholic Cardinal Monsignor Brusca and a construction team uncovering the grave of Oscar de la Valle, who in 1814 transported an urn full of Mater Lachrymarum's magical items to Viterbo, bringing death and destruction to all he encountered. The church buried La Valle in a coffin chained to the urn, so unearthing the coffin and breaking the chains reawakens the evil, setting Mater Lachrymarum's apocalyptic plans in motion. A priest sends the urn to his friend Michael Pierce at the Museum of Ancient Art in Rome, but an art-restoration student, Sarah Mandy (Asia Argento), and a museum staff member, Giselle Mares, come across it first. They break the urn's wax seal and examine its contents. As soon as Sarah leaves Giselle alone, Mater Lachrymarum and her demonic helpers murder Giselle, and Sarah soon finds herself trying to solve the mystery of Giselle's death while running for her life amidst a city spiraling into chaos. Michael and Sarah are lovers, so when Mater Lachrymarum's followers kidnap Michael's son, the stakes become personal. They become even more personal when Sarah discovers that she is the daughter of a white witch who was murdered by the Three Mothers and that she, too, is a white witch. With the assistance of her mother's spirit and an assemblage of religious and arcane do-gooders, Sarah proceeds from discovery to discovery. Since Mater Lachrymarum's minions hound her steps and murder all who help her, she leaves a trail of bodies in her wake, and the police, especially Detective Enzo Marchi, follow the trail. Sarah and Enzo both end up in the house Varelli built in Rome, and they find a secret passage that leads to the underground lair where Mater Lachrymarum and followers from around the world are having an orgy of sadistic sacrifice. Narrowly avoiding becoming sacrifices themselves, Sarah and Enzo destroy a garment from the urn that is the key to Mater Lachrymarum's power, which makes the house and the underground lair begin to crumble. A falling obelisk impales Mater Lachrymarum, and Sarah and Enzo barely escape the destruction, emerging from the underground lair victorious as a new day dawns on rescued Rome.

The emphasis on Rome provides one of *Mother of Tears*'s most significant departures, not only from the other films in the Three Mothers trilogy but from Argento's entire corpus. Whereas the early *gialli* show Rome as a city difficult to distinguish from any other modern metropolis, *Mother of Tears* features a Rome that tourists will recognize, full of domes, arches, and ruins. Whereas the first two films in the trilogy provide distinct urban locations for actions that primarily occur on the insides of bizarre and colorful structures, *Mother of Tears* returns again and again to the streets, filming mostly on location rather than on sets constructed to advertise their own artificiality. The political valence of *Suspiria*'s German setting is a subtle way to suggest the Three Mothers' fascistic plans for world domination; *Inferno*'s American setting is slightly less subtle in tying New York to Mater Tenebrarum's globalized power, but it is still not a subject directly discussed. By contrast, *Mother of Tears* makes Rome's political significance essential to the story. Providing crucial exposition, Sarah's helper Father Johannes (Udo Kier) explains that the witches "aim to make Rome fall again, to usher in the Second Age of Witches." Confirming Father Johannes's claims, a televised newscast later comments on the chaos, "They're calling it the Second Fall of Rome." Finally, the Three Mothers' hazy plan from the first two films becomes clear: they will bring in new Dark Ages by the same means that brought on the first Dark Ages, Rome's fall, so the story of *Mother of Tears* could occur nowhere else.

The importance of Rome in the Three Mothers' plans justifies the shift from *Suspiria* and *Inferno*'s colorfully constructed interiors to the abundant exterior locations shot for *Mother of Tears*. After the murder of Giselle, Mater Lachrymarum and her followers reclaim the urn and the magic objects inside, and they celebrate their triumph through a ceremony in which Mater Lachrymarum lowers the garment of power onto her naked, thoroughly photographed body. She chants words to accompany the mystic symbols on her new clothes, and as she raises her arms, the scene cuts to a woman on a bridge, surrounded by classical Roman architecture, pushing a stroller. She stops, picks up her baby, smiles, throws it over the side of the bridge (where it smacks into fatal stone and thuds into the water), and then breaks into tears. Next, a quick succession of cuts—to a stabbing on an exterior stairway, to hoodlums smashing a car, to two men strangling one another on a city street, back to the weeping mother—shows that people all over the city are descending into violence brought on by Mater Lachrymarum's spell. Flashes of public violence recur throughout the film, showing more and more people involved, and on one occasion a violent mob almost kills Sarah in the street. The violence brought on by Mater Lachrymarum's magic is both an aim and a means of multiplying the power to do more violence.

The growth of the witch's power through the violence on the streets of Rome provides the background for the journey that leads from Sarah's first encounter with the urn full of magic relics to Sarah finding and killing Mater Lachrymarum by destroying the most important of the relics. This journey is the film's plot, but the story uncovered within the plot duration is much more detailed and chronologically expansive. In fact, Sarah's quest, in which first Michael and later Enzo provide fact-gathering assistance, involves little more than uncovering backstory. The movie develops narrative interest with a few chases, random street violence, and the graphic murders of people who provide Sarah and Michael with information, but other than getting information, the protagonists never really *do* anything between the relic-finding beginning and relic-destroying end. Information gathering is, of course, the primary activity of protagonists in most mystery narratives, including *gialli,* but in such mysteries the information is about a variety of suspects, and the information's purpose is to mislead with red herrings as much or more than it is to enlighten with real explanations. In *Mother of Tears,* the information is not only all relevant to the bona fide Mother of Tears, but it is also all collected for its own sake, because knowing about the Mother of Tears is intrinsically valuable. Instead of art for art's sake, *Mother of Tears* focuses on story for story's sake.

After Sarah and Giselle go through the magic items in the urn, the first major source of storytelling is a priest whom Michael meets at the hospital where Monsignor Brusca is recovering from a stroke suffered shortly after unearthing Oscar de la Valle's grave. As the priest begins the legend of La Valle's discovery of the urn in 1814, the scene cuts to black-and-white sketches of what the priest describes: first, wolves crowded around the town where La Valle and the urn resided, digging up and destroying fresh corpses in the graveyard; then, La Valle boarded a coach for the Vatican, and everywhere he went, "children died, crops burned, whole villages were devastated"; finally, La Valle ended up in Viterbo, sick, blind, and dying. In quick succession after the revelation of this part of the backstory, more random violence plagues Rome, Michael's son is kidnapped, and punk-looking witches from all over the world begin arriving in Rome's airport. The second revelation of backstory, five minutes of film-time after the first, occurs in a library, where Sarah scours books with pages titled "Les Sciences Occultes" that provide artistic renderings of three-headed beasts and other mystical marvels. Thinking aloud as she reads, Sarah says, "Three Furies, three Fates, three Graces, Diana, three-headed, the Triad—why are there always three?" Her reading thus gives the Three Mothers the strong mythical context that they also have in De Quincey's original essay. A call from Michael interrupts Sarah's research and spurs her on toward another major source of storytelling, Father Johannes, on the path to whom she is chased by some of the witches earlier shown arriving in Rome.

While waiting for her meeting with Father Johannes, Sarah meets an intermediate source of information, Marta, who recognizes her as "Elisa Mandy's daughter." Marta provides information about Elisa's role in the backstory, which is crucial because it links Sarah to *Suspiria*. Up until this point, Sarah has believed that her parents died in a car crash in Freiburg, but Marta corrects the misinformation: "Your mother dared to fight a very powerful black witch, Mater Suspiriorum, the Mother of Sighs." Father Johannes enters the room and joins the conversation. In addition to explaining Mater Lachrymarum's goals, he gives the backstory even more depth, telling the story of the Three Mothers' thousand-year reign and their settlement in Freiburg, New York, and Rome. "Mater Tenebrarum and Mater Suspiriorum died many years ago," Father Johannes says, and catching on, Sarah says, "The Mother of Sighs—she murdered my parents." "Yes," Father Johannes continues, "but not before your mother had injured her horribly. After fighting your mother, she was reduced to a shell of her former self. A young dancer named Suzy Banyon finally managed to kill her." Not only does this part of the story create a link to the first film of the Three Mothers trilogy; it also provides more story than *Suspiria* offers by itself. If anyone ever wondered why Suzy Banyon, utterly lacking in magical ability, could kill such an uber-witch during a relatively short and easy exchange, here is the answer: Suzy's triumph might not *seem* to make sense in the first film, but it actually does make sense because prior to the film, Mater Suspirorum was weakened by a white witch with real power.

Sarah's acquisition of sense-making information is interrupted by more chases and the deaths of Father Johannes, Marta, and Marta's lover Elga, but it continues when Sarah goes to meet Mr. Guglielmo De Witt, who identifies himself as an alchemist and builds a connection to *Inferno* comparable to the connection that Father Johannes and Marta build to *Suspiria*. As he subjects Sarah to a mystical eye examination, from which he learns about her journey so far, he explains alchemy's combination of white and black magic as well as of witchcraft and science. "Centuries ago, a great Roman alchemist, Varelli, lived for a time in this villa," De Witt says as he leads Sarah into his home library. "He was also a gifted architect, and near the end of his life, he built the residences for the Three Mothers." At this point, De Witt produces a copy of Varelli's book *The Three Mothers,* and close-ups of its pages show the same text and page design shown at the beginning of *Inferno.* A voiceover and music that sound very similar to the sound that opens the previous film even accompany Sarah's reading. With this last piece of information, Sarah now knows everything that the viewers of all three films know about the Three Mothers, and the journey has given all of this knowledge a context that allows the previous two films to make a great deal more sense than they make on their own. Varelli's book also gives Sarah the last clue she needs to head toward her final confrontation with the Mother of Tears, the location of the witch's house in Rome and the Latin phrase, "What you see does not exist, and what you cannot see is truth," which guides her to the underground lair's hidden entrance.

By having Sarah's journey be a journey of storytelling, *Mother of Tears* not only does the opposite of the previous two films in the series—providing an abundance of story that allows the film's events to make rational sense—but it also recasts the previous films, allowing them to make sense as well. Instead of the excess of nonsense that turns the previous films into attacks on rational storytelling itself, the last film in the series makes so much sense that everything around it starts to make sense, too. The sound track colludes in this effort by combining themes from the previous films' scores with a much more conventional horror-film score that uses choral motifs to highlight the grandly religious, apocalyptic terror. Instead of being overtly antinarrative, *Mother of Tears* embraces narrative with the grandest narrative possible, one that makes sense of one thousand years of evil and then posits as its possible ending the end of the world. The scope is, in a word, biblical. It's not just a narrative; it's a supernarrative.

This supernarrativity is what perhaps most distinguishes the third film in the Three Mothers trilogy from the first two, and it lies behind much of the film's critical reception. A review by Dennis Harvey in *Variety* demonstrates:

It has taken Dario Argento nearly three decades to complete his "Three Mothers" horror trilogy commenced by 1977's "Suspiria"—his first, best and most widely popular post-giallo effort—and 1980's visually striking if muddled "Inferno." Whether viewers will think "Mother of Tears: The Third Mother" was worth the wait depends on if they are willing to settle for laughs over chills: This hectic pileup of supernatural nonsense is a treasure trove of seemingly unintentional hilarity. Although lacking helmer's usual aesthetic panache, this "Mother" is a cheesy, breathless future camp classic.

"Nonsense" in this review differs from the "muddled" nonsense of *Inferno*. It is of a class with "laughs," "hilarity," and "camp"; it refers to the film's undeniable aura of silliness, which radiates from its alarming excesses. In addition to the excess of story, *Mother of Tears* offers an excess of violence, which comes closer to the spirit of the earlier films but greatly surpasses them. Giselle gets her jaw ripped apart by a medieval torture device; she is also eviscerated with a knife and strangled with her own intestines. The Japanese witch who leads a group of witches from the airport gets her head smashed like a melon by a train's bathroom door. Father Johannes gets his throat slashed and his face mutilated by a meat cleaver. Michael's very young son gets torn apart and cannibalized. Elga gets her eyes gouged out by another medieval torture device, and Marta gets skewered by a spear that enters her vagina and exits her mouth. The list could continue. For visual flair, none of these deaths matches *Suspiria*'s close-up of a knife entering a still-beating heart, but together they might rival Peter Jackson's *Dead Alive* (1992) for the title of Goriest Film Ever. The extremes are extreme enough to be ludicrous, nauseating enough to be laughable.

Another laughable extreme appears in the film's treatment of gender issues. In *Deep Red,* the relationship between the amateur detective Marcus and his partner-in-sleuthing Gianna provides a humorous counterpart to the subtexts related to sex and sexuality that appear in Carlo's storyline. Playboy Marcus is smaller than Gianna, and since she is a confident professional, he often feels a need to assert his masculinity, even accepting her teasing offer to arm wrestle (he loses). Although the confusion about gender roles between Mark and Gianna plays for comedy, the playful subversion of those roles is ultimately serious, and as *Tenebre*'s exchange between Peter Neal and the reporter Tilde demonstrates, Argento listens to the critics who call his work sexist. Charges of sexism leveled against *Suspiria* and *Inferno* likely stem from their unwavering depictions of the feminine as either evil or an object of sexualized violence, depictions consistent with Barbara Creed's discussion of female abjection and the monstrous-feminine, which derives much of its monstrous power from the reproductive (i.e., mothering) capacity of the female body. The antagonists are, after all, witches led by a triad of cruel matriarchs, and their mostly female victims tend to be in their nightclothes when torn to pieces. Instead of backing down after thirty years of having the Three Mothers films called sexist, Argento ramps up the depiction of female abjection in *Mother of Tears.* The women in this film are not only violent; they are bad mothers. Under the influence of the Mother of Tears, one woman throws her baby off a bridge, witches eat Michael's son, and Father Johannes's assistant Valeria murders her own child with a cleaver before turning on Father Johannes. The ultimate bad mother, the Mother of Tears (a "wicked stepmother," as Varelli says in his book *The Three Mothers,* quoted in *Inferno*), becomes a cipher for bad motherhood, for women failing to live up to their God-given roles as nurturing givers of life.

While *Mother of Tears* takes the depictions of feminine evil to an even higher level, it also adds an element missing from the earlier films: *good* mothers who contrast with the bad. The ultimate good mother is Elisa, whose commitment to nurturing her progeny continues from beyond the grave. Sarah's devotion to her good mother appears several times, particularly when she weeps over pictures of her dead parent and when, after Marta briefly summons Elisa's spirit, grown-up Sarah shouts, "Don't leave me, Mommy!" to the fading shade. Mommy does not actually leave Sarah at that point; she stays to help until she must sacrifice herself to save Sarah by dragging Michael (turned into an undead servant of Mater Lachrymarum) into the fiery netherworld. Although she is not as dedicated as Elisa, Marta is also a good-mother figure. Her voice and eyes effuse sympathy when she tells Sarah the truth about her parents, and when the younger woman is in need, Marta and her partner Elga take Sarah into their home. That Marta and Elga are both lesbians and good-mother figures extends Argento's history of sympathetic portrayals of homosexuals. The lesbians' difference from the reproductive mothers who throw their babies off bridges and hack them up with meat cleavers defines good motherhood not as giving birth but as truly nurturing and caring for the young.

The effect of the ludicrous extremes of good and bad motherhood, extremes that do not necessarily ally reproduction with goodness, ultimately connect to extreme representations of patriarchy and heteronormativity. Heternormativity appears in the deaths of the good lesbian mothers: Marta's death from a spear driven through her vagina is a grotesque phallic punishment of her sexual deviance; it allies phallic aggression with heteronormative oppression, which is itself allied with Mater Lachrymarum's forces of bad motherhood. The extremity of the punishment reflects the extremity of the normative forces, which condemn themselves through the excess of the violence they do. The death of the Mother of Tears herself echoes the punishment that her minions visit upon Marta: when Sarah destroys the magic garment, Mater Lachrymarum stands naked and helpless before her followers for an instant and then is skewered by a giant obelisk that comes crashing into her lair. The phallic obelisk highlights the irony of a woman participating in phallic aggression that can—and does—subdue her as well. The aggression and violence reveal the evils of heternormative and patriarchal forces, which collapse on their purveyors just as the Three Mothers' houses collapse when their power is overcome. Mater Lachrymarum's death by obelisk is poetic justice to the Nth degree.

While the critical possibilities of such justice have a subversive allure, their ludicrous degree is problematic for any reading of the film that tries to establish a consistent political rhetoric. The extremes surrounding good and bad motherhood go so far that they do not seem sincere. When an adult shouts "Don't leave me, Mommy!" to her mother's ghost, the film's mommy issues—amplified by the fact that the exchange between mother and daughter is played by real-life mother and daughter Daria Nicolodi and Asia Argento—become so saccharine that they are almost as nauseating as the spear skewering Marta from orifice to orifice. The excess of the film's gore and supernarrativity combines with the excessive polarization of feminine roles to make *Mother of Tears* appear exaggerated on every level—sensory, narrative, and interpretive. In the context of such exaggeration, definitively labeling the film's exploitative imagery as feminist or antifeminist, queer or antiqueer becomes impossible. The result of the exaggeration is, as Dennis Harvey claims in *Variety*, pure camp. Nathan Lee, in a review in the *New York Times* titled "Supernatural Stew, Served with Camp," refers to the film's premise as "magnificent nonsense." Susan Sontag's classic 1964 essay "Notes on 'Camp'" describes camp as "a certain mode of aestheticism," which "is the spirit of extravagance" that as a taste responds to "the strongly exaggerated" (43). It relies on "seriousness that fails," or what Harvey calls "unintentional hilarity." Given Argento's turn toward dark humor in his *Masters of Horror* TV films *Jenifer* (2005) and *Pelts* (2006), immediate predecessors to *Mother of Tears*, intentionality behind the humor is debatable. Whether or not it is intentional, the failed seriousness of the film's aesthetic treatments of storytelling, violence, and gender issues makes its narrative absurd, not nonsensical in terms of irrationality but in terms of silliness. Exploring an avenue of aestheticism different from those explored in the earlier films, *Mother of Tears* uses the grandest narrative possible, a campy narrative so sweeping that it adds sense where it was formerly absent, and the result is silliness. While *Suspiria* and *Inferno* attack narrative through nonsensical irrationality, *Mother of Tears* attacks narrative by having rationality create nonsense. *Mother of Tears* is an inversion of the previous films with the same result: narrative's claim to primacy in film experience is laid low.

The particular mode of silly narrative that *Mother of Tears* employs resonates with some of the most popular novels-turned-films of its decade. David Edelstein of *New York* magazine claims that Sarah's "odyssey has a little *Harry Potter*, a little *Da Vinci Code*," and several Web commentators compare the film to Dan Brown's *Angels and Demons*, which also features characters running around Rome to stop a deadly plot.[10] What these texts have in common with *Mother of Tears* is the depiction of the forces of good fighting against conspiracies of bad so immense that the outcome of the fight could change the world forever. Their scope, which is critical to their appeal and success, is appropriately millennial, grand not despite postmodernity's skepticism about grand narratives of truth but *because* of that skepticism. Conspiracy narratives focus on paranoid reason's uncanny production of sense behind seemingly disconnected phenomena. In religious conspiracies, skeptical questioning of the overarching truths of religion's belief in the supernatural, as in the adaptations of Dan Brown's novels, often produces the possibility of newer, greater truths. *Mother of Tears* takes on the grandness of these texts' millennial scope and extends them to the point where their seriousness visibly fails, and in doing so it approaches satire of millennial sensibilities.

Similarly, the extreme gore, particularly in the scenes involving medieval torture devices, evokes another of the decade's most popular series, the *Saw* films that helped make "torture porn" part of the American film vocabulary. Those uberviolent films acknowledge Argento through their random puppets and carefully choreographed set pieces, and Argento, in turn, acknowledges them through a kind of one-upmanship, a demonstration that a master from an earlier generation can still outdo his cinematic progeny. The relationships between *Mother of Tears* and its higher-grossing contemporaries show Argento's film to be both of its time and apart from it, participating in its discourses while maintaining an ironic distance that highlights contemporaries' weaknesses while celebrating their triumphs.

Although the campiness and grandness of its narrative sets *Mother of Tears* apart, the film still bears many elements of Argento's signature style. A standout example is the scene in which Sarah explores the house Varelli built for Mater Lachrymarum, which, as Lee notes in the *New York Times*, consists mainly of a three-and-a-half minute "Steadicam tracking shot of thrilling complexity: the camera follows [Sarah] up and down stairs, through delicate variations of light and shadow"; it also moves gracefully from low to high angles to capture her disorientation as she navigates the labyrinthine halls and stairways. Although it gravitates toward a camp aestheticism, *Mother of Tears* does not completely abandon the traditional aestheticism—the appreciation for the beauty possible through cinematography—that characterizes the other films in the trilogy. Its use of elaborate set pieces and an amateur detective ties it to the first and second films and to the earlier *gialli*. Indeed, except for when professional detectives replace the amateurs, as in *The Stendhal Syndrome*, these elements run through all of Argento's feature films, *giallo* and supernatural alike (one could even argue that these elements are present in his lone comedy, *The Five Days of Milan*).

This continuity troubles the division of *giallo* and supernatural films into separate genres or subgenres. In *Broken Mirrors/Broken Minds*,

McDonagh includes an interview in which she says to Argento, "Your own films fall into two groups—the naturalistic thrillers and the supernatural horror films." Argento replies, "I think that's an artificial distinction; I don't see a great difference between them. The realistic pictures are not very realistic, even though they're about psychopaths rather than witches" (235–36). This reply suggests that in addition to troubling gender, sexuality, science, rationality, and narrative, Argento implicitly troubles genre.

As Argento's comment about his unrealistic realism indicates, strong genre boundaries do not divide his films into distinct categories. While the move from *Deep Red* to *Suspiria* is a turn toward the supernatural, the amateur sleuthing of Suzy, Rose, Mark, and Sarah in the Three Mothers trilogy imports aspects of the *giallo* into the context of supernatural horror. Furthermore, *Deep Red* and *Suspiria* share *The Bird with the Crystal Plumage*'s interest in reconstructed memory: just as *Bird*'s Sam and *Deep Red*'s Marcus see things of critical importance that they work to remember up until the films' climaxes, Suzy hears the soon-to-be-victim Pat say something, a hint about how to access the witches' hidden lair, that she struggles to understand until a critical moment when she is able to use the memory to find Mater Suspiriorum. Such recurring elements make genre boundaries permeable, but *Phenomena,* the film that Argento made between *Tenebre* and *Opera,* goes even further, becoming an experimental hybrid of *giallo* and supernatural horror that constitutes an attack on rational narrative worthy of the Three Mothers.

Phenomena

In contrast to its initial American title, *Creepers,* which emphasizes the film's interest in bugs, the lasting title *Phenomena* emphasizes the importance of seeing the film as a collection of strange happenings rather than as a deliberately plotted narrative. It is also a collection of Argento's styles and subjects, a microcosm of his works. Some critics regard it as the "nadir" of Argento's career (Gracey 94), and others regard it as one of his "most successful films" (Cozzi 86). In an interview on the Anchor Bay DVD, Argento calls *Phenomena* his "most personal" film as well as his "best." Regardless of its success as a film on its own, as part of Argento's entire oeuvre it stands as the effort that comes closest to using an incoherent story to articulate a coherent philosophy of what film as an art form should accomplish.

One major thread of the story has Jennifer Corvino (Jennifer Connelly—in the DVD interview, Argento explains that he used the name Jennifer to help Connelly identify with the part), the adolescent daughter of a celebrity, becoming an amateur detective in the case of a serial killer who is victimizing the students in her all-girls boarding school. This aspect of the story is pure *giallo*, and it plays out through familiar stalk-and-kill set pieces that overshadow but do not obscure a typical whodunit mystery with (barely) human culprits. However, Jennifer is not a normal amateur detective. The story's second major thread follows her as she tries to cope with her supernatural influence over insects, which swarm to protect her in times of distress and can telepathically communicate crucial information, such as the locations of dead bodies, to help her solve mysteries. Jennifer therefore has a place among other young people with psychic powers from then-recent supernatural horror films like *Carrie* (1976), *The Fury* (1978), *The Shining* (1980), and *Firestarter* (1984). With her supernatural defenses, Jennifer is more like Sarah from *Mother of Tears* than Suzy from *Suspiria* or one of the sleuths from the first five *gialli*, but unlike Sarah, Jennifer needs her powers to battle people who kill through ordinary means. The stories of the Three Mothers engage everyone with the supernatural, but the story of *Phenomena* confines the supernatural to a single character in an otherwise naturalistic mystery. The supernatural and natural phenomena interact as Jennifer interacts with her world, but one never entirely subsumes the other, so horror neither subsumes nor is subsumed by *giallo*.

The failure of the supernatural and the natural to subsume one another results from a struggle that plays out in *Phenomena*'s aesthetic as well as its story. Professor John McGregor (Donald Pleasance), a wheelchair-bound entomologist who helps Jennifer understand her power, turns a conversation about insects and the wind into an eerie reflection on the realm that he and his young female friend occupy:

> A very particular wind, typical of this part of the country. It comes from the Alps. The blasts of warm air cause snow avalanches, make the flowers grow, the hatching of the larvae. Some people get headaches; when it blows, there are those who say it causes madness. It's a strange part of the country, the Swiss Transylvania.

As Professor McGregor speaks, the camera slowly zooms in, giving his carefully delivered words greater import. On the sound track, the wind blows steadily, underscoring the ubiquity and power of what the professor describes. What he says is, strictly speaking, scientific: warm air causes avalanches and provokes the maturation of flowers and insects, which can trigger intense allergic as well as psychological reactions. Calling the region the "Swiss Transylvania," however, gives it a pall of supernatural significance. Thanks to Bram Stoker, Transylvania for many connotes vampires, but as Stoker indicates in the opening pages of *Dracula,* the Romanian forests had rich traditions of superstition long before they captured the Irish novelist's imagination. A wind with the power to alter lives, especially in a region already shrouded in superstition akin to the Transylvanian, could seem unnatural, and as the backdrop for Jennifer's supernatural relationship with insects, it seems like magic.

Cinematography and sound conspire to arouse such superstitious feeling, beginning with the film's opening frames, which capture sublime mountains and swaying trees as a bus approaches on a narrow road. The whistling wind conveys the vastness of the surroundings, and the bus retrieves a line of passengers before it putters away, leaving Vera (Fiore Argento) behind. Goblin's soft, haunting score rises, accenting the wind, and while the credits roll, a high crane shot explores the trees, leaving Vera beneath them, and then rejoins her as she heads toward a house tagged by sound and seclusion as a bad place. As she approaches the entrance, quick cuts show chains attached to a wall, jerking as if someone, or some*thing,* held by them were fighting to be free. The chains conjure the inhuman, the idea of a monster about to escape captivity in a mystical world of majestic mountains and dark woods.

The creature escapes and stalks Vera through point-of-view shots that hide his appearance. He eventually kills her, stabbing her with scissors, shoving her through glass (an effect shot by the cinematographer Romano Albani at 340 frames per second), and sending her severed head tumbling down a waterfall. The actions are inhuman, but the perpetrator is eventually revealed as human, at least mostly. An uptight schoolmistress at the academy Jennifer attends, Frau Bruckner (Daria Nicolodi), turns out to be protecting the killer, her deformed son. Although the connection to the schoolmistress is not made until after Jennifer falls into Frau Bruckner's clutches, a police detective, Inspector Geiger, visits an insane asylum to learn about the killer's genesis. The member of the hospital staff who tells the tale gives the asylum supernatural associations that fit with the Swiss Transylvanian surroundings: "The further down one goes in this place, the more monstrous the inmates become. It's probably the same in hell." When Inspector Geiger eventually visits Frau Bruckner's home, they discuss the killer's conception; she shows the detective a large scar on her chest as she recalls being grabbed by one of the asylum's inmates and raped through the bars of his cell. Frau Bruckner tells Jennifer that the child born from the rape "doesn't want to see his reflection . . . he stays in his room with his crazy thoughts." The boy's violent origin in a place compared to hell combines with his madness and aversion to mirrors to give him a mythical aura, a monstrosity that exceeds humanity and therefore belongs in the "dark fairy tale" that Argento's cowriter Franco Ferrini claims the film to be.

While the child's origins and actions suggest the fantastic, his grotesque appearance is grounded in science. The effects specialist Sergio Stivaletti, interviewed on the Anchor Bay DVD, explains that his studies in medicine inspired the design for the killer's mask—it is based on Patau syndrome, also known as trisomy 13. According to the U.S. National Library of Medicine, trisomy 13 "is a chromosomal condition associated with severe intellectual disability and physical abnormalities in many parts of the body . . . heart defects, brain or spinal cord abnormalities, very small or poorly developed eyes (microphthalmia), extra fingers and/or toes, an opening in the lip (a cleft lip) with or without an opening in the roof of the mouth (a cleft palate), and weak muscle tone (hypotonia)" ("Trisomy 13") Although few children survive this condition as long as Frau Bruckner's son, this medical description accounts for the boy's appearance as well as his mental instability (figure 23).

Viewed in these terms, the boy is less a fairy-tale monster than a marvel of extreme science, one of many extreme scientific phenomena that Argento puts on display in his aptly named film.

In his DVD interview, Argento claims that even Jennifer's power over insects has a basis in science, pointing to a German news story about police detectives experimenting with insects to help them solve crimes as well as to his consultant, a French entomologist named Leclerk, "who explained everything about how the world of insects applies to the world of criminals." Leclerk's diegetic stand-in, Dr. McGregor, explains

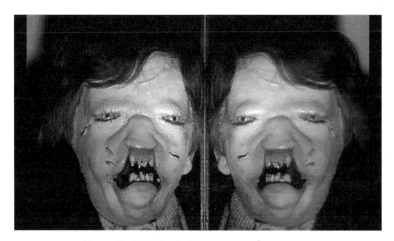

Figure 23. The killer in *Phenomena,*
whose features stem from the medical
condition trisomy 13, is both a fairy-tale
monster and a marvel of extreme science.

to Jennifer, "Extra-sensory perception—the paranormal powers that
are unusual in human beings—are perfectly natural in insects. Some
species communicate with each other over vast distances by telepathy.
. . . It's perfectly normal for insects to be slightly telepathic." Exuding
adolescent angst, Jennifer replies, "Yeah, it's normal for insects, but am
I normal?" Instead of providing an answer, Argento cuts to a scene of
Jennifer being picked on at school that culminates with her summoning
a swarm of flies that crowd around the school building, silencing her
cruel peers with terror.[11] This sequence grounds Jennifer's blossoming
power in scientific precedent and human development. Parallel to Frau
Bruckner's son, Jennifer is a developing adolescent who is ostracized for
exhibiting a genetic rarity. Like *Deep Red,* which introduces the psychic
Helga through a scientific discussion of extrasensory phenomena that
include insect telepathy, *Phenomena* positions its phenomena on the
fringe, the borderline between scientific rationality and supernatural
madness. On this borderline, the phenomena can be simultaneously
fantastic and scientific, irrational and rational.

Phenomena's flirtations with the irrational go much farther than
Deep Red's, earning association with the Three Mothers trilogy through

narrative elements that defy good sense. Several threads in the film's hybrid *giallo*/supernatural storyline demonstrate its tenuous relationship with the laws of sensible storytelling. First, the film is a mystery that features detectives and clues, but the ratiocination that Sherlock Holmes made central to the mystery genre gets pushed to the superfluous margins. Inspector Geiger exemplifies rational clue following, and it gets him all the way to Frau Bruckner's house. His efforts, however, go unrewarded: Frau Bruckner easily subdues him, and his greatest contribution ends up being that he buys Jennifer a little time to escape. Like the clue following and memory reconstructing of the *giallo* detectives, Geiger's ratiocination is in vain. Jennifer, however, finds her way to the killer's abode not by conventional, rational clue following but by using a special fly, the Great Sarcophagus, that when placed in a box acts as a compass for locating decomposing corpses. Her process also leads to trouble, but she ends up as the film's victorious survivor. These two threads—Inspector Geiger's ratiocination and Jennifer's mystical clue following—diminish classical mystery narrative to irrelevance.

Inspector Geiger's efforts also combine with efforts made by Morris Shapiro, a representative of Jennifer's celebrity father who tries to help her, in another challenge to traditional storytelling. Geiger arrives at Frau Bruckner's house just as Jennifer is figuring out that the schoolmistress is a villain; when Jennifer hears his approach, she lights up at the prospect of rescue. His potential as a rescuer does not disappear when Bruckner subdues him. Trying to flee, Jennifer enters a room where Bruckner has chained Geiger to a wall, and she falls into a pool of maggots and rotting human flesh. When Bruckner comes to finish Jennifer off, Geiger heroically mutilates his own hand to free himself from his chains, but though he tackles the madwoman to help Jennifer escape, Bruckner's reappearance after his attack indicates his failure to be a true savior. Similarly, Morris looks like a potential savior for Jennifer. As she endures abuses at Bruckner's hands, cross-cut scenes show Morris discovering Jennifer's location and driving to her rescue. After Geiger tackles Bruckner, Jennifer flees the house and runs down to the lake, where she has a final battle with Bruckner's deformed son. Surviving the battle with help from her insect friends, Jennifer walks away from the lake and greets Morris's approaching car with a relieved smile. Morris emerges, and they run toward each other with open arms, but before they unite, he is suddenly decapitated by a piece of sharp sheet metal, which Bruckner wields offscreen in her surprise return. Geiger and Morris's failures as rescuers for the young damsel in distress poke fun at such possibilities for narrative resolution as well as the traditional gender roles they involve. In the hybrid world of *Phenomena*, such predictable conclusions and roles have no place.

The actual end of Jennifer's trials ties off a final thread that deals a final blow to traditional narrative expectations. Early in the film, police visit Dr. McGregor to get a forensic analysis of Vera's decomposing head. During their visit, Dr. McGregor introduces them to Inga, a monkey who is trained to help the wheelchair-bound scientist perform daily tasks. With police looking on, Dr. McGregor scolds Inga for handling a scalpel, which the monkey claims to have found outside. Later, Frau Bruckner breaks into Dr. McGregor's home to murder him. Throughout the sequence, Inga screams, trying to find a way in to help her master, but all she can do is witness the crime. Later, Inga finds a straight razor in a garbage can, and in another sequence shown from Bruckner's unidentified point of view, Inga assaults the schoolmistress's car. By the time Bruckner decapitates Morris, Inga is long forgotten, so the film delivers one last surprise when the monkey leaps into the frame, knocks down Bruckner, and mutilates her face and neck with the straight razor. In place of a masculine hero, *Phenomena* provides a monkey as Jennifer's savior. The girl watches the mutilation in horror, and the film ends.

Just as Dr. McGregor gives Jennifer's influence over insects a context of scientific sense, the monkey's storyline provides the means (her training as a companion) and the motive (avenging the murder of her master) that cause her attack on Bruckner. That a monkey would do such things might be hard to believe, but Inga's storyline puts her behavior at least on the border of plausibility. The use of a real monkey in most of Inga's scenes bolsters this plausibility: to perform in the film, the monkey who plays Inga had to be about as smart as her character. She performed well overall, with problems arising only when she wandered off into the forest (retrieved within hours) and bit off the tip of Jennifer Connelly's finger (sewn back on successfully). The monkey phenomenon, like all the others in the film, has enough diegetic and nondiegetic explanation to suspend disbelief, but Inga's attack on Bruckner nevertheless plays as a shocking absurdity. Every bit of weirdness shown in the film's Swiss

Transylvanian setting, taken by itself, fits rationally with its context, but taken all together, these phenomena are overwhelming and therefore hard to believe. As McDonagh states, the film's "excess of plot elements is a little difficult to deal with" (184). Making things even more difficult, the Goblin score plays alongside heavy-metal tracks by Iron Maiden, Motorhead, and other popular musicians from the 1980s—music with lyrics that interrupt the flow of the narrative to alienating ends. *Giallo*, supernatural thriller, rational narrative, irrational randomness, scientific explanation, fantastic fairy tale, mock-heroic ending, monkey-ex-machina, bugs, decay, heavy metal, and a pool of maggots and gore: other than as an aesthetic assault on the senses, what approach could comprehend all of *Phenomena* at once?

The film provides an answer. In addition to having an uncanny influence over insects, Jennifer has a problem with somnambulism. Jennifer walking mindlessly around the school—on crumbling ledges, through woods, to a car of young men ready to take advantage of her, and toward her first meeting with Dr. McGregor—provides some of the film's most suspenseful moments. When she begins her journey, she sees a long white hallway lined with bluish doors (figure 24). It appears from her point of view: the shot centers on nebulous white at the hallway's end, and cross-cut with images of Jennifer sleepwalking, the camera tracks through the hall at increasing speed. More than a decade prior to *Phenomena*, Italian television featured *Dario Argento's Door into Darkness*, a show that presents each episode as another door opened upon a narrative possibility. In Jennifer's dream, each door is a possibility for her journey, so it is also a possibility for the film. The odd, excessive collection of elements that is *Phenomena* is a series of opened doors, of imaginings held together by thread after thread of causally motivated narrative. The causation and explanation provided in *Phenomena* appear in such excess that they mock narrative's reliance on such things. They lack the grandiose narrative of *Mother of Tears* as well as the elusive narratives of *Suspiria* and *Inferno*, but they still suggest that the primary purpose of film is not thinking but looking. Processing each opened door in relation to the others challenges or defies sense, but looking through each door, experiencing the dream, is a reward in itself. Taking the point of view of the dreamer, *Phenomena* equates Jennifer with Argento, the dreamer behind the film, and with viewers, the dreamers in front of the

Figure 24. In *Phenomena,* Jennifer's
sleepwalking sequence begins with a
point-of-view shot of a dream-world hallway.

film. The film, then, is the dream, and dreams do not need a reason to
be. Neither do (or does) certain *Phenomena.* Reason and narrative are
ancillary to what film can accomplish. If Argento's films have a coherent
philosophy, it is an imperative: *look,* they say, and *dream.*

Against Conventions: From *Trauma* to *Giallo*

With the exception of the Three Mothers trilogy, Argento has not sub-
jected his films to the parades of sequels typical of horror's masterworks.
The Internet Movie Database reports that plans for a sequel to *Phenomena* got close to production in 2001, but the project got scuttled because
of Argento's contractual obligations. Similarly, the movie that became
The Card Player (2004) was planned as a sequel to *The Stendhal Syndrome,* but since Asia Argento was unavailable to reprise her role, it was
rewritten as a stand-alone. Although Argento's works have few sequels,
the highly repetitive conventions of the *giallo,* some of which Argento
helped to ossify, relate each successive *giallo* in an auteur's oeuvre to its
predecessors. Similarly, repeated conventions are what make sequels to
American slasher films, descendents of the Italian *giallo,* recognizable.
For example, most of the films in the two *Halloween* series (eight films

in the first series, 1978–2002; two going on three in the second, 2007–12) are recognizable because of the return of a killer in a mask that looks like William Shatner with a hangover. Most of the films in the *Friday the Thirteenth* series (eleven films, one remake, 1980–2009) are recognizable because of the return of a killer in a hockey mask; all of the films in the *Nightmare on Elm Street* series (eight films, one remake, 1984–2010; subtract one from either *Friday* or *Nightmare* if double-counting 2003's *Freddy vs. Jason* is objectionable) are recognizable because of the return of a killer with a burnt face and a razor-fingered glove. Similarly, most *gialli* are recognizable because of the return of a killer in a trench coat, hat, and black gloves, so perhaps *all* of Argento's *gialli*, from *Bird* to *Giallo* (1970–2009), should be considered as a single series akin to a series of slashers.

Mikel Koven's *La Dolce Morte* compellingly links the *giallo* to the slasher, and whether or not Argento's *gialli*—or perhaps even all *gialli*—deserve to be considered as a large-scale serial raises theoretical questions about genre, sequels, serials, and remakes that are beyond the scope of this essay. However, for consideration of Argento's works as a whole, the similarities of films within the *giallo* and related traditions have critical importance, and the differences that stand out among those similarities are the key to understanding Argento's development after 1990.

As writer and producer, Argento continued beyond *Phenomena* to work on supernatural horror films directed by men who had previously worked as his assistants; these films include Lamberto Bava's *Demons* (1985) and *Demons 2* (1986), Michele Soavi's *The Church* (1989) and *The Sect* (1991), and Sergio Stivaletti's *Wax Mask* (1997, originally planned as a collaboration with fellow horror maestro Lucio Fulci). These collaborations combined with Argento's own growing reputation to strengthen the international status of Italian horror more generally, helping Argento's protégés as well as directors such as Mario Bava, Lucio Fulci, Sergio Martino, and Aldo Lado to receive much broader recognition. Despite Argento's reputation as a horror auteur, since 1990, almost all of his directorial features—*Trauma* (1993), *The Stendhal Syndrome* (1996), *Sleepless* (2001), *The Card Player* (2004), *Do You Like Hitchcock?* (2005), and *Giallo* (2009)—are naturalistic crime stories that fall into either the *giallo* tradition or what Koven identifies as the closely related *poliziotto* tradition. Of the features that do not fit this description—*Mother of Tears* (2007),

The Phantom of the Opera (1998), and *Dracula 3D* (2012, projected)—the first is the completion of his famous supernatural trilogy, and the latter two are adaptations of classic gothic fiction. These films—in addition to Argento's supernaturally tinted entries for the *Masters of Horror* TV show *Jenifer* (2005) and *Pelts* (2006)—are worthy of consideration, but this essay concludes by considering how the *giallo* and *giallo*-like films reveal a productive tension between Argento's later works and the works from his so-called golden era, which arguably ended with *Opera* (Gracey 139).

Trauma

As its title suggests, *Trauma* focuses on connections among violent experience, repression, and memory—connections explored in the memory reconstructions of *Bird with the Crystal Plumage* and *Deep Red.* In these earlier films, memory reconstructions turn out to be irrelevant to solving the crimes. The heroes' struggles with memory reconstruction are complemented by the villains' struggles with traumas—Monica's memory of her sexual assault in *Bird* and the memory of the murder of Carlo's father that Carlo and Marta share in *Deep Red*—which provide psychoanalytically informed explanations for the killers' actions that the films ultimately dismiss. Thus the films represent memory issues in psychoanalytic terms, not to reveal great truths about memory, but to belittle psychoanalytic truth claims. At first glance, *Trauma* seems to come from the same mold as these earlier films. It has an emphasis on memory that appears alongside uberviolent set pieces (including a decapitation by elevator that recalls Marta's death in *Deep Red*), hints of the supernatural (including a full-blown séance, also recalling *Deep Red*), unusual attention to animals (including a lizard, also from *Deep Red*), gripping camera movements (including killer-cam point-of-view shots, pervasive in earlier films), and other familiar elements that Argento helped turn into *giallo* conventions. In the interview on the Anchor Bay DVD of *Trauma*, Argento refers to the film as "pure Argento," reinforcing the tendency to receive it as a conventional Argento film.

However, unlike the earlier films that emphasize memory, *Trauma* does not treat all of its psychological content with the same dismissiveness. This content takes pride of place in the title, which suggests that the film is not about a single trauma (indeed, it features many) but about trauma as a phenomenon to be explored. Etymologically, "trauma" comes from the Greek word for "wound," and like most Argento films, *Trauma* features plenty of wounding, mostly dealt by the killer known as the Headhunter, who uses a handheld device rigged with a mechanically contracting wire noose that slices easily through necks. "Trauma" more commonly connotes psychological damage resulting from a violent incident. Cathy Caruth summarizes Freud's take on the phenomenon:

> The wound of the mind—the breach in the mind's experience of time, self, and the world—is not, like the wound of the body, a simple and healable event, but rather an event that . . . is experienced too soon, too unexpectedly to be fully known and is therefore not available to consciousness until it imposes itself again, repeatedly, in the nightmares and repetitive actions of the survivor. (3–4)

As the story unfolds, *Trauma* reveals several such incidents in the lives of sixteen-year-old Aura Petrescu (Asia Argento) and her mother Adriana (Piper Laurie), who turns out to be the killer.

Aura enters the film on the verge of jumping off a bridge, across which her fellow protagonist David is driving. He stops to prevent her suicide, and they form a relationship, first that of an adult (David) trying to help a child (Aura) who shares his history of drug addiction, then that of forbidden love. Their second meeting occurs after Aura has endured the trauma of seeing (she believes) both of her parents decapitated by the Headhunter (she has actually seen her mother carrying away her father's severed head). Not long after this incident, David learns that Aura suffers from anorexia, and he turns to a friend who works with him on a television news show for information. "How did she end up that way?" David asks, and his friend explains, "Trouble with her parents. It's said these girls will even have a classic dream. In the dream her father's leaning over her, about to kiss her." Five minutes of film time later, David's friend's voice elaborates on the subject in David's memory while David drives through an unnamed American city (Minneapolis): "There's something like eight million of them out there," meaning eight million women with anorexia. Taking David's perspective, the camera emphasizes glimpses of dangerously skinny women he sees while he drives. The memory-voiceover continues, "Deeply attached to an unstable mother, she'll dream her father is leaning over her about to kiss her."

At this point, the scene cuts to a man's face looming over the camera, identifiable in context as Aura's father leaning over her as a very young child, about to kiss her. Another cut shows Aura as she is in the present, eyes closed, dreaming the dream that David's friend describes and inhabiting her younger self as she waits happily for the kiss. The scene cuts back to the looming face, but before the father's kiss connects, he starts screaming and clutching at his throat. Aura, still inhabiting her younger self, stretches her mouth in a silent scream, and then older Aura, in her bed, awakes from the nightmare. Unclear in its immediate context, Aura's dream of her father being strangled and of her own silent scream reflects what Caruth describes as "the complex ways that knowing and not knowing are entangled in the language of trauma and in the stories associated with it" (4). In this moment of dreaming, Aura both does and does not know what her unconscious tells her in dreams, what her conscious mind represses: her mother is abusive, her father's murderer. The trauma of growing up with such a mother is the cause of her anorexia, a silent scream about the wound in her mind.

Behind Aura's traumatic childhood and present-day experiences lies yet another trauma, the one that prompts Adriana's murder spree. At the film's end, when Adriana has imprisoned and is preparing to kill Aura and David, David asks, "Why did you kill them?" Adriana responds, "Because . . . Nicholas," speaking the name of her baby boy, whose death the film has implied but not yet explained. The scene cuts to a flashback of Adriana in childbirth, doctor and nurses surrounding her. A rainstorm outside causes a sudden power surge that startles the doctor, who is working with a scalpel between Adriana's raised legs. He accidentally decapitates the baby, which explains not only Adriana's trauma but also her motive and modus operandi: many of her victims have been the medical staff involved in the incident, and she has killed them by decapitating them in the rain. In Adriana's flashback, the medical staff gives her shock therapy in an attempt to erase her memory and save their careers. This detail reveals that the traumatic memory has been willfully repressed by Adriana's psyche as well as by medical intervention; as a result of this repression, the memory has been reasserting itself in a repetition compulsion so strong that Adriana will kill only in the rain, the circumstance most strongly associated with her baby

Nicholas's death. She even goes as far as to create rain—setting off a motel's fire alarm and sprinkler system—to supply the conditions necessary to behead a member of the medical staff. Thus Adriana perfectly represents the cycle of trauma and repetition that Freud describes, a cycle so powerful that it ends up involving Aura in her own repetitive, destructive behavior, the life-refusing patterns of anorexia.

While *Trauma* is true to a psychoanalytic representation of trauma, as in the earlier films, Argento does not affirm psychoanalysis as a valid science. This refusal of affirmation occurs in two threads. The first involves what Aura witnesses at her family's estate: she thinks she sees the Headhunter carrying away her parents' severed heads, but like Sam in *The Bird with the Crystal Plumage* and Marcus in *Deep Red*, she feels that something is wrong with the memory. When she finally reconstructs what she really saw, her mother's living head beside her father's severed one, the reconstruction is too late—she and David are already Adriana's prisoners. The belatedness of the reconstruction is consistent with the earlier films; it refuses to validate psychoanalytic approaches to memory. The second refusal involves a psychiatrist, Dr. Judd, who works at the clinic where Aura's family has confined her. Dr. Judd pursues Aura after the murder of her father, bent on recommitting her to his clinic, and in one chase, he gets into a fatal car accident that reveals the severed heads of all the victims in the trunk of his car. The police conclude that he is the Headhunter, but when Adriana is revealed as the killer, Aura figures out Dr. Judd's true motive. Earlier in the film, Dr. Judd gives Aura a highly unorthodox and abusive "treatment" to help her with her memories, a psychedelic drug that causes visually elaborate hallucinations and reveals precisely what Dr. Judd does *not* want her to know: that she once saw him having sex with her mother. Combined with the discovery of Adriana's guilt, the revelation that Dr. Judd has had an affair with Adriana supplies his motive for covering up her crimes and carrying the evidence in his car. In the end, the psychiatrist is an abusive accomplice to murder, so as the film's representative of his profession, he puts psychiatry and psychoanalysis in a very bad light.

In its negative representation of psychoanalysis, *Trauma* is consistent with Argento's earlier films, but unlike *Bird* and *Deep Red*, which classify their psychologically damaged people as murderers who come to very bloody ends, *Trauma* is highly sympathetic to the psychological disorders that the flawed science of psychoanalysis would try to address. In the DVD interview, Argento explains that one inspiration for the film was a niece who struggled with anorexia. Argento and his coauthors on the *Trauma* script became very interested in the subject, so they researched it and discovered that anorexia is a significant and in their view under-represented social problem. The film, then, fills a gap by showing the truth about anorexia. In a sense, the core of the film is Argento's own family trauma, and the film is his own therapy, working through the traumatic experience with his daughter Asia in the role of the anorexic niece. *Trauma* suggests this strong relationship between film and therapy when Dr. Judd's psychedelic memory treatment leads to an image of Aura unraveling a VHS tape, a symbol for the unraveling of her memory that leads to revelations. Film, not psychoanalysis, is once again Argento's source of truth and meaning, but this time the truth has a personal and social mission. The result is a surprisingly traditional narrative film. It is easy to follow, has a staid color palette, and uses editorial cuts that rarely disrupt the story's continuity.

Trauma, then, is true to Argento conventions in every way but one: story is more salient and more important than visual experience. As McDonagh notes, "Enthusiasts treasure his films for their weirdness and their overwhelming visual beauty, precisely those things *Trauma* lacks" (224). The hallucinations and the murders have some of Argento's typi-cal visual flair, but they ultimately only advance the plot. The traditional prioritization of story is for Argento very unconventional, so the creation of what looks like a typical American thriller (it was shot in the United States, mostly using American crew and equipment) is for Argento an experimental move. By differing from his usual approach in this critical way, he challenges the conventions his earlier films helped create by making them compatible with traditional film narrative. Ironically, this breaking of his own mold can only happen through a film that looks like it could have come from somebody else's.

The Stendhal Syndrome (Revisited)

Argento's next film, *The Stendhal Syndrome*, accomplishes a great deal more in the visual arena; it was the first major Italian production to use CGI (Gracey 127). Because Anna Manni is a policewoman, the film belongs more to the *poliziotto* than the *giallo*, but it involves many *giallo* conventions. More importantly, it picks up where *Trauma* left off with serious treatment of character psychology; a psychoanalyst is an important character, and as Argento explains in an interview on the Blue Underground Blu-ray disc, the character represents the real-life psychoanalyst Graziella Magherini, whose book on the Stendhal Syndrome inspired Argento's story. In addition to once again giving psychological content pride of place by using a psychological condition as the film's title, Argento invests a great deal of screen time in showing Anna's psychological response to her rape. Like Monica Ranieri, Anna identifies with her attacker and becomes a murderer. In a sense, *The Stendhal Syndrome* dramatizes the perspective of the killer that is dismissed as irrelevant at the end of *The Bird with the Crystal Plumage*. One result is slower pacing, as the transformation from cop into killer is detailed. Another is that the psychologically troubled protagonist, again played by Asia Argento, becomes highly sympathetic. This sympathy develops from her storyline, so once again, Argento works against his own conventions by making the film's bizarre visuals secondary to plot.

Sleepless

Sleepless spends less time on psychology, making a different departure from the patterns of Argento's earlier films. To some, *Sleepless* seemed not to have departed at all; it begins the Neo-Animal Trilogy, which includes his next two feature-length films, *The Card Player* and *Do You Like Hitchcock?* and brings back even more of the classic *giallo* elements defined by Argento's first three features. An interview for the BBC by Almar Haflidason begins, "'Sleepless' seems to mark a return in style to some of your most acclaimed thrillers like 'Tenebre' and 'Deep Red,'" to which Argento responds, "This is a detective film, a 'giallo,' that has the same atmosphere as those movies. I wanted to get back to my style of twenty years ago after a long period of exploring horror and fantasy themes." Most elements of the plot are indeed a throwback to the films from the 1970s and 1980s, with much more in common with the first five *gialli* than any of the 1990s films. Although one of the protagonists, Ulisse Moretti, is a retired policeman, neither he nor his younger counterpart, Giacomo, is currently part of the police, so they are amateur detectives in a line of descent from *Bird*'s Sam Dalmas. The earlier films focus on protagonists seeing something that they need to reconstruct in their memories; Giacomo remembers hearing something that he struggles to identify and succeeds only after his confrontation with the killer, his friend Lorenzo, is under way. In *Deep Red*, Gabriele Lavia plays Carlo, who as the prime suspect for the murders draws attention away from the real culprit, his mother; in *Sleepless*, Gabriele Lavia plays Mr. Betti, who as the prime suspect for the murders draws attention away from the real culprit, his son (as Mr. Betti holds a gun on Giacomo and his girlfriend Gloria, for a moment he speaks and acts almost *exactly* like Carlo holding a gun on Marcus and Gianna). *Sleepless*'s title lacks the animal references of the titles in the first Animal Trilogy, but the killer chooses victims based on their similarity to animals and kills them in ways that mimic a farmer killing animals in a children's book, *The Death Farm*. During the stalk-and-kill set pieces, the pacing is fast, the editing is frenetic, and the Goblin score uses jolting metal riffs. The killer even uses a child-sized puppet that recalls the puppet from *Deep Red*. The list could go on: the movie is littered with classic Argento *giallo* fare.

What makes *Sleepless* one of the best of Argento's later works is not these much-heralded returns to form: it is the casting and performance of Max von Sydow as Moretti. Born in 1929, von Sydow is a veteran actor from many films by Argento's favorite, Ingmar Bergman, and even though Jennifer Connelly (in *Phenomena*) and Adrien Brody (in *Giallo*) are both Oscar winners, von Sydow is arguably the most celebrated actor ever to appear in an Argento film. His performance gives Moretti dimensions that would usually be superfluous in an Argento film. The film's dialogue mostly focuses on the mystery of the "dwarf killer," who in the present day seems to have picked up a murder spree from the 1980s that ended when a dwarf blamed for the crimes, Vincenzo, turned up dead. When conversations turn to the past, they tend to focus on the childhood experiences of Giacomo and Lorenzo. Moretti says very little about his past or his feelings—only a few lines about his failing memory and his recollections of his investigation of the murders in the 1980s. Nevertheless, von Sydow's layered tones, careworn facial expressions, and deep-feeling eyes give Moretti weight from a violence-stricken life and paternal caring for young Giacomo, whom he has known since his mother was a victim in the 1980s, that direct speech need not acknowledge. The closest acknowledgment occurs at the beginning of the film, set in the 1980s, when Moretti promises the boy Giacomo that he will find his mother's killer, "even if it takes me all my life." More than anything, von Sydow's performance conveys *age*, the wear of a lifetime of such dedication, oldness beyond the character's considerable years.

Moretti's weariness is one of three main ties to the film's title. The other two are more overt. The first relates to the killer's patterning of murders after the morbid children's rhyme (written by Asia Argento) in *The Death Farm,* which states that only after killing all the farm animals can the farmer finally go to sleep. Lorenzo's murders in the 1980s, when he was only a boy, stopped before he could complete the sequence of killings in the rhyme, which suggests that during the seventeen years until his killings resume in the present day, he has been (at least figuratively) sleepless. The second significance of the title *Sleepless* relates to Mrs. de Fabritiis, the mother of Vincenzo, who was wrongly accused of the crimes because witnesses saw that the killer had a small body. Seventeen years later, after Moretti suggests that he now believes Vincenzo could be innocent, Mrs. de Fabritiis says, "I haven't slept for seventeen years," conveying her unwavering concern over the accusations, her longing for closure, and, as she later admits, her guilt over killing Vincenzo to save him from the ignominies of prison. *Sleepless* marks the toll of time's passage again and again, giving the difference between the early 1980s and the early 2000s special significance.

After nearly two decades, Lorenzo resumes his murders, Moretti resumes his investigation, and Argento resumes the style he developed in *Deep Red* and *Tenebre* for the murder-and-investigation *giallo.* This parallel between the recursiveness of Argento's career and the timeline of his film may or may not be intentional, but the backward-looking orientation sets *Sleepless* apart from the aggressively present-focused and, in *Tenebre,* even future-focused orientations of the earlier films to which *Sleepless* invites comparison. *Sleepless*'s departure from Argento conventions is acknowledgment of time and history, and with that acknowledgment comes a need for clarity, akin to Moretti's need to address unfinished business and Mrs. de Fabritiis's need for closure. This clarity manifests in yet another entirely rational storyline that, like *Trauma,* gets fully and clearly explained: Moretti and Giacomo put all the clues together so that every one of the murders makes sense as either a performance of *The Death Farm* or an attempt to elude capture. Even the killer's use of a child-sized puppet, which is bizarre and mysterious in *Deep Red,* makes sense in *Sleepless* because it helps the killer evade discovery by perpetuating the belief that the killer is a dwarf. The film refuses to leave even a single loose end: as the credits roll, a minor plot point, the disappearance of Vincenzo's bones from the cemetery, is resolved when police discover them among Lorenzo's belongings. In *Sleepless*, the wisdom of age explains away the randomness of *Deep Red* and *Tenebre*; no lack of resolution will keep viewers awake.

The Card Player

Even while looking backward, Argento demonstrates a firm grasp on the present by showing an interest in how technology can shape narrative. In *Sleepless*'s first set piece, Angela, a sex worker, discovers evidence that a client is a killer, so she flees his apartment and nervously takes the train home. A cell phone call lets her know that the killer is on her trail; several more calls intensify his game of cat-and-mouse as he stalks and finally kills her on the train. This use of a cell phone recalls a single scene in *The Stendhal Syndrome*, in which the original killer, Alfredo, calls his police-woman victim, Anna, to taunt her and then surprise her by revealing that he is calling from within the same room. Such cell-phone stalking relates Argento's films to the popular *Scream* series (1996–2011), which took its inspiration from the phone stalker in *When a Stranger Calls* (1979). It also provides a bridge to Argento's next film, *The Card Player*, which lets technology shape its narrative by focusing on ways a stalker can wreak havoc with a computer. Like *The Stendhal Syndrome*, *The Card Player* is a *poliziotto*; it takes place almost entirely in the world of law enforcement (a world that is lit, in a major experiment for Argento, almost entirely with natural and location lights). The killer kidnaps young women and uses them as the stakes in games of Internet poker that he plays with the police. Streaming video shows the young women suffering on one side of the screen, while the card games unfold on the other. When the police lose a hand of cards, a woman loses a body part. Refusing to play or losing too many times means a woman dies; enough wins mean she goes free. Seizing on a current fad for video poker and anticipating the computer terror of the big-production effort *Untraceable* (2008), Argento's use of technology in his story makes *The Card Player* unmistakably contemporary even as it replays the black-gloved-killer and other conventions that he has been using for decades.

Online stalking opens up new possibilities for a sadistic killer, and the titular Card Player uses many of them to his advantage. First and foremost, computers hide his identity. The Card Player can interact with the police at great length, and even though the police use high-tech means to try to trace his identity and location, he is never in any real danger of being discovered while he is online. Second, the killer can broaden the impact of his cruelty. Pre-Internet, the only person hurt by every second of a torturous murder was the victim, but with streaming video, the Card Player can torment the police, too: they must watch as the women suffer and feel agonizing suspense over every slowly dealt digital card that will determine the killer's next move. The Card Player's police victims include the commissioner, whose daughter Lucia (Fiore Argento) is one of the streaming victims, as well as Anna, who is singled out to be his primary adversary. Anna eventually learns that the Card Player is Carlo, a fellow policeman who is in love with her and wants revenge for being rebuffed. Third, he can create alibis for himself by misrepresenting the timing of his games. The software the Card Player uses for video poker creates the illusion that he is playing the game live, but Anna and her Irish partner John finally discover that the games are prerecorded, which allows the Card Player to be in the same room with his adversaries while they think he is at a faraway computer.

These advantages help the Card Player to mislead the police as well as the film's audience about his identity, location, and timing, so incorporating the Internet into the story creates many opportunities for suspense and surprise. It also creates distinctive opportunities for visual representation, such as an image that combines the policeman-killer's reflection with the online poker game and streaming video (figure 25). In superimposing Carlo's face as if it were a reflection on the computer screen as he plays an online game, this image avoids a typical shot/reverse editing pattern to establish the relationship between the player and the game. It also collapses three different spaces and activities into a single moment in space and time: the space occupied by the victim and killer (in streaming video), the space occupied by the police (reflected on the screen), and the intermediate space of the Internet-based game all appear simultaneously. The simultaneity encourages viewers (both the police and the film's audience) to interpret the streaming video and the game as live. It is actually prerecorded, but this fact is hidden until later in the

Figure 25. In *The Card Player,* the titular killer
challenges police to poker games over the
Internet; this image exemplifies the opportunities
for layered visuals that this scenario creates.

film, as is Carlo's identity as the killer. The illusory simultaneity of the
actions in the image puts Carlo in two places at once, which is a logical
impossibility of the sort often captured in the illusions painted by M. C.
Escher, for whom Argento shows his appreciation in *Suspiria.* The logical impossibility gives Carlo his alibi: since he cannot be in two places at
once, he cannot be the killer.

The illusion captured in this image makes technology treacherous.
The online game and video are fooling the police just as the film of the
online game, video, and players are likely fooling *The Card Player*'s
audience. This moment in the film is an image (the shot) of an image
(the computer screen) of an image (the streaming video). The combination of technologies captured in these inset images exemplifies what Jay
Bolter and Richard Grusin call "remediation." Bolter and Grusin identify
a tendency of new media to remediate, or incorporate, the old. For example, Internet media remediate video through streaming video content.
Remediation works through a combination of immediacy, a sense of
transparency that allows the user to connect directly with content, and
hypermediacy, elements that foreground the process of mediation. In
the video-poker example, the immediacy works through the suggestion,

an illusion, that the user is actually playing a game with the Card Player, but hypermediacy appears through aspects of the interface, most visibly the screen within a screen created by the streaming video, that call attention to the elements on the screen as computer-generated. Argento also participates in the flipside of remediation, older media incorporating the new, by including this Internet game (new medium) in his film (older medium). The illusion that gives Carlo his alibi—the suggestion that everything occurs simultaneously—stems from the logic of immediacy. The logic of hypermediacy, the fact that the game's inclusion of streaming video is a mediation of a mediation, is what allows both Argento and the Card Player to construct the illusion.

Argento's films have always been self-conscious, from the first meditations on spectatorship in *Bird with the Crystal Plumage* forward. The inclusion of new media in *The Card Player* as illusion makers central to the story asks viewers to think about the media and remediation involved in what they are watching. *The Card Player*, then, takes Argento's now-conventional self-consciousness and gives it a new rhetorical form through new technology. At the same time as the film shows layer upon layer of technology, it does not show what viewers familiar with Argento's work most expect—elaborate, gory violence. While the violence done to the Card Player's victims is extreme, it occurs beyond the frame of the streaming video provided to police, so it is also beyond the images delivered to the film's audience. Argento has described this omission as part of a goal to "'show extreme sadism without any blood'" (qtd. in Jones 307). Another of the film's goals is to depict evil, which he has described as "'present in its various forms and its different masks in all my work. In *The Card Player*, and I feel keenly about this, the new dimension is technology, its power to be employed by evil in its most sinister, phantasmagorical and ambiguous aspects'" (qtd. in Jones 302). The former goal serves the latter: the sadism's bloodlessness keeps attention on its delivery, the technology, which when captured in Argento's frame becomes the self-conscious villain of the piece.

Do You Like Hitchcock?

Argento ratchets up self-consciousness even further in his next feature-length film, *Do You Like Hitchcock?* Although he prefers to cite Fritz Lang and Ingmar Bergman as influences, by 2005 Argento had lived for decades with the moniker the Italian Hitchcock. Made for Italian television, *Do You Like Hitchcock?* is more than an homage to the original Master of Suspense who gave Argento his nickname. It is a film about a young man, Giulio, who studies film and starts seeing elements from Hitchcock's films everywhere in his real life. When someone brutally murders the mother of Sasha, a woman he has spied on from his rear apartment window, he begins to suspect that Sasha and her acquaintance Federica have made a deal to trade murders à la the main characters in Hitchcock's *Strangers on a Train* (1951). Becoming an amateur detective, he gets embroiled in a plot that condenses elements from *Strangers* as well as Hitchcock's *Rear Window* (1954) and *Dial M for Murder* (1954), with shades of *Vertigo, Psycho,* and several other films thrown in for good measure. Giulio's suspicions turn out to be true, and after the women's accomplice Andrea (a man) almost kills him, he and his girlfriend Arianna bring the conspirators to justice.

Do You Like Hitchcock? is a mosaic of references to other films, both Hitchcock's and Argento's. Virtually every shot contains some kind of wink to the audience. Some of those winks are obvious: Giulio often visits his video store, where Andrea is the clerk, which provides the camera opportunities to capture movie posters as well as rows of films that have packaging advertising their titles. The most visible movie posters are for Hitchcock's *Marnie* (1964) and *Psycho,* but also Argento's own *The Card Player.* Movie packaging tags *Vertigo* as well as films by Luchino Visconti (whose 1943 film *Ossessione* is a forerunner of the *giallo*), Bernardo Bertolucci (who cowrote Sergio Leone's 1968 *Once upon a Time in the West* with Argento), William Friedkin (whose 1973 film *The Exorcist* whetted appetites for supernatural horror à la *Suspiria*), and Quentin Tarantino (whose kinetic, uberviolent style owes a well-acknowledged debt to earlier filmmakers like Argento). Beyond these obvious winks, Argento includes shots that look like re-creations of shots from Hitchcock films. For example, Giulio gazing out his window allows for *Rear Window* re-creations, and Giulio in the shower allows for a humorous *Psycho* re-creation. Re-creations also extend to memorable Argento moments—for example, shots of Giulio almost being drowned in hot bathwater and Andrea being hit by a car both recall *Deep Red.*

The sum of these references suggests that the film is less about Hitchcock than it is about Argento as a filmmaker both empowered and haunted by his forerunners. At the beginning of the film, Giulio is writing a thesis about German expressionism, and his apartment walls and viewing habits bring expressionist films such as *The Golem* (1920) and *Nosferatu* (1922) into the picture. This interest tags Argento's roots in expressionist greats like his oft-cited Fritz Lang, and when at the end of the film Giulio says he is now doing a thesis on Russian cinema of the Stalin era, the film suggests that he has moved on from his interest in expressionism just as Argento left his more expressionistic style behind with *Suspiria* and *Inferno*. Such suggestions make reading Giulio as a stand-in for Argento very tempting, but considering that Giulio has a very close relationship with his mother (shades of Norman Bates) and a girlfriend who seems to play a mothering role, such a reading would also be very awkward. Giulio's Freudian characterization ultimately points toward his fictionality; for Argento, Freud is good fun when constructing fictions, but taking Freud as a key to truth would be an error, especially if the truth sought is the truth about Dario.

The most telling wink at the audience in *Do You Like Hitchcock?* appears at the very end, when Giulio returns to his window-gazing habits and spies a new neighbor moving into Sasha's now-vacant apartment. The titillatingly bare-breasted neighbor is reading a novel with a yellow cover—a *giallo*, Mary Roberts Rinehart's *A Light in the Window*. The ending suggests that now that Giulio has survived a Hitchcock plot, he will soon be embroiled in a new wave of Hitchcock-inspired films, a life in *giallo*. If *Do You Like Hitchcock?* were to have a sequel, it might very well be *Do You Like Argento?* To date, it has no such sequel, but the idea of a life in *giallo* becomes literalized in Argento's most recent (at the time of this writing) crime thriller, provocatively titled *Giallo*.

Giallo

A movie called *Giallo* directed by the man who helped to create the *giallo* film tradition suggests the possibility of a summative, authoritative statement about what being *giallo* means; one might look to a film called *Giallo* for the quintessence of *giallo*. Instead, Argento delivers a film that is so ambivalent about *giallo* that it hardly qualifies for the genre. Indeed, it does not fully qualify for the Argento oeuvre discussed in this essay: it is the only feature he has directed without being one of the original screenwriters. Its original authors, Sean Keller and Jim Agnew, did, however, write it with Argento in mind. In an interview with James Gracey, Keller explains:

> We both loved the *gialli* of the sixties and seventies and thought that a super-stylistic homage to the work of Argento, Bava, and (Sergio) Martino would be a refreshing change to the horror scene. We wrote a script that was a kitchen-sink *giallo.* It has everything: opera, cats, black-gloved killers, flashbacks, red herrings, jazz, beautiful women dying horribly. . . . We called it *Yellow.* (Gracey 176)

Thus the film was conceived as the sort of quintessence that its title suggests, but once it fell into Argento's hands, it changed: "A number of cuts were made by the director, and amongst these was the removal of the traditionall *giallo* villain garb of dark leather raincoat, fedora, and black leather gloves" (Gracey 183). Argento's changes did not wipe out the script's *giallo*-ness entirely, but they did increase the distance from *giallo* conventions already inherent in the main character, Inspector Enzo Avolfi (Adrien Brody), whose job as a policeman makes him more proper to *giallo's* near cousin, the *poliziotto.* The un-*giallo* aspects of *Giallo* give the film an overarching ambivalence toward the tradition referenced in its name.

For the knowing viewer, this ambivalence announces itself at the very beginning of the film. After the credits, the camera pans over the city of Turin's beautiful skyline. The scene cuts to a close-up of a man's hands, which are handling a syringe and a liquid—villainous portents—*without* wearing the typical *giallo* killer's black leather gloves. The absence of this critical component, particularly important in Argento films because the gloves allow him to use his own hands in such close-ups, plays as a pointed break with tradition. The hands belong to a killer who calls himself Yellow, not a deliberate reference to crime thrillers but to his jaundiced skin, because of which he has suffered ostracism and abuse since childhood. The revelation of the hands is a surprise break, but its consequences are not as far-reaching as the revelation of the killer's face. Yellow's face appears first in patches framed by the rearview mirror of his taxi, then in a direct profile shot, and finally, from the midpoint of the film onward, in many complete headshots. Enzo and Linda, the sister of Yellow's latest abductee Celine, follow clues toward his name and location, but the audience gets to see and know him far better and far earlier than a typical *giallo* would allow.

Knowing Yellow, getting inside his head, provides the film's primary conceit: Enzo is the sort of cop—clichéd now because of the popularity of *Manhunter* (1986), *The Silence of the Lambs* (1991), and other adaptations of Thomas Harris novels—who walks a fine line between good and evil because to catch killers, he has to think like them ("To catch a killer, you must think like a killer" is the tagline on the cover of the Maya Entertainment *Giallo*). An equation between Enzo and Yellow is anything but subtle. With the help of a great deal of make-up, Adrien Brody plays both roles; the name credited for Yellow, Byron Deidra, is an anagram for his. After getting to know how hard, cold, and calculating Enzo is, Linda finally pronounces, "You're just like him!" Thus she vocalizes a comparison that the film has already made by having both Yellow and Enzo decorate their homes (for Enzo, his office is his home) with photos of mutilated women and by having Enzo reveal that in his childhood, he brutally murdered the man who murdered his mother. This clichéd doubling prevents "police" and "killer" from lining up easily with "good" and "evil," leaving audiences with no option but ambivalence toward the film's primary candidate for hero.

Giallo confirms ambivalence as the film's dominant affect with an ending that has Enzo selfishly kill Yellow before Yellow tells Linda where Celine is trapped. The final shot shows an oblivious policeman patrolling a parking deck. He walks by a van that has Celine bound and gagged in its back, kicking and moaning to be free. The patrolman stops as if he hears something, but he gets interrupted by a brief cell-phone call, after which he turns toward the van. The camera moves toward the van, closer and closer to a pool of Celine's dripping blood. On this image, the film freezes, and the credit "Written and Directed by Dario Argento" appears. Does the policeman save Celine? Just like the moral status of Enzo's methods for hunting killers, the answer is indeterminate.

The indeterminacy and ambivalence that characterize the ending and the detective/killer pairing also apply to the film's treatments of beauty and violence. When Linda first comes to Enzo for help finding her sister, she leaves him a picture, and as he examines it on his own, he remarks, "Too beautiful. He hates beautiful things." This remark shows that Enzo has developed at least enough insight to understand his quarry's preoccupation with beauty, but Yellow's relationship with beauty and beautiful women is not as simple as hatred. During his abduction of Celine, he knocks her out with an injection, strokes her head and hair, and says "beautiful." He also says "beautiful" in an earlier sequence, as he subdues his previous victim, Keiko. His tone when he utters this word is of appreciation rather than loathing. The appreciation is, of course, warped, as it is a prelude to degradation. Yellow keeps his victims over a period of days, destroying their beauty with tortures that a table full of tools mostly leaves to the imagination. With Celine already in reserve, he approaches Keiko's still-living face, which is lacerated in several places, and says, "So ugly . . . kiss kiss, no more." He proceeds to mutilate her lips. Yellow delights in taking beauty and its sexual advantages away from his victims. He does not destroy beauty because he hates it; he destroys beauty because he loves it, envies it, and resents it. His feeling is a type of ambivalence. He has several monologues in front of a mirror, and he bleaches his own skin to remove his yellow ugliness. Keying into his psychology, Celine tries to demoralize him by calling him ugly, echoing the cruelty of prettier schoolchildren shown taunting him in flashbacks, but she only incites his anger. Her understanding does not give her a usable strategy, but she is nevertheless right to conclude that beauty and his lack of it are his motives for killing.

Yellow's warped appreciation of beauty, an appreciation that leads him to destroy it, recalls what is perhaps the most frequently quoted thing Argento has ever said about his philosophy of moviemaking: "I like women, especially beautiful ones. If they have a good face and figure, I would much prefer to watch them being murdered than an ugly girl or man." If this quotation aptly describes Argento's feelings, then he and Yellow both like seeing the destruction of beautiful women. This proclivity is not their only commonality: Yellow takes pictures of his victims, so he and Argento both like *photographing* the destruction of beautiful women. The art of Yellow and the art of the *giallo* are the same in that they focus on capturing the degradation of beautiful female flesh. Yellow likes the images he captures very much: he likes to look at them on his computer while he sucks on a pacifier and masturbates. Through this revelation *Giallo* suggests that his destructiveness is a product of arrested development. His reduction of beauty into indistinct ugliness suggests an anal fetish, his pacifier suggests an oral fetish, and his masturbation suggests a genital fetish—he is stuck in all three phases of Freudian development at once! This diagnosis, like all psychoanalytic diagnoses in Argento's films, rings hollow, but the film raises it as a possibility, just as it raises the possibility of condemning the *giallo* tradition in film by equating it with Yellow's murderousness.

In the interview translated at the end of this book, Élie Castiel asks Argento what he has to say about the fact that women are usually the victims in his films. Argento responds, "I don't agree. I think that in my films there's an equitable justice in victim selection. As many women as men are murdered. Moreover, women are often the ones who solve the mysteries." This claim about equity modifies, or perhaps simply corrects, the earlier statement about liking to see beautiful women murdered; it suggests that Argento does not agree with the equation of his work and feelings with the behaviors of someone like Yellow. Yellow is the worst possible construction that could be put on the combination of beauty and violence that Argento captures in his *gialli*—and in all his films. If Yellow has a strong relationship with the *giallo* tradition in film, then, he is an image of the tradition as its most ardent critics portray it—he is the killer that *Opera*'s Inspector Santini wants Betty to be. Yellow even looks a little bit like Argento, albeit in a horrifically distorted way. If Yellow looks like Argento, either figuratively or literally, he is Argento as he appears in the horrifically distorting eyes of his critics. The ambivalence and indeterminacy that suffuse *Giallo* extend to the relationship between Yellow and Argento and between Yellow and the *giallo* tradition. The former both is and is not the latter.

As the most recent film in a long line of works that both are and are not repetitions of the conventions that Argento made part of the *giallo* tradition, *Giallo* makes a rhetorical statement about the way Argento's later works reflect on their origins. The last two decades of Argento's filmmaking have engaged in overt negotiations with the first two, exploring tensions and finding new ways to develop without completely abandoning their roots. Argento has never reached a point where he is satisfied, where he is willing to stop pushing himself to grow into new artistic territory. He seems unlikely to reach such a point for as long he keeps making films. If fate is kind, he will continue to craft provocative combinations of beauty and violence for many years to come.

Notes

1. For more about horror's connection to psychoanalysis, see Steven Schneider, ed., *Horror Film and Psychoanalysis: Freud's Worst Nightmare.*

2. See Mikel J. Koven's *La Dolce Morte* for a complete discussion of amateur detectives in *giallo* cinema.

3. The spelling of the title is debatable; it might more properly be *Tenebrae,* as the film shows the cover of Peter Neal's novel of that name with this spelling. I have chosen to use the spelling on the widely available Anchor Bay DVD, which is the primary spelling on the Internet Movie Database.

4. The problems inherent to norms established by the Catholic church take center stage in many *gialli,* such as Lucio Fulci's *Don't Torture a Duckling* (1972), which features a classically gothic killer priest. While *Christiano's* allusion to the church isn't completely isolated in Argento's work—*The Church* (1989), which he wrote and produced, is a case in point—it never emerges as the major concern that it becomes in films such as Fulci's. I am inclined to associate Argento's retreat from engagement with Catholicism, an omnipresent concern for Italian filmmakers, with the internationalism of his films, but supporting this association lies beyond the scope of the present argument.

5. One can find politics in anything, but arguing that the early *gialli* have a conscious political agenda is difficult. While I don't think these films have specific political agendas, I am not claiming that they don't have a political unconscious (à la Fredric Jameson) or that they're otherwise insusceptible to political interpretation. Everything is. For example, in "Intimations (and More) of Colonialism: Dario Argento's *L'Uccello dale piume di cristallo,*" Frank Burke provides an interesting reading of (post)colonial politics in *The Bird with the Crystal Plumage.*

6. Anna Powell, drawing on the philosophy of Gilles Deleuze, argues that *Suspiria* extends the sensory reach of film beyond sight and sound into touch through its emphasis on painful and abject imagery, from the razors that kill Sara to a disgusting rain of maggots that falls in the dance academy (142–45).

7. For more detailed accounts of aestheticized murder in literature and film, see Joel Black's *The Aesthetics of Murder* and Steven Jay Schneider's "Murder as Art/The Art of Murder."

8. Here a longer discussion of the Sublime tradition in gothic/horror fiction and in art more generally—spurred by the eighteenth-century thinker Edmund Burke—might be appropriate, but it would also take us too far away from Argento's films, which, as I've already noted, combine the Sublime and the beautiful in various ways. In short: in contrast to the beauty of intricately managed gardens, the sublimity of mountains and other things much grander than humanity has the potential to demonstrate our insignificance in an edifying way. Among sources of the Sublime, Burke includes death and its reminders, particularly corpses (which Julia Kristeva names as the ultimate in abjection and

describes in *Powers of Horror* as having functions very similar to the Sublime). The Sublime can excite just the sort of passion that Pater describes, and so the consciousness of death—raised by corpses, gore, and other gruesome, violent spectacles—occasioned by the horror film could dilate our short interval of existence, enhancing our moments as they pass.

9. The most typical sole survivor is what Rose seems set up to be—the Final Girl, described by Carol Clover in *Men, Women, and Chain Saws.* Clover discusses the Bad Place of the horror film, a convention for which Mater Tenebrarum's house certainly qualifies, but she doesn't discuss what happens when the Bad Place replaces the Final Girl as the protagonist.

10. For comparisons of *Mother of Tears* to *Angels and Demons,* see, for example, http://whiggles.landofwhimsy.com/2006/05/mother-of-tears-cast-and-crew -rumours.html and http://forum.cinefacts.de/90105-argentos-la-terza-madre -mother-tears.html (accessed February 26, 2012).

11. For more about *Phenomena* and adolescent development, see Donald Campbell's "Visions of Deformity: Dario Argento's *Phenomena.*"

Interviews with Dario Argento |

By Élie Castiel

Élie Castiel, "Dario Argento," *Sequences: La Revue de Cinema* 167 (November-December 1993): 8–9.

ÉLIE CASTIEL: Your cinematic career began when you assisted Sergio Leone with *Once upon a Time in the West.* Did this first experience in film influence your career?

DARIO ARGENTO: First of all, I'd like to correct your claim. I didn't begin as an assistant for Sergio Leone, but rather I cowrote the script for the film you mentioned, with the collaboration of Bernardo Bertolucci. As for the influence of this experience, it's clear that early connections leave their marks. If you watch *Once upon a Time in the West* today, you'll already find certain themes that I approach in the films I make now, such as mystery.

EC: After this first experience with the Western genre, you move to the police thriller, and next the horror film, or fantasy, if you prefer.

DA: I don't consider changing style or genre to be a change in itself, but a different way of presenting characters. You can find the same topics in one genre or another.

EC: When you break into horror with *Profondo Rosso* [*Deep Red*], it's evident that your approach is more parodic than otherwise. But little by little, it seems like you're taking yourself more seriously.

DA: I don't completely agree with this statement, although I approached each film with a different energy and atmosphere from the previous film. I film above all by instinct.

EC: In *Suspiria,* you approached, among others, the topics of mysticism and superstition. Did you do much research?

DA: I've never believed in magic or sorcery. But during the years when I was filming *Suspiria,* I thought these topics would make good stories for the horror genre. I got interested, then, in the subject and did some research.

EC: For as long as the horror film has existed, it has been linked with eroticism and sadism. Along these lines, what responsibility do you have to the audience?

DA: You have to admit that there's not a lot of eroticism in my films. What concerns me above all is that the audience appreciate the work that I do. As for sadism, it's an integral part of the genre. My responsibility to the moviegoers is to try to satisfy their curiosity.

EC: What about the question of voyeurism?

DA: The cinema itself is a voyeuristic art, a gaze fixed on the world and the individual. Moviegoers are also voyeurs, often narcissists, but who also often like to look at and contemplate others. My films often approach this phenomenon.

EC: Your first three films include the name of an animal in the title. In the following films, objects replace beasts.

DA: Objects have assumed an important place in our lives. And a film director ought to have the responsibility to create resonance with everything he films. Moreover, objects are important in the genre films I've made. You'll notice that animals, especially cats, are found in almost all my films, which is a way of returning to my roots in my first film.

EC: The victim in your films is often a woman. What do you have to say on this subject?

DA: I don't agree. I think that in my films there's an equitable justice in victim selection. As many women as men are murdered. Moreover, women are often the ones who solve the mysteries.

EC: Your style is often baroque. Did the Italian filmmaker Mario Bava influence you?

DA: Yes, he influenced me for the same reason as Fritz Lang with his expressionism. I really love to work with shadow and lights. Color can also convey subtleties. The American film noir of the forties also inspired me.

EC: Do you think there's a future for the horror film, or have we already reached a saturation point?

DA: There will always be an audience for this genre of films, for as long as the cinema continues to exist. Human beings often need strong sensations.

EC: And you, do you think you'll change genres one day?

DA: Not at the moment. I am very comfortable working in horror. I have no intention to change. The possibilities are enormous.

By Stephane Derderian

Stephane Derderian, "Entretien avec Dario Argento," *L'avant-scene Cinema* (March 2007): 6–9.

STEPHANE DERDERIAN: Was the original title *Deep Red* always intended to refer to the film's bloodiness?

DARIO ARGENTO: At the time when I produced it, the film was the bloodiest one I had ever made. After my Animal Trilogy, I wanted to do something different, bloodier, more psychological, harder, and scarier, too.

SD: It's the first time that there are well-defined characters, too. Was the relationship between the characters played by Daria Nicolodi and David Hemmings built up while you were shooting?

DA: No. Nothing developed while we were shooting. Before I'm ready to shoot, everything is already on paper. I always prepare my films in advance: I make a storyboard, I sketch out each of the characters, etc. But it's not just the characters that are important: the film is also very psychoanalytical. During shooting, I have to determine the composition of the shots, but that's the only new job it's incumbent on me to do. Concerning characters, everything's already written down.

SD: How did you work with the editor, Franco Fraticelli? Did you have all the cuts in mind from the beginning?

DA: We had already made four films together. He was well acquainted with the way I work. I gave him the script and the storyboards; he knew exactly what I wanted.

SD: Visual memory is a subject that often comes up in your films (*The Bird with the Crystal Plumage, Tenebre, Trauma*). What does this subject represent for you?

DA: I'm obsessed with memory. We have a tendency to change facts and stories because of our memory. It is greatly influenced by our personality, by our culture, and by our environment. That's why, in *The Bird with the Crystal Plumage*, Tony Musante's memory plays little tricks on him. He saw a girl dressed in white and a man in a hat dressed all in black. But he didn't pay close enough attention to what he saw. Well, in our unconscious, black symbolizes evil, and white symbolizes purity. As a result, there was this confusion that took place this time because it was the woman who was trying to murder her husband. You can see this problem of memory again in *Deep Red*. Memory often betrays us. For example, if we see something happen in the street, and if there are four different witnesses, there will be four different points of view. I had talked with a chief of police about this subject, and he explained to me that at the time of a murder, it is absolutely necessary for the witnesses to give their depositions within forty-eight hours, because after that, the memory starts to change things. It can twist the facts because of our personal experience.

SD: When you were shooting *Deep Red*, were you sure that the viewer wouldn't see the face of the murderer?

DA: I had the idea for this challenge while I was writing the film. Franco Fraticelli, my editor, wasn't very keen; he was convinced that people would see the killer. In fact, in the reflection in the mirror, the position of the killer is fixed, whereas David Hemmings is moving. The viewer's attention is necessarily going to follow the one that's moving while he goes down the hallway; the viewer won't pay attention to the left side of the image.

SD: You show the killer . . . this is not the case in *The Bird with the Crystal Plumage*.

DA: Indeed, yes, I wanted to press our luck a little bit further!

SD: This film is the longest of your career—more than two hours. Did the length concern you during shooting or editing?

DA: While writing the script, one conducts a timing. My assistant saw that it was going to be longer than usual. It was decided that I would make it just like I had written it.

SD: Like Jean-Pierre Marielle, the antiques dealer from *The Bird with the Crystal Plumage*, the character played by Gabriele Lavia is homosexual.

DA: Homosexuals are part of our everyday life. In my profession, I work with homosexuals. I also have homosexual friends. I think they logically have a place in my films. They are part of our society, which is made up of heterosexuals and homosexuals. And for that matter, in *Tenebre* there is also a lesbian couple.

SD: In *Deep Red*, some sound effects and some isolated bits of dialogue stand out, like in *Suspiria*. Does the sound track merit as much attention as the image?

DA: Sound isn't as important as the image, but I treat it like an actor. It's a little like dealing with the crew and the director. When I shoot, I stop the dialogue, and I can raise the music, or vice versa. Music is a very important character in all my films.

SD: There is talk in the film about spiritual mediums, like in *Trauma*. What are your relationships with them and with esotericism?

DA: I am very interested in esotericism. It is the subject of *Suspiria* and *Inferno*. *Inferno* is esotericism taken to the extreme. On the other hand, mediums are very interesting characters in as much as they make a kind of spectacle. I simply think that in the majority of cases they're charlatans. I don't truly believe in sorcery, but I think that certain mediums have divinatory powers . . . when they touch you, for example. Some of them have the potential to enter into contact with things that are beyond us. . . .

SD: What are the real motives that drive David Hemmings to take on this investigation?

DA: It's a game for him. He understands that he is very close to the truth, but there's something that prevents him from reaching it, and that's what pushes him to make this investigation. He talks about it, by the way, several times through the course of the story.

SD: There is something very original, very modern in the structure of your films: people don't look for a suspect as much as they look for a truth. How did this come about?

DA: When I write, I practice a kind of automatism. I have a film in mind that makes an impression like a sort of universal truth. It's like I have a blank page in front of me, and the story before my eyes. I wait until things play themselves out. Then I commit myself to faithfully reproducing what I read in front of me. It's the entire film that unfolds before my eyes . . . there's not a single element in the image that wasn't in the script.

SD: Don't you suggest that the viewers could themselves become investigators?

DA: An investigation doesn't have to involve a murder. But also the problems that present themselves to us in our lives. We have a duty to search for more profound truths.

SD: Is the psychology of the murderer less important than the psychology of the investigator?

DA: Indeed, in my films I favor the investigator. The murderer is like a ubiquitous ectoplasm with a more simplistic psychology. Murderers want to kill and can do incredible things. When the investigators throw themselves into pursuing the murderer, we naturally follow them.

SD: In *Tenebre*, you present murder as an act of liberation.

DA: In my other films, the murderer wants to satisfy a murderous impulse. In the case of *Tenebre*, there's something more profound. That's why I included a quotation from Conan Doyle, who studied the behavior of murderers quite a lot.

SD: In *Deep Red, The Bird with the Crystal Plumage,* and above all *The Stendhal Syndrome,* the world of painting is very present. . . .

DA: Not only painting, but also architecture, sculpture, and works of art in general. They greatly influenced me when I was a child or teenager. One time during my childhood, I was a victim of the Stendhal Syndrome myself. I was with my family in Athens, and we visited the Parthenon. I had something like vertigo. I became very sick. I had a feeling like climbing a mountain, going up very high. I'd thought, therefore, of talking about the syndrome in a film. Then I read a book by an Italian psychiatrist and analyst at the Hospital of Florence. They had a lot of cases of the Stendhal Syndrome in Florence, which is a very beautiful city, with magnificent architecture. I read the book while I was in the United States casting for *Two Evil Eyes.* I then discovered what had happened to me and that I could easily tell the story.

Feature Films and Television
Directed by Dario Argento

This list includes the principal cast as well as some characters discussed in the critical essay. Some of Argento's works were filmed without sound, with dialogue tracks dubbed in multiple languages later. Cast members spoke Italian, English, and other languages during shooting. Some films were shot in Italy, some in the United States, and some elsewhere. The "original" language of a title or film is therefore a vexed issue. For consistency, this filmography first lists titles most frequently used for the films in English-speaking markets today. Other titles, including the Italian when it differs from the first title listed, appear second.

The Bird with the Crystal Plumage (1970)
Alternate Titles: *L'uccello dalle piume di cristallo, The Phantom of Terror, The Bird with the Glass Feathers, The Sadist with Black Gloves*
Italy, West Germany
Production: Central Cinema Company Film (CCC), Glazier, Seda Spettacoli
Distribution: Universal Marion Corporation, Columbia Broadcasting System, Twenty-First Century Film Corporation, Blue Underground, VCI Entertainment
Producer: Salvatore Argento
Director: Dario Argento
Assistant Director: Roberto Pariante
Writer: Dario Argento
Adapted from *The Screaming Mimi,* by Fredric Brown
Cinematographer: Vittorio Storaro
Production Designer: Dario Micheli
Costume Designer: Dario Micheli
Makeup: Giuseppe Ferranti

Editor: Franco Fraticelli

Music: Ennio Morricone

Cast: Tony Musante (Sam Dalmas), Suzy Kendall (Julia), Enrico Maria Salerno (Inspector Morosini), Eva Renzi (Monica Ranieri), Umberto Raho (Alberto Ranieri), Renato Romano (Professor Carlo Dover), Werner Peters (Antique Dealer)

96 min.

The Cat o' Nine Tails (1971)

Alternate Title: *Il gatto a nove code*

Italy, France, West Germany

Production: Labrador Films, Seda Spettacoli, Terra-Filmkunst, Transconta S.A.

Distribution: National General Pictures, Columbia Broadcasting System, Anchor Bay Entertainment, Reel Media International, Blue Underground

Producer: Salvatore Argento

Director: Dario Argento

Assistant Director: Roberto Pariante

Writers: Dario Argento, Luigi Collo, Dardano Sacchetti

Cinematographer: Erico Menczer

Production Designer: Carlo Leva

Costume Designer: Carlo Leva, Luca Sabatelli

Visual Effects: Luciano Vittori

Editor: Franco Fraticelli

Music: Ennio Morricone

Cast: James Franciscus (Carlo Giordani), Karl Malden (Franco Arno), Catherine Spaak (Anna Terzi), Pier Paolo Capponi (Police Supt. Spini), Horst Frank (Dr. Braun), Rada Rassimov (Bianca Merusi), Aldo Reggiani (Dr. Casoni), Carlo Alighiero (Dr. Calabresi), Vittorio Congia (Righetto, the cameraman), Cinzia de Carolis (Lori), Werner Pochath (Manuel), Tino Carraro (Prof. Fulvio Terzi)

112 min.

Four Flies on Grey Velvet (1971)

Alternate Title: *4 mosche di velluto grigio*

Italy, France

Production: Marianne Productions, Seda Spettacoli, Universal Productions France

Distribution: Paramount Pictures, Mya Communication, Ryko Distribution

Producer: Salvatore Argento

Director: Dario Argento

Assistant Director: Roberto Pariante

Writers: Dario Argento, Luigi Cozzi, Mario Foglietti
Cinematographer: Franco Di Giacomo
Production Designer: Enrico Sabbatini
Wardrobe Assistant: Giovanni Viti
Special Effects: Cataldo Galiano
Editor: Francoise Bonnot
Music: Ennio Morricone
Cast: Michael Brandon (Roberto Tobias), Mimsy Farmer (Nina Tobias), Jean-Piette Marielle (Gianni Arrosio), Bud Spencer (Godfrey/God), Aldo Bufi Landi (Pathologist), Calisto Calisti (Carlo Marosi)
104 min.

Door into Darkness (1973)
Alternate Title: *La porta sul buio*
Episodes: "The Neighbor" (Il Vicino di casa), "The Tram" (Il Tram), "Eyewitness" (Testimone ocular), and "The Doll" (La Bambola)
Italy
Production: Seda Spettacoli, Radiotelevisione Italiana (RAI)
Distribution: Mya Communication
Producer: Dario Argento
Directors: Luigi Cozzi ("The Neighbor"), Dario Argento ("The Tram," "Eyewitness"), Roberto Pariante ("Eyewitness"), Mario Foglietti ("The Doll")
Writers: Luigi Cozzi ("The Neighbor," "Eyewitness"), Dario Argento ("The Tram," "Eyewitness"), Mario Foglietti ("The Doll"), Marcela Elsberger ("The Doll")
Cinematographer: Elio Polacchi
Production Designer: Dario Michele
Costume Designer: Dario Michele
Editors: Amedeo Giomini and Alberto Moro ("The Neighbor"), Amedeo Giomini ("The Tram," "Eyewitness," "The Doll")
Music: Giorgio Gaslini
Cast: Dario Argento (himself/host); "The Neighbor": Aldo Reggiani (Luca), Laura Belli (Stefania), Mimmo Ralmara (The Neighbor); "The Tram": Paola Tedesco (Gioila), Enzo Cerusico (Commisario Giordani), Corado Olmi (Officer Morini), Emilio Marchesini (Marco Roviti); "Eyewitness": Marilù Tolo (Roberta Leoni), Riccardo Salvino (Guido Leoni), Glauco Onorato (Police Inspector), Altea De Nicola (Anna); "The Doll": Mara Venier (Daniela Moreschi), Robert Hoffman (Doctor), Erika Blanc (Elena Moreschi), Gianfranco D'Angelo (Police Commissioner), Umberto Raho (Psychiatrist)
228 min. ("The Neighbor": 58 min.; "The Tram": 54 min.; "Eyewitness": 55 min.; "The Doll": 61 min.)

Summary: Argento introduces the first episode by saying that all episodes share "a common atmosphere of fear, anguish, unease. They're crime stories, but they're new and different." In "The Neighbor," a young couple with a baby move into their new apartment and discover that their upstairs neighbor has murdered his wife. Hitchcock-like cat-and-mouse suspense ensues until the neighbor captures the couple, who are saved barely in time when their crying baby gets the attention of men outside. Argento's introduction to "The Tram" sums up the premise: "A murder happens in front of everyone, but no one sees anything—how come?" Focusing entirely on the investigation, this episode is a love letter to classic mysteries. The solution, that the tram's lights blinked out at a critical moment, is less important than dismissive treatment of a Freudian explanation of the killer's motive (as in *Bird*) and last-minute commentary about criminality and socioeconomic class. "Eyewitness" explores minutiae of memory à la *Bird* and *Deep Red*. Roberta thinks she saw a murder but ultimately learns that the presumed victim, Anna, faked the scene as part of a plot with Roberta's husband, Guido, to murder Roberta and blame Anna's supposed killer. In a clear homage to Mario Bava's *Blood and Black Lace* (1964), "The Doll" focuses on an escaped mental patient stalking and killing a woman in a clothing factory. The episode uses intense point-of-view shots and a misleading narrative to surprise audiences with a gender twist, also reminiscent of *Bird* (a man suggested to be the killer is actually in pursuit of the female killer, whose motive is to kill her sister, who always stole everything from her). The main mystery of this episode is the mystery of what the camera actually shows: camera technique and narrative confusion create the uncertainty that drives the story.

The Five Days of Milan (1973)
Alternate Title: *Le cinque giornate*
Italy
Production: Seda Spettacoli
Distribution: e-m-s the DVD Company
Producer: Salvatore Argento
Director: Dario Argento
Assistant Directors: Sofia Scandurra, Franco Gambarana
Writers: Dario Argento, Nanni Balestrini, Luigi Cozzi, Enzo Ungari
Cinematographer: Luigi Kuveiller
Production Designer: Giuseppe Bassan
Costume Designer: Elena Mannini
Special Effects: Aldo Gasparri
Editor: Franco Fraticelli
Music: Giorgio Gaslini

Cast: Adriano Celentano (Cainazzo), Enzo Cerusico (Romolo Marcelli), Marilu Tolo (The Countess), Luisa De Santis (Pregnant Woman), Glauco Onorato (Zampino), Carla Tato (The Widow), Sergio Graziani (Baron Tranzunto)

122 min.

Summary: This dark comedy follows odd-couple-like Cainazzo and Romolo through a series of adventures against the backdrop of the Italian Revolution of 1848. Titles for different segments emphasize the picaresque structure. The film opens with a cannon shot freeing Cainazzo and other criminals from prison. In a sequence that evokes the Argento-favorite Charlie Chaplin in *Modern Times* (1936), Cainazzo hides himself behind an Italian flag as he flees down the street, and he ends up leading a small army that mistakes him for a patriot. The first titled scene, "The Fatal Encounter," introduces Cainazzo to Romolo. Together they flee from various explosions. In "A Difficult Childbirth," they help a pregnant woman to deliver. They soon find themselves loading guns against a barricade garrisoned by a countess who drinks tea while the lower classes fight. In "The Milanese, My People," the countess treats fighters to sexual favors. Cainazzo and Romolo plan a heist as a way to profit from revolutionary chaos. "The Big Job" shows Argento's increasingly politicized treatment of the revolution in a series featuring city leaders from across Italy planning Milan's fate. In "The Duke," Cainazzo and Romolo encounter a noble who ironically tries to explain politics to the confused men: "There's no royalty here. We're all brothers. Just call me Sir Baron." Upset by Italian treatment of prisoners, Austrians perpetrate a massacre. Argento's trademark extreme violence makes the tone become increasingly somber. Separated from his pal, Cainazzo fears that Romolo is dead. "The Last Words and Other Events" features a fight over the dying words of a revolutionary hero. "Long live Italy"? "Milan to the Milanese"? Cainazzo says the last words were really, "Fuck off, all of you." Cainazzo and Romolo reunite and save the widow of a traitor from being executed. In "The Widow's Bread," Romolo has a romance with the widow, and Cainazzo leaves, only to be captured by Austrians. He meets Zamponi, a thief acquaintance hailed throughout the film as a revolutionary hero who has really been working for the Austrians all along. Zamponi releases him, and he meets up with Romolo again. Trying to stop the rape of a woman caught in bed with an Austrian, Romolo accidentally kills an Italian leader. Romolo is executed by a firing squad. Grieving, Cainazzo takes the stage during a revolutionary celebration and proclaims, "We've been tricked!" *The Five Days* offers a combination of bawdy humor and political satire that is smart, gripping, and far more accessible and coherent than its reputation or Argento's others works suggest.

Deep Red (1975)
Alternate Titles: *Profondo Rosso, The Deep Red Hatchet Murders, The Hatchet Murders*
Italy
Production: Rizzoli Film, Seda Spettacoli
Distribution: Howard Mahler Films, Anchor Bay Entertainment, EastWest Entertainment, Reel Media International
Producer: Salvatore Argento
Director: Dario Argento
Assistant Director: Stefano Rolla
Writers: Dario Argento, Bernardo Zapponi
Cinematographer: Luigi Kuveiller
Production Designer: Giuseppe Bassan
Costume Designer: Elena Mannini
Special Effects: Germano Natali, Carlo Rambaldi
Editor: Franci Fraticelli
Music: Giorgio Gaslini, Goblin (Walter Martino, Fabio Pignatelli, Claudio Simonetti)
Cast: David Hemmings (Marcus Daly), Daria Nicolodi (Gianna Brezzi), Gabriele Lavia (Carlo), Macha Meril (Helga Ulmann), Giuliana Calandra (Amanda Righetti), Glauco Mauri (Prof. Giordani), Clara Calamai (Marta)
126 min.

Suspiria (1977)
Italy
Production: Seda Spettacoli
Distribution: International Classics, Magnum Entertainment, Anchor Bay Entertainment, Blue Underground, Genius Products
Producer: Claudio Argento
Director: Dario Argento
Assistant Director: Antonio Gabrielli
Writers: Dario Argento, Daria Nicolodi
Cinematographer: Luciano Tovoli
Production Designer: Giuseppe Bassan
Costume Designer: Pierangelo Cicoletti
Special Effects: Germano Natali
Editor: Franco Fraticelli
Music: Dario Argento, Goblin (Agostino Marangolo, Walter Martino, Fabio Pignatelli, Claudio Simonetti)
Cast: Jessica Harper (Suzy Banyon), Stefania Casini (Sara), Flavio Bucci (Daniel), Miguel Bosé (Mark), Barbara Magnolfi (Olga), Susanna Javicoli (Sonia), Eva Axén (Pat Hingle), Rudolf Schündler (Prof. Milius), Udo Kier

(Dr. Frank Mandel), Alida Valli (Miss Tanner), Joan Bennett (Madame Blanc)
98 min.

Inferno (1980)
Italy
Production: Produzioni Intersound
Distribution: Twentieth-Century Fox Film Corporation, Anchor Bay Entertainment, Blue Underground, CBS/Fox, Fox Video
Producer: Claudio Argento
Director: Dario Argento
Assistant Directors: Lamberto Bava, Andrea Piazzesi
Writer: Dario Argento
Cinematographer: Romano Albani
Art Director: Giuseppe Bassan
Costume Designer: Massimo Lentini
Special Effects: Germano Natali
Editor: Franco Fraticelli
Music: Keith Emerson
Cast: Leigh McCloskey (Mark Eliot), Irene Miracle (Rose Eliot), Eleonora Giorgi (Sarah), Daria Nicolodi (Elise Stallone Van Adler), Sacha Pitoeff (Kazanian), Alida Valli (Carol, the Caretaker), Veronica Lazar (The Nurse), Gabriele Lavia (Carlo), Feodor Chaliapin Jr. (Professor Arnold/Dr. Varelli), Leopoldo Mastelloni (John, the Butler), Ania Pieroni (Musical Student), James Fleetwood (Cook), Fulvio Mingozzi (Cab Driver)
107 min.

Tenebre (1982)
Alternate Titles: *Unsane, Tenebrae*
Italy
Production: Sigma Cinematografica Roma
Distribution: Bedford Entertainment, Fox Hills Video, Anchor Bay Entertainment
Producer: Claudio Argento
Director: Dario Argento
Assistant Directors: Lamberto Bava, Michele Soavi
Writer: Dario Argento
Cinematographer: Luciano Tovoli
Production Designer: Giuseppe Bassan
Costume Designers: Pierangelo Cicoletti, Carlo Palazzi, Franco Tomei
Special Effects: Giovanni Corridori
Editor: Franco Fraticelli

Music: Massimo Morante, Fabio Pignatelli, Claudio Simonetti
Cast: Anthony Franciosa (Peter Neal), Christian Borromeo (Gianni), Mirella
    D'Angelo (Tilde), Veronica Lario (Jane McKerrow), Ania Pieroni (Elsa
    Manni), Eva Robins (Girl on Beach), Carola Stagnaro (Detective Altieri),
    John Steiner (Christiano Berti), Lara Wendel (Maria Alboretto), John
    Saxon (Bullmer), Daria Nicolodi (Anne), Giuliano Gemma (Detective
    Germani)
110 min.

Phenomena (1985)
Alternate Title: *Creepers*
Italy
Production: DACFILM Rome
Distribution: New Line Cinema, Media Home Entertainment, Anchor Bay
    Entertainment, The Roan Group, EastWest Entertainment
Producer: Dario Argento
Director: Dario Argento
Assistant Directors: Michele Soavi, Bettina Graebe
Writers: Dario Argento, Franco Ferrini
Cinematographer: Romano Albani
Production Designers: Maurizio Garroni, Nello Giorgetti, Luciano Spadoni,
    Umberto Turco
Costume Designers: Giorgio Armani, Marina Malavasi, Patrizia Massaia
Special Effects: Antionio Corridori
Editor: Franco Fraticelli
Music: Claudio Simonetti, Bill Wyman, Simon Boswell
Cast: Jennifer Connelly (Jennifer Corvino), Daria Nicolodi (Frau Bruckner),
    Dalila Di Lazaro (Headmistress), Patrick Bauchau (Inspector Rudolf
    Geiger), Donald Pleasance (Professor John McGregor), Fiore Argento
    (Vera Brandt), Federica Mastroianni (Sophie), Mario Donatone (Morris
    Shapiro), Tanga (Inga)
110 min.

Opera (1987)
Alternate Title: *Terror at the Opera*
Italy
Production: ADC Films, Cecchi Gori Group Tiger Cinematografica
Distribution: South Gate Entertainment, Orion Classics, Anchor Bay
    Entertainment, Blue Underground
Producer: Dario Argento
Director: Dario Argento
Assistant Directors: Antonio Gabrielli, Paolo Zenatello, Alessandro
    Ingargiola, Michele Soavi

Writers: Dario Argento, Franco Ferrini
Cinematographer: Ronnie Taylor
Production Management: Verena Baldeo, Alessandro Calosci, Fabrizio Diaz, Olivier Gérard
Costume Designer: Lia Francesca Morandini
Special Effects: Sergio Stivaletti, Germano Natali, Giovani Corridori
Editor: Franco Fraticelli
Music: Renato Agostini, Antonio Corridori, Giovanni Corridori, Massimo Cristofanelli, Germano Natali, Sergio Stivaletti
Cast: Cristina Marsillach (Betty), Ian Charleson (Marco), Urbano Barberini (Inspector Alan Santini), Daria Nicolodi (Mira), Coralina Cataldi-Tassoni (Giulia), Antonella Vitale (Marion), William McNamara (Stefano)
107 min.

Two Evil Eyes (1990)
Alternate Title: *Due occhi diabolici*
Italy, U.S.A.
Production: ADC Films, Gruppo Bema
Distribution: Taurus Entertainment Company, Anchor Bay Entertainment, Blue Underground, Cinefear, Fox Video, Image Entertainment, Media Home Entertainment
Producer: Achille Manzotti
Director: Dario Argento ("The Black Cat"), George A. Romero ("The Facts in the Case of Mr. Valdemar")
Writers: Dario Argento, Franco Ferrini ("The Black Cat"); George A. Romero ("The Facts in the Case of Mr. Valdemar")
Adapted from "The Black Cat" and "The Facts in the Case of Mr. Valdemar," by Edgar Allan Poe
Cinematographer: Peter Reniers
Production Designer: Cletus Anderson ("The Black Cat")
Costume Designer: Barbara Anderson
Special Effects: Tom Savini
Editor: Pasquale Buba ("The Black Cat")
Music: Pino Donaggio
Cast: "The Facts in the Case of Mr. Valdemar": Adrienne Barbeau (Jessica Valdemar), Ramy Zada (Dr. Robert Hoffman), Bingo O'Malley (Ernest Valdemar), Tom Atkins (Detective Grogan); "The Black Cat": Harvey Keitel (Roderick Usher), Madeleine Potter (Annabel), John Amos (Detective Legrand), Sally Kirkland (Eleonora), Kim Hunter (Mrs. Pym), Martin Balsam (Mr. Pym), Julie Benz (Betty)
120 min.
Summary: This is an anthology in the style of Romero's *Creepshow* (1982), but with only two episodes, both adaptations of tales by Edgar Allan Poe.

First, Romero's "The Facts in the Case of Mr. Valdemar" updates Poe's tale by having a wife scheme to get her dying older husband's money by having his doctor hypnotize him into signing it over. The man dies while hypnotized, which strands his consciousness in an in-between realm where "the others" eventually turn his body into the living dead and bring about the wife and doctor's deaths. The doctor dies while using self-hypnosis to sleep, thus becoming another zombie. Argento's "The Black Cat" combines a variety of Poe's tales (several of which are indicated in characters' names) as the photographer Roderick Usher records brutal deaths reminiscent of "The Pit and the Pendulum" and others. A resilient black cat torments him until, in a fit of rage, he murders his wife. The cat is immured with the body; it escapes and dies by Usher's handsaw. In a nice touch of Argento extremity, kittens the cat had while in the wall reveal the crime to police—they have survived by eating the corpse. Fleeing, Usher accidentally hangs himself. A grotesque dream sequence evokes witchcraft, and Usher's morbid photography makes him yet another Argento stand-in who raises questions about those who enjoy violent spectacle.

Trauma (1993)
Italy, U.S.A.
Production: ADC Films, Overseas FilmGroup
Distribution: Republic Pictures, Anchor Bay Entertainment
Producer: Dario Argento
Director: Dario Argento
Assistant Directors: Rod Smith, Philip Elins, Daniel Carrey
Writers: Franco Ferrini, Gianni Romoli, Dario Argento, T. E. D. Klein, Ruth Jessup
Cinematographer: Raffaele Mertes
Production Designer: Billy Jett
Costume Designer: Leesa Evans
Special Effects: Tom Savini, Greg Funk, Will Huff, Christopher P. Martin
Editor: Bennett Goldberg
Music: Pino Donaggio
Cast: Christopher Rydell (David Parsons), Asia Argento (Aura Petrescu), Piper Laurie (Adriana Petrescu), Frederic Forrest (Dr. Judd), Brad Dourif (Dr. Lloyd), Hope Alexander-Willis (Linda Quirk), Sharon Barr (Hilda Volkman), Isabell O'Connor (Georgia Jackson), Jacqueline Kim (Alice)
106 min.

The Stendhal Syndrome (1996)
Alternate Title: *La sindrome di Stendhal*
Italy
Production: Cine 2000, Medusa Produzione

Distribution: Blue Underground, Troma Team Video
Producers: Dario Argento, Giuseppe Colombo
Director: Dario Argento
Assistant Directors: Nicolo Bongiorno, Fabrizio Campanella, Filip Macelloni,
    Daniele Persica, Luigi Cozzi
Writers: Dario Argento, Franco Ferrini
Cinematographer: Giuseppe Rotuno
Production Designer: Giuseppe Rotunno
Costume Designer: Lia Francesca Morandini
Special Effects: Sergio Stivaletti
Editor: Angelo Nicolini
Music: Ennio Morricone
Cast: Asia Argento (Detective Anna Manni), Thomas Kretschmann (Alfredo
    Grossi), Marco Leonardi (Marco Longhi), Luigi Diberti (Inspector
    Manetti), Paolo Bonacelli (Dr. Cavanna), Julien Lambroschini (Marie),
    John Quentin (Anna's Father)
119 min.

The Phantom of the Opera (1998)
Alternate Title: *Il fantasma dell'opera*
Italy
Production: Medusa Film, Cine 2000
Distribution: A-Pix Entertainment
Producers: Giuseppe Colombo, Aron Sipos
Director: Dario Argento
Assistant Directors: Peter Racz, Alessandro Ingargiola, Enrico Tubertini
Writers: Gerard Brach, Dario Argento
Adapted from *The Phantom of the Opera,* by Gaston Leroux
Cinematographer: Ronnie Taylor
Production Designers: Massimo Antonello Geleng, Csaba Stork
Costume Designer: Agnes Gyarnathy
Special Effects: Sergio Stivaletti, Peter Szilagyi
Editor: Anna Rosa Napoli
Music: Ennio Morricone
Cast: Julian Sands (The Phantom), Asia Argento (Christine Daae), Andrea Di
    Stefano (Baron Raoul De Chagny), Nadia Rinaldi (Carlotta Altieri), Istvan
    Bubik (Ignace, the Rat Catcher)
99 min.
Summary: Few would call this film the best adaptation of Leroux's novel, but
    it is certainly among the strangest. An understudy to the famous Carlotta in
    a Paris production of *Carmen,* Christine gets her chance at the lead thanks
    to an intervention by the legendary Phantom, who was raised by rats in the
    tunnels beneath the opera house. A love triangle forms with the Phantom,

Christine, and Christine's suitor Raoul, but Christine favors the unusually handsome Phantom, going to him and having sex with him willingly. Their supernaturally enhanced (they communicate telepathically) relationship goes to extremes; as the Phantom proclaims, "Hate and love are one." Reluctantly assisted by Raoul, they end up running from an angry mob as well as from a rat catcher, whose rat-killing gadgets and antics provide many moments that go beyond comic relief into surreality. The final battle between the rat catcher and the Phantom ends badly for both. Considered by many to be Argento's worst, it does have a few wonderfully hallucinatory moments—one involves a rat trap and a lot of writhing naked people.

Sleepless (2001)
Alternate Title: *Non ho sonno*
Italy
Production: Cecchi Gori Group Tiger Cinematografica, Medusa Produzione, Opera Film Produzione
Distribution: Artisan
Producer: Dario Argento
Director: Dario Argento
Assistant Directors: Ricardo Cannone, Giulietta Ravel, Marzio Casa, Luca Grivet Brancot
Writers: Dario Argento, Franco Ferrini, Carlo Lucarelli
Cinematographer: Ronnie Taylor
Production Designer: Massimo Antonello Geleng
Costume Designer: Susy Mattolini
Special Effects: David Bracci, Gastone Callori, Massimo Cristofanelli, Gabriele Magri, Vittorio Magri, Barbara Morosetti, Franco Ragusa
Editor: Anna Rosa Napoli
Music: Goblin (Agostino Marangola, Massimo Morante, Fabio Pignatelli, Claudio Simonetti)
Cast: Max von Sydow (Ulisse Moretti), Stefano Dionisi (Giacomo), Chiara Caselli (Gloria), Gabriele Lavia (Mr. Betti), Rossella Falk (Laura de Fabritiis), Paolo Maria Scalondro (Manni), Roberto Zibetti (Lorenzo)
117 min.

The Card Player (2004)
Alternate Title: *Il cartaio*
Italy
Production: Medusa Produzione, Opera Film Produzione
Distribution: Anchor Bay Entertainment
Producer: Dario Argento
Director: Dario Argento
Assistant Directors: Fabrizio Bava, Francesco Perri, Marco Santoro

Writers: Dario Argento, Jay Benedict, Franco Ferrini, Phoebe Scholfield
Cinematographer: Benoit Debie
Production Designers: Marina Pinzuti Ansolini, Massimo Antonello Geleng
Costume Designers: Patrizia Chericoni, Florence Emir
Special Effects: Sergio Stivaletti, Danilo Bollettini, Franco Ragusa
Editor: Walter Fasano
Music: Claudio Simonetti
Cast: Stefania Rocca (Anna Mari), Liam Cunningham (John Brennan), Silvio Muccini (Remo), Adalberto Maria Merli (Police Commissioner), Claudio Santamaria (Carlo Stumi), Fiore Argento (Lucia Marini)
103 min.

Do You Like Hitchcock?
Alternate Title: *Ti piace Hitchcock?*
Italy, Spain
Production: Film Commission Torino-Piemonte, Genesis Motion Pictures, Institut del Cinema Catala (ICC), Opera Film Produzione, RAI Trade, Television de Catalunya
Distribution: Anchor Bay Entertainment
Producers: Carlo Bixio, Joan Antoni Gonzalez, Fabrizio Zappi
Director: Dario Argento
Assistant Directors: Leopoldo Pescatori, Guido Foa
Writers: Dario Argento, Franco Ferrini
Cinematographer: Frederic Fasano
Production Designers: Francesca Bocca, Valentina Ferroni
Costume Designer: Fabio Angelotti
Special Effects: Sergio Stivaletti, Gastone Callori, Marco Monetta, Silvano Scasseddu, Franco Simeone
Editor: Walter Fasano
Music: Pino Donaggio
Cast: Elio Germano (Giulio), Chiara Conti (Federica), Elisabetta Rocchetti (Sasha), Cristina Brondo (Arianna), Ivan Morales (Andrea), Edoardo Stoppa (Inspector), Elena Maria Bellini (Giulio's Mother), Milvia Marigliano (Sasha's Mother)
93 min.

"Jenifer" (from the TV show *Masters of Horror,* 2005)
U.S.A.
Production: Starz Productions, Nice Guy Productions, Industry Entertainment, IDT Entertainment
Distribution: Showtime Networks, Anchor Bay
Producers: Ben Browning, Adam Goldworm
Director: Dario Argento

Assistant Director: Raj Uppal
Writer: Steven Weber
Adapted from the short story by Bruce Jones
Cinematographer: Attila Szaly
Production Designer: David Fischer
Special Effects: Sarah Graham
Editor: Marshall Harvey
Music: Claudio Simonetti
Cast: Steven Weber (Frank Spivey), Carrie Fleming (Jenifer), Brenda James
    (Ruby), Harris Allan (Pete)
58 min.
Summary: Police detective Frank Spivey comes upon a shabbily dressed man
    about to murder what appears to be a beautiful woman, Jenifer. He shoots
    the man dead and soon learns that Jenifer has a hideously deformed,
    predatory face. She scratches him, which may be the means through which
    she makes him incapable of resisting her, even after he discovers that she
    likes to murder and eat people. Gradually, he loses his family and career,
    becoming just like the shabbily dressed man in the beginning. On the brink
    of murdering Jenifer, he is shot by a hunter, and the cycle begins again.

"Pelts" (from the TV show *Masters of Horror,* 2006)
Canada, U.S.A.
Production: Starz Productions, Nice Guy Productions, Industry
    Entertainment, IDT Entertainment
Distribution: Showtime Networks, Anchor Bay
Producers: Ben Browning, Adam Goldworn
Director: Dario Argento
Assistant Directors: Ian Samoil, Darren Robson, Ania Musiatowicz
Writer: Matt Venne
Adapted from the short story by F. Paul Wilson
Cinematographer: Attila Szalay
Production Designer: David Fischer
Costume Designer: Lyn Kelly
Special Effects: Howard Berger
Editor: Jacqueline Cambas
Music: Claudio Simonetti
Cast: Meat Loaf (Jake Feldman), Link Baker (Lou Chinaski), Emilio Salituro
    (Sergio), Elise Lew (Sue Chin Yao), Ellen Ewusie (Shanna), John Saxon
    (Jeb "Pa" Jameson), Michal Suchanek (Larry Jameson), Brenda McDonald
    (Mother Mayter)
58 min.
Summary: Jeb Jameson and his son Larry trap raccoons on the forbidden
    land of Mother Mayter (an Argento wink at audience members who know

the Three Mothers), discovering that the creatures have exceptionally fine fur. Unfortunately, these magical raccoons' pelts carry a curse that drives their handlers to commit extreme acts of violence and self-mutilation. Jake Feldman, a coat maker, retrieves the pelts from the Jameson home (father and son are dead) and decides to have his sweatshop make a fur coat to win him the love of a stripper, Shanna. The coat gets made, and Jake, Shanna, and others die in some of the most extreme gore in the Argento oeuvre.

The Mother of Tears (2007)
Alternate Titles: *La Terza Madre, The Third Mother*
Italy, U.S.A.
Production: Film Commission Torino-Piemonte, Medusa Produzione, Myriad Pictures, Opera Film Produzione, Sky
Distribution: Myriad Pictures, Genius Products
Producers: Claudio Argento, Dario Argento, Marina Berlusconi, Giulia Marletta
Director: Dario Argento
Assistant Directors: Leopoldo Pescatori, Luca Padrini, Nicola Rondolino
Writers: Jace Anderson, Dario Argento, Walter Fasano, Adam Gierasch, Simona Simonetti
Cinematographer: Frederic Fasano
Production Designers: Francesca Bocca, Valentina Ferroni
Costume Designer: Ludovica Amati
Special Effects: Sergio Stivaletti, Danilo Bollettini
Editor: Walter Fasano
Music: Claudio Simonetti
Cast: Asia Argento (Sarah Mandy), Cristian Solimeno (Detective Enzo Marchi), Adam James (Michael Pierce), Moran Atias (Mater Lachrymarum), Valeria Cavalli (Marta Calussi), Philippe Leroy (Guglielmo DeWitt), Daria Nicolodi (Elisa Mandy), Coralina Cataldi-Tassoni (Giselle Mares), Udo Kier (Father Johannes), Jun Ichikawa (Katerina), Tommaso Banfi (Father Milesi), Franco Leo (Monsignor Brusca), Silvia Rubino (Elga)
102 min.

Giallo (2009)
U.S.A., U.K., Spain, Italy
Production: Hannibal Pictures, Giallo Production, Footprint Investment Fund, Media Films, Opera Produzione
Distribution: Maya Entertainment
Producers: Adrien Brody, Rafael Primorac, Richard Rionda Del Castro
Director: Dario Argento
Assistant Directors: Fabrizio Bava, Jim Agnew, Stefano Ruggeri

Writers: Jim Agnew, Sean Keller, Dario Argento
Cinematographer: Frederic Fasano
Production Designer: Davide Bassan
Costume Designer: Stefania Svizzeretto
Special Effects: Sergio Stivaletti
Editor: Roberto Silvi
Music: Marco Werba
Cast: Adrien Brody (Inspector Enzo Avolfi and Yellow), Emmanuelle Seigner
(Linda), Elsa Pataky (Celine), Robert Miano (Inspector Mori), Valentina
Izumi (Keiko)
92 min.

Dracula 3D (2012, projected)
Italy, France, Spain
Production: Enrique Cerezo Producciones Cinematograficas S.A., Film
Export Group, Les Films de l'Astre
Distribution: Film Export Group
Producers: Enrique Cerezo, Roberto Di Girolamo, Sergio Gobbi, Franco
Paolucci, Giovanni Paolucci
Director: Dario Argento
Writers: Dario Argento, Antonio Tentori, Stefano Piani, and Enrique Cerezo
Cinematographer: Luciano Tovoli
Production Designer: Massimo Antonella Geleng
Adapted from *Dracula,* by Bram Stoker
Special Effects: Sergio Stivaletti
Editors: Daniele Campellis, Marshall Harvey
Music: Claudio Simonetti
Cast: Rutger Hauer (Abraham Van Helsing), Asia Argento (Lucy Westenra),
Thomas Kretschmann (Dracula), Marta Gastini (Mina Harker), Unax
Ugalde (Jonathan Harker)
Summary: Shot in Turin by a team of Argento veterans, this film reinterprets
the classic story, Argento-style. In the horror film magazine *Fangoria* 308
(November 2011), Roberto D'Onofrio's article "*Dracula 3D:* Profondo
Vampire" quotes interviews with Dario Argento, Thomas Kretschmann,
Asia Argento, and Unax Ugalde. After lovingly describing his use of an
Alexa and a Sony F3 camera (Argento is the first Italian director to use
the latter) for shooting the film entirely in 3D, Argento comments on
the Italian locations he selected to capture the original story's period
flavor, authentic castles of a sort currently unavailable in Transylvania,
where the film is set. Argento emphasizes that the film will be "a Dario
Argento movie," describing "gory killings, with blood splattering out of the
screen," and a Dracula whose powers of transformation have expanded to
include flies, a giant mantis, and "even a spider . . . a half-human spider!"

Kretschmann emphasizes that his Dracula is much more like Christopher Lee's than Gary Oldman's interpretation. He also comments on the strangeness of once again having to violate and torture Asia in front of her father; he recalls Dario telling him "to think of it as a *Stendhal* sequel." Asia herself seems happy to play Lucy rather than Mina, even though Mina's is traditionally the larger role: mentioning that her sister Fiore Argento and mother Daria Nicolodi have both died in her father's films, she seems proud of "a beautiful moment in the film, set in a crypt, where I die for the first time in a film directed by my father." Ugalde comments on Jonathan Harker's expanded presence and "darker interpretation," alluding to the film's extended treatment of Harker's "relationship with the Count."

"Alfred Hitchcock Quotes." *WDW: Who's Dated Who.com.* 2010; April 6, 2012. http://www.whosdatedwho.com/tpx_179/alfred-hitchcock/quotes.

Argento, Asia. Interview by Billy Chainsaw. *Dark Dreams: The Films of Dario Argento.* 2001; April 6, 2012. http://www.dark-dreams.co.uk/interviews/asia7.php.

———. Interview by Nick Dawe. *Dark Dreams: The Films of Dario Argento.* 2010; April 6, 2012. http://www.dark-dreams.co.uk/interviews/asia4.php.

Argento, Dario. "Interview with *Mother of Tears* Director Dario Argento." *Bloody Disgusting.* 2008; May 27, 2011. www.bloody-disgusting.com/interview/497.

———. Interview by Francesco Locane. *Dark Dreams: The Films of Dario Argento.* 2010; April 6, 2012. http://www.dark-dreams.co.uk/interviews/interview8.php.

Arnold, Gary. "'Suspiria': Upstaged Terror Gone Wild.'" *Washington Post,* August 24, 1977, B7.

Badley, Linda. "Talking Heads, Unruly Women, and Wound Culture: Dario Argento's *Trauma* (1993)." *Kinoeye* 2.12. (June 24, 2002); November 10, 2011. http://www.kinoeye.org/02/12/badley12.php.

Balmain, Colette. "Female Subjectivity and the Politics of 'Becoming Other': Dario Argento's *La Sindrome Di Stendhal (The Stendhal Syndrome,* 1996)." *Kinoeye* 2.12. (June 24, 2002); May 27, 2011. http://www.kinoeye.org/02/12/balmain12.php.

Benshoff, Harry M. *Monsters in the Closet: Homosexuality and the Horror Film.* New York: Manchester University Press, 1997.

Bertellini, Giorgio, and Gian Piero Brunetta. "*Profondo Rosso/Deep Red.*" In *The Cinema of Italy.* London: Wallflower, 2004. 213–22.

The Bird with the Crystal Plumage. Dir. Dario Argento. DVD. Blue Underground, 2005.

Black, Joel. *The Aesthetics of Murder: A Study in Romantic Literature and Contemporary Culture.* Baltimore: Johns Hopkins University Press, 1991.

Bolter, Jay David, and Richard Grusin. *Remediation.* Cambridge: Massachusetts Institute of Technology Press, 2000.

Bondanella, Peter. *A History of Italian Cinema.* New York: Continuum, 2009.

Burke, Frank. "Intimations (and More) of Colonialism: Dario Argento's *L'uccello Dalle Piume Di Cristallo* (*The Bird with the Crystal Plumage*, 1970)." *Kinoeye* 2.11 (June 10, 2002); May 27, 2011. http://www.kinoeye.org/02/11/burke11 .php.

Burke, Frank, Annette Burfoot, and Susan Lord. "Dario Argento's *The Bird with the Crystal Plumage*: Caging Women's Rage." In *Killing Women: The Visual Culture of Gender and Violence.* Ed. Annette Burfoot and Susan Lord. Cultural Studies Series No. 6. Waterloo, Ont.: Wilfred Laurier University Press, 2006. 197–217.

Campbell, Donald. "Visions of Deformity: Dario Argento's *Phenomena* (1985)." *Kinoeye* 2.12 (June 24, 2002), May 27, 2011. http://www.kinoeye.org/02/12/ campbell12.php.

Caruth, Cathy. *Unclaimed Experience.* Baltimore: The Johns Hopkins University Press, 1996.

Castricano, Jodey. "For the Love of Smoke and Mirrors: Dario Argento's *Inferno* (1980)." *Kinoeye* 2.11 (June 10, 2002); May 27, 2011. http://www.kinoeye .org/02/11/castricano11.php.

The Cat o' Nine Tails. Dir. Dario Argento. DVD. Blue Underground, 2007.

Clover, Carol J. *Men, Women, and Chain Saws: Gender in the Modern Horror Film.* Princeton, N.J.: Princeton University Press, 1992.

Colavito, Jason. *Knowing Fear: Science, Knowledge, and the Development of the Horror Genre.* Jefferson, N.C.: McFarland and Co., 2008.

Coldrey, Julian. "Mundanity before Murder: Further Comments on Dario Argento's *Profondo Rosso* (*Deep Red*, 1975)." *Kinoeye* 2.14 (September 23, 2002); May 27, 2011. http://www.kinoeye.org/02/14/coldrey14.php.

Comstock, George. "A Sociological Perspective on Television Violence and Aggression." *American Behavioral Scientist* 51.8 (2008): 1188–89.

Cooper, L. Andrew. *Gothic Realities: The Impact of Horror Fiction on Modern Culture.* Jefferson, N.C.: McFarland, 2010

———. "The Indulgence of Critique: Relocating the Sadistic Voyeur in Dario Argento's *Opera*." *Quarterly Review of Film and Video* 22.1 (2005): 63–72.

Cozzi, Luigi. *Giallo Argento: All about Dario Argento's Movies.* Rome: Profondo Rosso, 2006.

Craig, J. Robert. "Dario Argento's Palette of Death: Color Response in His 'Three Mothers' Films." *Journal of Evolutionary Psychology* 16.1–2 (1995): 53–60.

Crane, Jonathan Lake. *Terror and Everyday Life: Singular Moments in the History of the Horror Film.* Thousand Oaks, Calif.: Sage Publications, 1994.

Creed, Barbara. *The Monstrous-Feminine: Film, Feminism, Psychoanalysis.* New York: Routledge, 1993.

Darnton, Nina. "*Inferno,* Mythic Horror Tale." *New York Times,* August 15, 1986, C14.

Dario Argento. Cine Cult Series. Milan: Mediane Library, 2007.

"Dario Argento: Master of Horror." *Dario Argento's Door into Darkness.* Dir. Luigi Cozzi. DVD. Mya Communication, 2009.

Dario Argento's World of Horror. Dir. Michele Soavi. VHS. Synapse Films, 1986.

Deep Red. Dir. Dario Argento. DVD. Blue Underground, 2007.

Delorme, Stephane. "Sous Le Gore, Le Frisson D'argento." *Cahiers du Cinema* 564 (2002): 42–43.

De Quincey, Thomas. "On Murder, Considered as One of the Fine Arts." In *Project Gutenberg EBook of Miscellaneous Essays, by Thomas De Quincey.* January 13, 2004; May 27, 2011. http://www.gutenberg.org/ebooks/10708.

———. *Suspiria de Profundis.* In *Confessions of an English Opium Eater and Other Writings.* New York: Oxford University Press, 2008. 87–181.

Doane, Mary Ann. "*Caught* and *Rebecca*: The Inscription of Femininity as Absence." In *Feminist Film Theory: A Reader.* Ed. Sue Thornham. New York: New York University Press, 1999. 70–82.

Edelstein, David. Review of *Mother of Tears*, dir. Dario Argento. *New York*, May 30, 2008; May 27, 2011. http://nymag.com/listings/movie/mother-of-tears-the-thir/.

Freedman, Jonathan L. *Media Violence and Its Effect on Aggression: Assessing the Scientific Evidence.* Toronto: University of Toronto Press, 2002.

Freud, Sigmund. *Beyond the Pleasure Principle. Bartleby.com.* January 29, 2011. http://www.bartleby.com/276/.

———. *Group Psychology and the Analysis of the Ego. Bartleby.com.* January 29, 2011. http://www.bartleby.com/290/.

———. *Leonardo Da Vinci. Bartleby.com.* February 18, 2011. http://www.bartleby.com/277/.

———. *The Interpretation of Dreams.* New York: Avon, 1980.

———. "The Psychogenesis of a Case of Homosexuality in a Woman." In *Freud on Women, A Reader.* Ed. Elisabeth Young-Bruehl. W. W. Norton and Co., 1990. 241–66.

———. "The Uncanny." Laurel Amtower's Homepage. February 18, 2011. http://www-rohan.sdsu.edu/~amtower/uncanny.html.

———. *Three Essays on the Theory of Sexuality.* Trans. James Strachey. New York: Basic Books, 1975.

Gallant, Chris. *Art of Darkness: The Cinema of Dario Argento.* Guildford: FAB, 2000.

Gerbner, George. "Reclaiming Our Cultural Mythology: Television's Global Marketing Strategy Creates a Damaging and Alienated Window on the World." *In Context: A Quarterly of Humane Sustainable Culture* 38 (Spring 1994): 40; November 8, 2011. http://www.context.org/ICLIB/IC38/Gerbner.htm.

Giallo. Dir. Dario Argento. DVD. Maya Entertainment, 2009.

Golden, Christopher. *Cut! Horror Writers on Horror Film.* New York: Berkley Books, 1992.

Gracey, James. *Dario Argento*. Harpenden, Hertz, U.K.: Kamera Books, 2010.

Grant, Barry Keith. *The Dread of Difference: Gender and the Horror Film*. Texas Film Studies Series. Austin: University of Texas Press, 1996.

Grant, Barry Keith, and Christopher Sharrett. *Planks of Reason: Essays on the Horror Film*. Rev. ed. Lanham, Md.: Scarecrow Press, 2004.

Halberstam, Judith. *Skin Shows: Gothic Horror and the Technology of Monsters*. Durham, N.C.: Duke University Press, 1995.

Harvey, Dennis. Review of *Mother of Tears*, dir. Dario Argento. *Variety*, October 8–14, 2007; March 1, 2012. http://www.variety.com/review/ VE1117934653?refcatid=31.

Hawkins, Joan. *Cutting Edge: Art-Horror and the Horrific Avant-Garde*. Minneapolis: University of Minnesota Press, 2000.

Haflidason, Almar. "Dario Argento, Part 1: Sleepless" (interview). British Broadcasting Corporation. October 2003; April 6, 2012. http://www.bbc .co.uk/films/2002/02/08/dario_argento_sleepless_interview.shtml.

Humphries, Reynold. "Trains of Thought: Dario Argento's *Non Ho Sonno* (*Sleepless*, 2000)." *Kinoeye* 2.12 (June 24, 2002); May 27, 2011. http://www.kinoeye .org/02/12/humphries12.php.

Hunt, Leon. "A (Sadistic) Night at the Opera: Notes on the Italian Horror Film." *Velvet Light Trap* 30 (1992): 65–75.

Hutchings, Peter. "The Argento Effect." In *Defining Cult Movies: The Cultural Politics of Oppositional Taste*. Ed. Mark Jancovich, Antonio Lazaro Reboll, Julian Stringer, and Andy Willis. New York: Manchester University Press, 2003. 127–41.

Inferno. Dir. Dario Argento. DVD. Blue Underground, 2007.

Inferno. Dir. Dario Argento. VHS. Anchor Bay, 2000.

Jones, Alan. *Profondo Argento: The Man, the Myths, and the Magic*. Surrey: FAB Press, 2004.

Knee, Adam. "Gender, Genre, Argento." In *The Dread of Difference: Gender and the Horror Film*. Ed. Barry Keith Grant. Austin: University of Texas Press, 1996. 213–30.

Koven, Mikel J. *La Dolce Morte: Vernacular Cinema and the Italian Giallo Film*. Lanham, Md.: Scarecrow Press, 2006.

Kristeva, Julia. *Powers of Horror: An Essay on Abjection*. Trans. Leon S. Roudiez. New York: Columbia University Press, 1982.

Lee, Nathan. "Supernatural Stew, Served with Camp." *New York Times*, June 6, 2008, E11.

Lowenstein, Adam. *Shocking Representation: Historical Trauma, National Cinema, and the Modern Horror Film*. New York: Columbia University Press, 2005.

McDonagh, Maitland. *Broken Mirrors/Broken Minds: The Dark Dreams of Dario Argento*. Expanded ed. Minneapolis: University of Minnesota Press, 2010.

Medved, Michael. "Hollywood's Four Big Lies." In *Screen Violence*. Ed. Karl French. London: Bloomsbury Publishing, 1996. 20–34.

Mendik, Xavier. "Transgressive Drives and Traumatic Flashbacks: Dario Argento's *Tenebrae* (*Unsane,* 1982)." *Kinoeye* 2.12 (June 24, 2002); May 27, 2011. http://www.kinoeye.org/02/12/mendik12.php.

Mendik, Xavier, Anne Mullen, and Emer O'Beirne. "A (Repeated) Time to Die: The Investigation of Primal Trauma in the Films of Dario Argento." In *Crime Scenes: Detective Narratives in European Culture since 1945.* Ed. Emer O'Beirne and Anne Mullenci. Amsterdam: Rodopi, 2000. 25–36.

Met, Philippe, David Boyd, and R. Barton Palmer. "'Knowing Too Much' about Hitchcock: The Genesis of the Italian Giallo." In *After Hitchcock: Influence, Imitation, and Intertextuality.* Ed. David Boyd and R. Barton Palmer: University of Texas Press, 2006. 195–214.

Mietkiewicz, Henry. "Surfacing Series Gives Birth to Book." *Toronto Star,* September 15, 1989, D19.

Modleski, Tania. *The Women Who Knew Too Much: Hitchcock and Feminist Theory.* 2d ed. New York: Routledge, 2005.

Moore, Ben. "'Suspiria' Remake Will Make Original's Scenes 'Artful,' Will Include 'Goblin' Score." *Screen Rant.* March 31, 2011; April 9, 2012. http://screenrant.com/suspiria-remake-artful-goblin-score-benm-108608/.

Mulvey, Laura. *Visual and Other Pleasures.* Bloomington: Indiana University Press, 1989.

Needham, Gary. "From Punctum to Pentazet, and Everything in Between: Dario Argento's *Il Gatto a Nove Code* (*The Cat o' Nine Tails,* 1971) and *Quattro Mosche Di Velluto Grigio* (*Four Flies on Grey Velvet,* 1972)." *Kinoeye* 2.11 (June 10, 2002); May 27, 2011. http://www.kinoeye.org/02/11/needham11_no2.php.

O'Neill, Phelim. "DVD Blu-ray Releases: *Suspiria.*" *The Guardian,* January 9, 2010, 23.

Pater, Walter. *The Renaissance. Project Gutenberg EBook of The Renaissance, by Walter Pater.* March 27, 2009; May 27, 2011. http://www.gutenberg.org/catalog/world/readfile?fk_files=1448865.

Paul, Louis. *Italian Horror Film Directors.* Jefferson, N.C.: McFarland, 2005.

Phenomena. Dir. Dario Argento. DVD. Anchor Bay, 2008.

Pinedo, Isabel Cristina. *Recreational Terror: Women and the Pleasures of Horror-Film Viewing.* Albany: State University of New York Press, 1997.

Poe, Edgar Allan. "The Philosophy of Composition." In *Edgar Allan Poe: Selected Prose and Poetry.* Rev. ed. New York: Holt, Rinehart, and Winston, 1950. 421–31.

———. "The Poetic Principle." In *Edgar Allan Poe: Selected Prose and Poetry.* Rev. ed. New York: Holt, Rinehart, and Winston, 1950. 415–20.

Powell, Anna. *Deleuze and the Horror Film.* Edinburgh: Edinburgh University Press, 2005.

Reich, Jacqueline, and Keala Jewell. "The Mother of All Horror: Witches, Gender, and the Films of Dario Argento." In *Monsters in the Italian Literary Imagination*. Ed. Keala Jan Jewell. Detroit: Wayne State University Press, 2001. 89–105.

Sarris, Andrew. "Notes on the Auteur Theory in 1962." In *Film Theory and Criticism*. 7th ed. Ed. Leo Braudy and Marshall Cohen. New York: Oxford University Press, 2009. 451–54.

Schneider, Steven Jay. *Fear without Frontiers: Horror Cinema across the Globe*. Godalming, U.K.: FAB, 2003.

———. "Murder as Art/The Art of Murder: Aestheticizing Violence in Modern Cinematic Horror." In *Dark Thoughts: Philosophic Reflections on Cinematic Horror*. Ed. Steven Jay Schneider and Daniel Shaw. Lanham, Md.: Scarecrow Press, 2003. 174–97.

———, ed. *Horror Film and Psychoanalysis: Freud's Worst Nightmare*. Cambridge Studies in Film. New York: Cambridge University Press, 2009.

Schneider, Steven Jay, and Frank Lafond. "Dario Argento: Resources Online and in Print." *Kinoeye* 2.12 (June 24, 2002); May 27, 2011. http://www.kinoeye.org/02/12/argentobibliography12.php.

Schneider, Steven Jay, and Tony Williams. *Horror International*. Contemporary Approaches to Film and Television Series. Detroit: Wayne State University Press, 2005.

Schulte-Sasse, Linda. "The 'Mother' of All Horror Movies: Dario Argento's *Suspiria* (1977)." *Kinoeye* 2.11 (June 10, 2002); May 27, 2011. http://www.kinoeye.org/02/11/schultesasse11.php.

Sconce, Jeffrey. *Sleaze Artists: Cinema at the Margins of Taste, Style, and Politics*. Ed. Jeffrey Sconce. Durham, N.C.: Duke University Press, 2007.

Sevastakis, Michael. "A Dangerous Mind: Dario Argento's *Opera* (1987)." *Kinoeye* 2.12 (June 24, 2002); May 27, 2011. http://www.kinoeye.org/02/12/sevastakis12.php.

Skal, David J. *Screams of Reason: Mad Science and Modern Culture*. New York: W. W. Norton, 1998.

Smith, Joan. "Speaking Up for Corpses." In *Screen Violence*. Ed. Karl French. London: Bloomsbury Publishing, 1996. 196–204.

Smuts, Aaron. "The Principles of Association: Dario Argento's *Profondo Rosso* (*Deep Red*, 1975)." *Kinoeye* 2.11 (June 10 2002); May 27, 2011. http://www.kinoeye.org/02/11/smuts11.php.

Sontag, Susan. "Notes on 'Camp.'" In *The Cult Film Reader*. Ed. Ernest Mathijs and Xavier Mendik. New York: Open University Press, 2008. 41–52.

Staiger, Janet. *Media Reception Studies*. New York: New York University Press, 2005.

The Stendhal Syndrome. Dir. Dario Argento. Blu-Ray. Blue Underground, 2008.

Thornham, Sue. *Feminist Film Theory: A Reader*. Edinburgh: Edinburgh University Press, 1999.

Trauma. Dir. Dario Argento. DVD. Anchor Bay, 2005.

"Trisomy 13." *Genetics Home Reference.* U.S. Library of Medicine. January 2009; April 9, 2012. http://ghr.nlm.nih.gov/condition/trisomy-13.

Williams, Linda. "Film Bodies: Gender, Genre, and Excess." In *Film Theory and Criticism.* 7th ed. Ed. Leo Braudy and Marshall Cohen. New York: Oxford University Press, 2009. 602–16.

Winter, Douglas. "Opera of Violence: The Films of Dario Argento." In *Cut! Horror Writers on Horror Film.* Ed. Christopher Golden. New York: Berkeley Books, 1992. 266–88.

Wood, Robin. "An Introduction to the American Horror Film." In *Planks of Reason: Essays on the Horror Film.* Ed. Barry Keith Grant. Metuchen, N.J.: Scarecrow Press, 1984. 164–200.

———. "Returning the Look: *Eyes of a Stranger.*" In *American Horrors: Essays on the Modern American Horror Film.* Ed. Gregory A. Waller. Urbana: University of Illinois Press, 1987. 79–85.

Index

computer-generated imagery (CGI), 18, 133

Comstock, George, 14

Connelly, Jennifer, 120, 125, 135

Cozzi, Luigi, 48, 92

Crane, Jonathan Lake, 10, 13

crane shots, 71, 121

Creed, Barbara, 77, 115

Creepers. See Phenomena

Dali, Salvador, 100

Dario Argento: Master of Horror, 92

Dario Argento's Door into Darkness, 24, 126, 157-58

Dario Argento's World of Horror, 7

Dark Dreams website, 21-22, 106

Dark Shadows, 77

Darnton, Nina, 103

Dawn of the Dead, 92

Dead Alive, 114

Death Proof, 4

Deep Red, 3-4, 24, 42, 47, 51-62, 66, 70, 73-74, 76, 84, 86, 104, 108, 114, 119, 123, 129, 132, 134-37, 141, 150-54, 158

Deleuze, Gilles, 147n6

Demons, 3, 128

Demons 2, 2, 128

De Palma, Brian, 7

De Quincey, Thomas, 88-93, 96-97, 112

desensitization, 14

Dial M for Murder, 141

Doane, Mary Ann, 6

Don't Torture a Duckling, 147n4

Door into Darkness. See Dario Argento's Door into Darkness

Doyle, Arthur Conan, 84, 154

Do You Like Hitchcock? 128, 134, 140-42

Dracula 3D, 2, 129, 170-71

dreams: in Argento's films, 50-52, 126-27, 130-31, 164; and Argento's style, 61-62, 75, 94-96

Edelstein, David, 117

Escher, M. C., 76, 139

Exorcist, The, 141

expressionism, 74-75, 86, 142, 151

fairy tales, 75, 77, 85, 96, 104, 122-23, 126

Fellini, Federico, 4, 66, 94-95, 102

feminism, 6, 62, 117

Firestarter, 120

Five Days of Milan, The, 2, 76-77, 118, 158-59

forensics, 32, 52, 125. *See also* science

Four Flies on Grey Velvet, 38, 42-53, 55, 59-62, 66

Frankenstein's monster, 11-12, 48-49

Fraticelli, Franco, 151-52

Freedman, Jonathan, 14

French cinema, 5

Freud, Sigmund: on dreams, 50-51, 61-62; on homosexuality and perversion, 36-37, 49, 53, 57-60, 66, 146; on memory, 31, 33, 68; on oedipal identification, 25-26, 35, 142; on trauma and repression, 56, 130, 132. *See also* gender; homosexuality; identification; psychoanalysis

Friday the Thirteenth, 11, 128

Friedkin, William, 141

Fulci, Lucio, 38, 128, 147n4

Fury, The, 120

Gallant, Chris, 7, 9, 70

gender: and identification, 6, 7, 9, 35, 48, 53, 60; and normativity, 33-34, 114, 117, 125, 158; and violence, 5-9, 146, 150

genetics, 38-43, 52, 123. *See also* science

genre: categorizing films, 1, 24, 49, 77, 95, 149-51; challenged in films, 2, 4, 106, 118-19, 124; history of, 11, 23-24, 37, 89-92, 128, 142; reflected on in films, 31, 62, 72 . *See also* giallo; slasher; supernatural, the

giallo: amateur detectives, 29, 37, 52-53, 62, 82-84, 106, 114, 118-20, 134, 141, 147n2; costumes, 30, 32, 36, 56; definition, 24, 49, 62, 103, 127-28, 133-36; evolution, 53-54, 119-20, 124, 126, 129, 141; reflected on in films, 62, 72, 84, 142-46

Giallo (film title), 2, 127-28, 135, 142-46

Goblin, 55, 76-77, 85, 121, 126, 135

L. Andrew Cooper is an assistant professor of film and digital media at the University of Louisville and the author of *Gothic Realities: The Impact of Horror Fiction on Modern Culture.*

Books in the series
Contemporary Film Directors

Philip Kaufman
  Annette Insdorf

Richard Linklater
  David T. Johnson

David Lynch
  Justus Nieland

John Sayles
  David R. Shumway

Dario Argento
  L. Andrew Cooper

The University of Illinois Press
is a founding member of the
Association of American University Presses.

Designed by Paula Newcomb
Composed in 10/13 New Caledonia LT Std
with Helvetica Neue LT Std display
by Celia Shapland
at the University of Illinois Press
Manufactured by Thomson-Shore, Inc.

University of Illinois Press
1325 South Oak Street
Champaign, IL 61820-6903
www.press.uillinois.edu